# Advance Praise for
## *Life, Marriage, and Religious Liberty*

"This book commemorates ten years since the release of the Manhattan Statement on *Life, Marriage, and Religious Liberty*. That ten years feels more like a quarter century. The pace of cultural change in the West has far exceeded reasonable estimates. I am grateful to see this volume addressing these critical issues through the written contributions of some of our finest thinkers and analysts. Martin Luther King, Jr. insisted the church must not simply reflect culture, but must act to influence it. Works such as this one can help us accomplish that goal."

—HUNTER BAKER, J.D., Ph.D., Dean, College of Arts and Sciences,
Union University

"*The Manhattan Declaration* was a landmark event in American history when it was issued in 2009. This splendid volume is a fitting reflection on the Declaration, and a welcome check-up on its health and influence ten years hence. *Life, Marriage, and Religious Liberty* is more than that, for it stands on its own as a collection of social commentaries by a score or so of America's most insightful and engaged scholars and journalists. It is in fact a trusty guide to those perplexed by the somersaults in our culture and politics over the last decade."

—GERARD V. BRADLEY, Professor of Law and Director, National Law Institute,
Co-editor, *The American Journal of Jurisprudence*,
University of Notre Dame Law School

# LIFE, MARRIAGE, AND RELIGIOUS LIBERTY

## What Belongs to God, What Belongs to Caesar

Essays for the Tenth Anniversary of
*The Manhattan Declaration*

Edited by
DAVID S. DOCKERY
AND JOHN STONESTREET

**FIDELIS**
BOOKS

A FIDELIS BOOKS BOOK
An Imprint of Post Hill Press

ISBN: 978-1-64293-257-7
ISBN (eBook): 978-1-64293-258-4

Cover Design by Cody Corcoran

Unless otherwise indicated all Scripture is from:
The Holy Bible, English Standard Version. ESV® Text Edition: 2016.
Copyright © 2001 by Crossway Bibles, a publishing ministry of
Good News Publishers.

FIDELIS
BOOKS

Post Hill
PRESS

**Post Hill Press**
New York • Nashville
posthillpress.com

Published in the United States of America

*in piam memoriam*

**Charles W. "Chuck" Colson (1931–2012)**

Mentor, Visionary, Leader,
and Courageous Follower of Christ

# CONTENTS

Preface (David S. Dockery and John Stonestreet) . . . . . . . . . . . . . . . . . ix

Introduction: What Belongs to God, What Belongs to Caesar:
A Personal Reflection on *The Manhattan Declaration*
(Timothy George) . . . . . . . . . . . . . . . . . . . . . . . . . . . . . . . . . . . . . xiii

Why *The Manhattan Declaration?* (Charles W. "Chuck" Colson) . . . . .xix


**PART ONE: Life**

Life is the Greatest Human Right (Randy Alcorn) . . . . . . . . . . . . . . . .3

Why Life at All Stages Belongs to God, Not the State
(Russell Moore and Andrew Walker) . . . . . . . . . . . . . . . . . . . . . . . . .13

How the Church Can Defend Life at All Stages (Trevin Wax) . . . . . . .26

How the Church Can Protect the Dignity of the Most Vulnerable
Among Us (Joni Eareckson Tada) . . . . . . . . . . . . . . . . . . . . . . . . . . .38

Why Being Pro-Life is also Pro-Woman (Frederica Mathewes-Green). . .51


**PART TWO: Marriage**

Why Marriage Matters Most: Sharing the Gospel Matrimony
(Timothy Cardinal Dolan) . . . . . . . . . . . . . . . . . . . . . . . . . . . . . . . .63

What Must We Do? An Evangelical Perspective (Rick Warren) . . . . . .73

The Vindication of *The Manhattan Declaration*, Then and Now
(Mary Eberstadt) . . . . . . . . . . . . . . . . . . . . . . . . . . . . . . . . . . . . . . .81

Why Marriage Belongs to God, Not to the State
(Jennifer Roback Morse) . . . . . . . . . . . . . . . . . . . . . . . . . . . . . . . . . .91

Marriage Equality, Marriage Reality (Ryan T. Anderson) . . . . . . . . . .103

**PART THREE: Religious Liberty**

Why Religious Freedom Matters: A Brief History (Michael Farris). . . . 117

Why Our Conscience Belongs to God, Not the State
(Chad Hatfield). . . . . . . . . . . . . . . . . . . . . . . . . . . . . . . . . . . . . .129

How the Church Can Protect Religious Freedom
and Rights of Conscience (R. R. Reno) . . . . . . . . . . . . . . . . . . . . . .136

The Child in Relation to Family and State (Bruce Ashford) . . . . . . . .147

Religious Freedom: A Contemporary Review (Kristen Waggoner) . . .159


Postscript: A Contest of Worldviews (Robert P. George). . . . . . . . . . .172


About the Contributors . . . . . . . . . . . . . . . . . . . . . . . . . . . . . . . . .184


ADDENDUM: *The Manhattan Declaration:*
A Call of Christian Conscience. . . . . . . . . . . . . . . . . . . . . . . . . . . . .191

# PREFACE

In the fall of 2009, guided by the leadership of Chuck Colson (1931–2012), more than 150 religious leaders came together to address the three key issues of the cultural moment: life, marriage, and religious liberty. At Colson's request, Timothy George, dean of the Beeson Divinity School, and Robert P. George, McCormick Professor of Jurisprudence at Princeton University, served as primary authors of a significant statement known as *The Manhattan Declaration*. We were privileged to be part of the collective that affirmed the *Declaration* and part of a smaller group who offered initial support for the project.

Included among the 150 religious leaders were Roman Catholics, Orthodox, and Evangelical Protestants from various denominations as well as non-denominational backgrounds. Deep theological differences would have made it difficult for those in this group to reach consensus about things such as the work of evangelism or church life, or even to share communion together. So, to be clear, *The Manhattan Declaration* was no attempt at a mushy ecumenism. Rather, the statement was an affirmation built around genuine shared conviction. Though, they also recognized their shared commitments to the Nicene Creed and their shared concerns regarding the issues of life, marriage, and religious liberty, among other important cultural and societal challenges. Within months, more than 550,000 people added their names in support of the *Declaration*.

Now, a decade later, we find ourselves at a somewhat different cultural moment, even as we maintain our commitments on these three key issues. A few years ago, the responsibility for the *Declaration* was handed to the Colson Center for Christian Worldview, under the direction of John Stonestreet, by *The Manhattan Declaration* Board. The ten-year anniversary of the statement provides an opportunity to not only renew and reaffirm the commitments articulated so clearly in 2009, but also to reflect on what those commitments require of us today. In that light, several people who were directly or indirectly influenced by the wide-ranging leadership of Chuck Colson have come together to speak afresh to these vital issues.

Building on their work as the primary authors of the original statement, Timothy George and Robert P. George have provided the bookend chapters for this volume. The Beeson dean has written an initial reflection while the McCormick Professor has offered a concluding and defining word regarding a contest of worldviews. Between these two brilliant chapters are thoughtful contributions related to themes of life, marriage, and religious liberty. We have provided a word from Chuck Colson, which was originally penned in 2010 shortly after the release of the *Declaration*.

Bestselling author Randy Alcorn has provided the opening chapter on the importance of life. Russell Moore and Andrew Walker, key leaders at the Ethics and Religious Liberty Commission have combined to address "Why Life at All Stages Belongs to God, Not the State." Their chapter includes important thoughts on a variety of ethical issues including abortion, infanticide, euthanasia, poverty, elderly care, and capital punishment. A younger voice, Trevin Wax, whose influence continues to grow, speaks to "How the Church Can Defend Life at All Stages." Readers will appreciate the powerful, personal insights from Joni Eareckson Tada, as she writes about "How the Church Can Protect the Dignity of the Most Vulnerable Among Us." Frederica Mathewes-Green courageously reflects on "Why Being Pro-Life is also Pro-Woman."

The second section of the book focuses on marriage, beginning with significant chapters on the importance of marriage. Timothy Cardinal Dolan has offered a Roman Catholic perspective and Rick Warren has provided an evangelical perspective. The ever-astute cultural observer Mary Eberstadt has offered a thoughtful contribution to the broader impact of *The Manhattan Declaration*. Jennifer Roback Morse has given us a fine piece on "Why Marriage Belongs to God, Not the State" and the persuasive work of Ryan Anderson follows with a timely response called "Marriage Equality, Marriage Reality."

The third section includes important chapters on the issue of religious liberty. The initial chapter in this section, authored by Michael Farris, provides a historical overview regarding "Why Religious Freedom

Matters." Chad Hatfield, president at St. Vladimir's Seminary, has offered a pastoral perspective on "Why Our Conscience Belongs to God, Not the State." R. R. Reno, editor of *First Things*, has provided a wonderful piece on "How the Church Can Protect Religious Liberty and the Rights of Conscience." Kristen Waggoner offers a thoughtful review of our culture's most recent religious freedom clashes, and theologian Bruce Ashford has penned the final chapter in this section with a reflection on children in contemporary society. *The Manhattan Declaration* is attached as an addendum.

The group of influential thinkers contributing to this book, each speaking from their respective and distinct theological, vocational, and ecclesiastical backgrounds, provide a symphonic, up-to-date commentary on the three primary principles affirmed in the *Declaration*. The chapters, while substantive and convictional, are best described as succinct and readable. The authors seek to be charitable to those with whom they differ, modeling kindness, humility, and civility. Genuine civility and kindness are much needed in our polarized and fragmented culture. Civility, rightly understood, is not merely a diplomatic posture nor a code of conduct, but a virtue. The volume is thus a chorus, which seeks to "hold fast what is good" (I Thess. 5:21) while faithfully "holding fast to the word of life" (Phil. 2:14-16). Speaking and living with convictional civility and convictional kindness reflects lessons we all learned from Chuck Colson.

While the authors attempt to reflect and model faithful cultural engagement, there remain real differences among us. We, editors and authors, represent different Christian traditions. We share substantial agreement on the issues of life, marriage, and religious liberty, but we speak from, and not always for, our different traditions and denominational perspectives, which create tensions when applied. As the various authors of this volume expand on the affirmations of *The Manhattan Declaration*, they offer implications not necessarily shared by every participant in this project. That does not diminish our shared affirmations regarding the importance of life, marriage, and religious liberty. As editors, we have chosen to allow these differences to stand. We hope our ability to work together for the common good on these vital matters provides a witness to others, even balancing our differences regarding the entailments with our shared affirmations. We pray this will itself be a witness to a watching world of how devoted men and women wrestle seriously with these matters of central importance while taking up the call to engage the culture in a way faithful to the best of the great Christian tradition.

As editors, we wish to acknowledge the important contributions of Lisa Weathers and Tim Padgett and thank them for their devoted efforts. We also express our gratitude to Gary Terashita at Fidelis Books for his overall guidance throughout this project. With thankful hearts, we dedicate this book to the memory of our dear friend and mentor Chuck Colson (1931–2012). It is our prayer this work will bear fruit for God's kingdom as we to seek to provide a resource that will serve the next generation while bringing glory to our great God.

*Soli Deo Gloria*

David S. Dockery, *President*
Trinity International University/Trinity Evangelical Divinity School

John Stonestreet, *President*
Chuck Colson Center for Christian Worldview

# INTRODUCTION

# What Belongs to God, What Belongs to Caesar

## A Personal Reflection on
## *The Manhattan Declaration*

### Timothy George

*The Manhattan Declaration: A Call of Christian Conscience* originated in the heart and vision of Charles Wendell Colson—Chuck to his many friends and admirers. Following the retirement of Carl F. H. Henry, I was invited to join the Prison Fellowship Board of Directors and to serve as chair of its Theology Committee. At our annual spring board meeting in June 2009, I was asked to bring a devotional message on the foundational principles of our ministry. Aware that 2009 was the seventy-fifth anniversary of the famous *Barmen Declaration*, a historic statement of faith set forth by courageous Christians at the dawn of the Nazi era in May 1934, I brought copies of this famous document to the meeting and distributed them to members of the board. I then offered a few comments on the meaning of Barmen focusing on its first article: "Jesus Christ, as he has tested for us in the Holy Scripture, is the one word of God which we have to hear and which we have to trust and obey in life and in death."[1] I pointed out that many of those who were present at Barmen that day,

---

[1] "The Theological *Declaration* of Barmen," *Church & Society* 85, no. 6 (1995): 124.

such as Pastor Martin Niemöller, experienced great suffering and persecution at the hands of the Nazis in the years following.

As soon as the meeting was over, Chuck declared, "The church needs a Barmen *Declaration* for today!" As scholars are wont to do, I recommended we give more reflection to this idea and assemble a committee to study it in depth. "No," Chuck retorted, "We have to get to work on this right away!" Immediately, we both thought of our friend Robby George, a devout Catholic scholar and leading public intellectual at Princeton. We joined forces and spent many hours that summer working on the draft of a statement supporting the sanctity of life, the dignity of marriage, and religious freedom for all.

By late September, we were ready to share what emerged with a wider circle of religious leaders, some fifty of whom assembled for a day-long meeting in New York City. On that occasion, someone suggested the document be called *The Manhattan Declaration*, and the name stuck. By November 20, 2009, some 150 Christian leaders enlisted in the cause, and *The Manhattan Declaration* was presented to the public at the National Press Club in Washington. Catholic, Protestant, and Orthodox leaders stood together side-by-side and declared our common commitment to what we believed to be three of the most pressing, and increasingly contested, moral issues of our time: the sanctity of life for every single person including the elderly, the weak, and the pre-born, each of whom is uniquely made in the image of God (*imago Dei*) and is inherently worthy of respect and protection; the historic institution of marriage between one man and one woman, not for the sake of traditionalism but for the flourishing of families and the nurturing of children, an institution which is the cornerstone of society across civilizations; and religious freedom, not only for Christians, but for all persons everywhere, and for religious institutions as well as for individuals, for synagogues, mosques, temples, and churches, and the work they do on behalf of the common good in education and benevolence.

Among my most vivid memories of Chuck Colson are the times I went with him to visit prisoners behind bars. Chuck never forgot he served a Savior who was crucified as a prisoner, one who knew what it was like to be stripped, sentenced, beaten, and mocked. He never forgot Jesus's words: "I was in prison and you visited me." The key issues addressed in *The Manhattan Declaration*, Chuck firmly believed, were directly related to his work for prison reform, restorative justice, and evangelism. Prison

Fellowship is a wonderful worldwide ministry dedicated to serving prisoners and their families. As a former prisoner, Chuck never doubted God called him to this work. But Chuck knew there was a prior concern to be addressed. He asked: "What is broken in our society—in the schools, churches, police system, in our financial and economic structures, in our systems of governance and civic accountability—what is amiss here that results in the incarceration of so many of our sons and daughters?" The answer to this question could not be found in politics alone, as Chuck saw it. The fundamental issue is not political but spiritual. What he advocated was a chastened form of civic virtue based on the fact Christians hold a dual citizenship, one in this world, and the other, as St. Paul said, in heaven (Phil. 3:20).

Over the years, Chuck Colson came to see the close connection between the despair he witnessed firsthand within the prisons and the "culture of death" in society on the outside. He knew genuine reform had to embrace the family, the community, and the church, the "mediating institutions" of society, as well as the state. He came to see the work he did, and continued to do, in the prisons would ultimately fail unless it was undergirded by a robust Christian worldview, an understanding of what we believe and how it applies to our lives.

This perspective was reinforced by the three great intellectual heroes to whom Chuck turned again and again. William Wilberforce was the young member of Parliament who devoted his life to abolishing the slave trade. He refused to divorce his evangelical faith from his public witness. And Abraham Kuyper, the Reformed theologian and Prime Minister of the Netherlands whom Chuck quoted more than anyone else. Kuyper said: "There is not one square inch in the whole domain of our human existence over which Christ, who is sovereign over *all*, does not cry: 'Mine, that belongs to me!'"[2] And there was Dietrich Bonhoeffer, a champion of faith and conscience in one of the darkest moments of human history. Bonhoeffer, a member of the Confessing Church and supporter of the *Barmen Declaration*, preached a gospel of costly grace. He wrote in 1937, "When Christ calls a man, he bids him come and die."[3]

---

[2] Abraham Kuyper, "Sphere Sovereignty," in *Abraham Kuyper: A Centennial Reader*, ed. James D. Bratt (Grand Rapids: Eerdmans, 1998), 488.

[3] Dietrich Bonhoeffer, *Discipleship*, vol. 4 of *Dietrich Bonhoeffer Works* (Minneapolis: Fortress Press, 2003), 87.

The early drafts of *The Manhattan Declaration* did refer to Barmen as a precedent inspiring our concern. But the reference to Barmen was deleted in the final form of *The Manhattan Declaration* for several good reasons. First, we did not make the claim in 2009, nor should we make it today, that our present historical moment is analogous to the repression Jews, Christians, and many others experienced in Hitler's Germany. Second, the *Barmen Declaration* was written and signed by only Protestant (Lutheran and Reformed) Christians, whereas *The Manhattan Declaration* intentionally included Roman Catholic, Evangelical Protestant, and Eastern Orthodox voices. None of us were interested in putting forth an easygoing ecumenism, one that blurs the theological convictions we hold dear. We understood ourselves to be *principled* Protestants, Catholics, and Orthodox believers and nothing we wrote in *The Manhattan Declaration* compromises our cherished confessional beliefs, this despite raucous criticism from some who claimed otherwise. But what we did share in common was massive: the spiritual patrimony of all Christians committed to the historic faith of the early church, expressed in the Trinitarian and Christological consensus of the classic creeds and confessions. What we wanted to say as clearly as we could, with charity and civility, is we discerned in our life together a movement of the Holy Spirit, one propelling us to stand together in a common struggle, to venture what I once called "an ecumenism of the trenches."[4]

Was *The Manhattan Declaration* a partisan political ploy? Some thought so and condemned it as a covert Republican initiative. However, there were Democrats, Republicans, and Independents alike among those who originally embraced *The Manhattan Declaration*. For example, the well-known social activist and pacifist Ronald J. Sider, wrote soon after the *Declaration* was released:

> *People like myself have often been identified as politically "liberal" or "progressive" because of our vigorous advocacy of justice for the poor, racial justice, full equality of women, peacemaking, and care for creation. Vigorously and publicly I continue to take such stands. But I also want to insist that I think it is absolutely crucial for people like myself to stand publicly with those sometimes identified as politically*

---

[4] Timothy George, "Introduction to the First ECT Statement," *First Things*, March 12, 2015, https://www.firstthings.com/web-exclusives/2015/03/introduction-to-the-first-ect-statement.

*"conservative" in order to defend the sanctity of human life, the histor-*
*ical definition of marriage, and religious freedom. This is not a political*
*ploy or a partisan agenda. It flows from a foundational moral commit-*
*ment. Finally, it flows from my confession that Jesus Christ is Lord of all.*
*I am a registered Democrat. But my commitment to Jesus Christ, to a*
*biblically balanced political agenda, and to a consistent ethic of life far*
*transcends any limited political interests.*[5]

Neither Barmen nor Manhattan were "political" statements in the sense of being tied to a particular political party or ideology. What is crucial is both statements refused to say there are areas of life which do not belong to Jesus Christ. Both affirmed the sovereignty of God and the Lordship of Jesus Christ. Both appealed to the authority of Holy Scripture. Each offered quotations from the Bible as the theological basis of its statements.

*The Manhattan Declaration* did not claim the three issues highlighted in its text were the only matters of pressing moral concern in our culture today. Indeed, we clearly recognized many other issues also call for Christian engagement, and we named some of these: care of creation, racial injustice, the proliferation of violence, the blight of poverty and hunger around the world, and a myriad of other human rights causes—from providing clean water in developing nations to providing homes for tens of thousands of children orphaned by war, disease, and gender discrimination.

But we did argue that the three issues of life, marriage, and religious freedom were basic foundational principles of justice and common good. We believed these three issues were inextricably linked and that to sacrifice any one of them would invariably lead to the weakening of the others.

Chuck Colson always hoped *The Manhattan Declaration*, which began as a document, would become a movement, one delivering a palpable effect on the three issues we addressed. To some extent, it did. Within a matter of months, more than 500,000 Christians—Orthodox, Catholic, and Evangelicals—signed *The Manhattan Declaration*. In some areas since then, there has been a forward movement in a good direction. I think of the masses of younger Christians who swarm the National March for Life each year. In others, sadly, there has been a stepping back

---

[5] Ronald Sider, "ePistle 11/18," Evangelicals for Social Action, November 18, 2009.

and loss of concern. After ten years, one thing is certain: the need for the Church of Jesus Christ, and indeed for all people of faith and goodwill, to speak clearly about life, marriage, and religious freedom is greater now than ever. In today's changing political and cultural landscape, the oft-quoted final words of *The Manhattan Declaration* are still operative: "We will fully and ungrudgingly render to Caesar what is Caesar's. But under no circumstances will we render to Caesar what is God's."

At the dawn of the New Year, 1943, just four months before he was arrested by the Gestapo, Dietrich Bonhoeffer addressed a personal letter to some of his closest friends. This letter has been published as *After Ten Years: A Reckoning Made At The New Year 1943*. Bonhoeffer reviewed the events of the past decade, including the fears, hopes, and aspirations, that gripped him and his friends during the turbulent times through which they lived. In one section of this letter, Bonhoeffer asked the question, "Who stands firm?" He answered in words we still need to hear and heed today:

> *Only the one whose ultimate standard is not his reason, his principles, conscience, freedom, or virtue; only the one who has prepared to sacrifice all of these when, in faith and in relationship to God alone, he is called to obedient and responsible action. Such a person is the responsible one, whose life is to be nothing but a response to God's question and call. Where are these responsible ones?*[6]

---

[6] Bonhoeffer, "After Ten Years," in *Letters and Papers from Prison*, vol. 8 of *Dietrich Bonhoeffer Works* (Minneapolis: Fortress Press, 2010), 40.

# Why *The Manhattan Declaration?*[1]

### *Charles W. "Chuck" Colson*

For the past several decades, I have devoted my teaching to a simple proposition: Christianity is more than a religion. And it is more than a personal relationship with Jesus Christ. Christianity is an all-encompassing worldview that shapes how we think and how we live in the world. It couldn't be otherwise.

"In the beginning was the Word," John tells us in the opening of his gospel. "And the word became flesh and dwelt among us." "Word" is the English translation of the Greek *Logos*. And as a translation, "Word" falls far short of the richness and totality of *Logos*. For John, for Greek speakers all the way back to Plato and beyond, *Logos* meant ultimate reality, all that was known or could be known, the glue that holds the universe together.

So, Christ is more than a founder of a religion. He is more than my personal savior (and I thank God every day that He is). He is the *Logos*. And if that's true, then, the brilliant Dutch politician and theologian Abraham Kuyper was right when he proclaimed, "In the total expanse of human life there is not a single square inch of which the Christ, who alone is sovereign, does not declare, 'That is mine!'"

If Christ cries out "Mine" about every aspect of life: Medicine, music, literature, science, family, law, politics, then we, the church, when we look at every aspect of life, must cry out "HIS!"

---

[1] This presentation by Chuck Colson originally appeared as the Foreword for the publication of *The Manhattan Declaration* (Stokesdale, NC: Life Books, 2010)

So, our duty is to bring Christ's truth to bear on every aspect of life. And at no time in my life do I remember a time when it was so important to do so.

What we are witnessing today in America is a titanic struggle between two antithetical worldviews: Secular naturalism and Christianity. The one side holds there is no God, that we humans are nothing but a complex amalgamation of atoms—glorified germs whose ancestors arose from the primordial soup. The other holds that God created the universe, His physical and moral laws are observable and knowable, and He created man in His image—endowing man with a sacred dignity and free will.

We see this struggle all around us. In the classroom, the courtroom, and on Capitol Hill. If man is nothing special, then why not abortion, why not cloning, why not experiment with human embryos? If there is no moral law, no ultimate truth, why not same-sex marriage, why not enshrine individual preference as the ultimate arbiter of human conduct, why not borrow money you can't repay—who cares how it might affect others?

This is why, last September, sixty Protestant, Catholic, and Orthodox leaders gathered in New York to fine-tune one of the finest expressions of Christian worldview I have ever seen: *The Manhattan Declaration*.

*The Manhattan Declaration*, grounded in scripture and the creeds all Christians confess, is a clarion call to conscience, a wake-up call to the church. And it deals with the three most crucial moral issues facing our nation and the church today: The sanctity of human life, marriage between one man and one woman, and the importance of religious freedom, or freedom of conscience.

The response has been phenomenal. I would not have imagined that within three short months, more than 500,000 people from every Christian denomination would sign the *Declaration*.

I have been asked by many, however, why it is the *Declaration* focuses on these three issues? What about other pressing issues? Social justice? The Environment? Others? My answer is these three issues are so foundational, so critical, every other Christian, indeed human, concern flows out of them.

First and foremost is human dignity. For thirty-four years I've gone into America's prisons to witness to the most marginalized among us, precisely because I believe every human being is made in God's image. When

I walk through the vile-smelling cell blocks, I don't see tattooed inmates; I see beautiful people, made in the image of God—the very people for whom Christ died on the cross.

It's that very understanding of the sacredness of all human life that sends me into the prisons. It's the belief in the sacredness of human life that led the early church to fight the Roman practice of infanticide and abortion; that put Christians in the forefront of fighting slavery, of promoting civil rights, and today, fighting human trafficking across the globe.

The sanctity of human life is the foundation of true social justice. It's the same with marriage between one man and one woman. As *The Manhattan Declaration* proclaims, "Marriage…is the first institution of human society—indeed it is the institution on which all other human institutions have their foundation."

And even though marriage is more honored in the breach than in observance today, it remains the bedrock institution no society can survive without. Again, *The Manhattan Declaration* speaks clearly:

> *Vast human experience confirms that marriage is the original and most important institution for sustaining the health, education, and welfare of all persons in a society. Where marriage is honored, and where there is a flourishing marriage culture, everyone benefits—the spouses, their children, the communities and societies in which they live. Where the marriage culture begins to erode, social pathologies of every sort quickly manifest themselves.*

Is it any wonder that more than 60 percent of our nation's prisoners grew up in households without a father? The statistics only confirm what I've seen inside our nation's prisons. I can't begin to count the number of men behind bars who have told me about their childhoods—and the fact they come from broken homes, with no dad. So, they find male role models in the gangs.

The third foundational issue is religious freedom, or freedom of conscience. American Christians can no longer ignore the fact this "first freedom" enshrined in the Bill of Rights is under assault. We see it in the news every day, whether it's a Methodist camp losing its tax-exempt status because it refused to allow a same-sex marriage ceremony, or Congress's steadfast refusal to protect the religious freedom of medical providers in the current spate of health-care "reform" bills.

Is the day coming when a Baptist daycare center could be forced to hire homosexuals? Or a Catholic adoption agency being driven out of business because it refuses to place orphaned children with same-sex couples? Well, the latter has already happened. And more is coming unless the church speaks out.

This is no time for the Church to step away from the fray, hiding behind the excuse we should "not get involved in politics." But while these are in one sense political issues, they are first and foremost profoundly moral issues that affect the common good. We neither love God nor our neighbor if we sit idly by as human dignity, traditional marriage, and religious freedom come under attack. And that is why I am so excited about *The Manhattan Declaration*. Never, in my lifetime at least, have Christians from all denominations come together to forcefully proclaim "Here we stand!"

Are you willing to join us in the closing affirmation of *The Manhattan Declaration*? "We will fully and ungrudgingly render to Caesar what is Caesar's, but under no circumstances will we render to Caesar what is God's."

# PART ONE

# Life

# Life is the Greatest Human Right

*Randy Alcorn*

The moral fabric of American society is woven around a premise stated in the *Declaration of Independence*: "We hold these truths to be self-evident, that all men are created equal, that they are endowed by their Creator with certain unalienable rights, that among these are life, liberty and the pursuit of happiness." Regrettably, some of the signers of the *Declaration of Independence* marginalized women and racial minorities. However, the notion of *all* human beings made equal by God was eventually reflected in our laws.

"We hold these truths to be self-evident" affirms that certain truths are so basic, so foundational we *must* hold to them if this country is to endure. The logical progression is since all people are created equal, there are God-given rights we are not free to ignore. The first most basic right is the right to life. For if someone's life is taken, it is impossible to exercise their rights to liberty or to pursue happiness.

The three most consequential moral human rights issues in American history each hinged on understanding what "all men are created equal" means. The first question: Does "all men" mean only the white race, or does it include blacks and other minorities? The second question: Does "all men" mean only males, or does it include females? Laws changed as our nation came to a correct answer to these questions. But the third question has every bit as much moral significance as the first two: Does "all men" mean only the bigger and older, or does it include preborn children, our littlest boys and girls?

*Without the right to life, there cannot be any other rights.* An aborted female child will never have any rights as a female. An aborted black child will never have any rights as a black person. No aborted child will ever have personal or civil or gender or ethnic rights of any kind.

The claim that abortion is a civil rights issue for women is one of the greatest ironies of the "pro-choice" movement. Abortion takes away the most basic right any person can have: the right to live. If anything ever warranted restatement it is this: once anyone's right to life is violated, no other rights can be upheld.

In her book *When Is It Right to Die?* Joni Eareckson Tada says, "True rights are based in God's moral law. Proverbs 31:8–9 reads, 'Open your mouth for the mute, for the rights of all who are destitute. Open your mouth, judge righteously, defend the rights of the poor and needy.' But take God out of the picture, and rights become nothing more than people's willful determinations dressed up in the language of 'rights' to give them a showy kind of dignity. Then the exercise of rights becomes nothing more than a national competition between who is more victimized than whom."[1] For all citizens of all countries, defending life from conception to death should take precedence, but for Christ-followers this is grounded in something far more authoritative than the *Declaration of Independence*, it is grounded in the inspired Word of God.

## What Scripture Says About Life

My home state of Oregon, which I love in many ways, became in 1997 the first jurisdiction in human history to legalize physician-assisted suicide. At that time, even the Netherlands, which commonly practiced it, and Nazi Germany, which practiced it in its involuntary form, were not so bold as to legalize it (though the Netherlands eventually did in 2001).

Oregon is also a state where unborn babies have been legally killed since 1969, four years before *Roe v. Wade*. In fact, every taxpayer in Oregon, including every pro-life taxpayer, helps pay for state-funded abortions. A 2018 ballot measure forbidding taxpayer funding to take the lives of the unborn, unless necessary to save the mother's life, was voted down by a nearly two-thirds majority. Many Christians in 1973 (including me as

---

[1] Joni Eareckson Tada, *When Is It Right to Die?* (Grand Rapids, MI: Zondervan, 2018), 71.

4

an eighteen-year-old) were nowhere to be found opposing abortion in 1973. Likewise, in Oregon we allowed physician-assisted suicide ballot measures to pass in 1994 and 1997. Sadly, many Christians—I had conversations with some of them—actually voted for it. Fast-forward twenty years and consider the issues facing our society today. Never has it been more important for believers to understand what God's Word says about human life and our responsibility to defend it from beginning to end.

Scripture teaches God created all life, maintains all life, and rules over all life. Except in instances where God delegates His authority over life to men (e.g. capital punishment in Genesis 9:3,6), the prerogative to take life is God's and His alone: "See now that I, even I, am he, and there is no god beside me; I kill and I make alive; I wound and I heal; and there is none that can deliver out of my hand" (Deut. 32:39). He warns us, "You shall not murder" (Matt. 19:18) (See also Gen. 2:7; Deut. 8:3; 30:20; I Sam. 2:6; Job 27:3; Ps. 30:3; 104:30; Eccles. 12:7; Isa. 38:16; Acts 17:25,28; Rom. 4:17; I Tim. 6:13; James 4:15).

Human life is unique and preeminent in all of God's creation. We are made in God's image, and our life is so valuable in God's sight that God made the ultimate sacrifice to provide eternal life for us (Gen. 1:27; John 3:14-16). Our worth is determined not by mental or physical capacities, or tangible contribution to society, but by our intrinsic God-given nature.

## Defending Life at Its Beginning

As the climax of God's creation, Scripture proclaims mankind's intrinsic worth—far greater than any animal placed under his care. God endows us with personhood at the moment of creation, which is the moment of conception, before which there was not a human being and after which there is. Scripture teaches the psychosomatic unity of the whole person: body, soul, and spirit (1 Thess. 5:23). Wherever there is a genetically distinct living human being, there is a living spirit.

Rocks and trees and animals and human organs do not have moral natures, good or bad. Morality can be ascribed only to a person. As a member of the human race, each person sinned "in Adam," and is therefore a sinner from his very beginning (Rom. 5:12–19).

David says, "Behold, I was brought forth in iniquity." Then he goes back even further, to the actual beginning of his life, saying "and in sin did my mother conceive me" (Ps. 51:5). *Each person has a sinful nature from the point of conception.* This demonstrates there is a person present, for who but an actual person can have a sinful nature?

The Hebrew word used in the Old Testament to refer to the unborn (Ex. 2 1:22–25) is *yeled,* a word that "generally indicates young children, but may refer to teens or even young adults."[2] Hebrews did not have or need a separate word for unborn children. They were just like any other children, only younger. In the Bible there is no such thing as a potential or "almost" child.

When Rebekah was pregnant with Jacob and Esau, Scripture says, "The children struggled together within her" (Gen. 25:22). Jacob was given prominence over his twin Esau "though they were not born yet" (Romans 9:11). The unborn are regarded as "babies" in the full sense of the word. God tells Jeremiah, "Before I formed you in the womb, I knew you" (Jer. 1:5). He could not know Jeremiah in his mother's womb unless Jeremiah, the person, was present. The Creator is involved in an intimate, knowing relationship not only with born people, but also with unborn people.

"Thus says the Lord who made you, who formed you from the womb and will help you…" (Isa. 44:2). What each person is, not merely what he or she might become, is present in their mother's womb. Psalms 139:13–16 depict God's involvement with each preborn person. God created David's "inward parts," not at birth, but before birth. David says to his Creator, "You knitted me together in my mother's womb" (v. 13). Each person is not manufactured on a cosmic assembly line, but personally formed by God from the point of conception. All the days of his life have been planned out by God before any have come to be.

In Luke 1 there are references to the unborn John the Baptist, including his responding to the presence of the preborn Jesus in His mother Mary (v. 41). The word translated *baby* in these verses is the Greek word *brephos*. It's the same word used for the already born baby Jesus (Luke 2:12, 16) and for the babies brought to Jesus to receive His blessing (Luke 18:15–17). It's also the same word used in Acts 7:19 for the newborn babies killed by Pharaoh. To the writers of the New Testament, like the Old, whether born or unborn, a baby is simply a baby.

---

[2] Lawrence O. Richards, *Expository Dictionary of Bible Words* (Grand Rapids, MI: Zondervan Publishing House, 1985), 156–7.

The Bible is very clear: every child in the womb is created by God. Furthermore, Christ loves that child and proved it by becoming like him—He spent nine months in His own mother's womb. Finally, Christ died for that child, showing how precious He considers him to be.

Christ's disciples failed to understand how valuable children were to Him and they rebuked those who tried to bring them near Him (Luke 18:15–17). But Jesus called the children to Him and said, "Let the little children come to me, and do not hinder them, for the kingdom of God belongs to such as these." He did not consider attention to children a distraction from His kingdom business, but an integral part of it.

God says children are a blessing and gift (Ps. 127:3–5). Society treats children more and more as liabilities. We must learn to see children as God does. King Jesus will say to us, "Truly, I say to you, as you did it to one of the least of these my brothers, you did it to me" (Matt. 25:40). As we intervene on behalf of His littlest children, we should realize it is Christ for whom we intervene. But we must also come to terms with what else he said: "Truly, I say to you, as you did not do it to one of the least of these, you did not do it to me" (v. 45).

## Human Rights and Abortion

As Christians, we should oppose abortion because it destroys a human life. It thereby violates God's explicit command "You shall not murder" (Ex. 20:13). Regardless of personal religious beliefs, however, we should all publicly oppose abortion for the same reason we oppose slavery and rape—*it is a fundamental violation of human rights.*

An Oregon abortionist said, "Not everybody is meant to be born. I believe, for a baby, life begins when his mother wants him." So, a human life becomes real only when and if a specific person values it? Imagine the implications of that philosophy if it were applied to teenagers, spouses, the elderly, the disabled, or racial minorities. How many women have been unwanted by their husbands? Does this make them less human? Is it right for their rights be violated because they are unwanted?

The Fourteenth Amendment says the state shall not deprive any person of life without due process of law. When that was written, the word *human* was a synonym for *person* and could just as easily have been used. The Supreme Court admitted in *Roe v. Wade:* "If the suggestion of personhood [of the unborn] is established, the appellant's [pro-abortion] case, of course, collapses, for the fetus's right to life is then guaranteed specifically by the [fourteenth] amendment."[3]

To solve this problem, the court chose to abandon the historic meaning of personhood. In years following, a long series of subjective and artificial distinctions have been made by pro-choice advocates to differentiate between *humans* and *persons*.

Changing the meaning of words doesn't change reality. The only objective questions we can ask are these:

*Is it human; that is, did it come from human beings?*
*Is it a genetically unique individual?*
*Is it alive and growing?*

If the answers are *yes*, then "it" is in fact a "he" or "she," a living person, who possesses rights and constitutionally and morally deserves legal protection.

In the *New York Times,* pro-choice writer Barbara Ehrenreich said, "A woman may think of her fetus as a person or as just cells depending on whether the pregnancy is wanted or not. This does not reflect moral confusion, but choice in action."[4]

This Alice-in-Wonderland approach says a woman's choice is not made in light of scientific and moral realities. Instead, her choice is the only important reality, overshadowing all matters of *fact*. If society generally operated this way, we could justify every killing any time. The real issue would not be the worth of the person killed, but the free choice of the one doing the killing. The article went on to say, "Moreover, a woman may think of the fetus as a person and still find it necessary and morally responsible to have an abortion."[5] This logical conclusion, if carried out in our society, *would ultimately mean the end of all human rights and social justice.* The old arguments that the fetus is just a lump of flesh have been replaced by "This may be a human child, but I still feel good about killing her." (Remember, over half the children who are killed by abortion are females, who have all their rights taken from them.)

---

[3] *Roe v. Wade*, 410 U.S. (1973).

[4] Cited by John Leo in "The Moral Complexity of Choice," *U.S. News & World Report*, 11 December 1989, 64.

[5] C. Everett Koop, Action Line: Christian Action Council Newsletter 9, no. 5 (July 12, 1985), 3.

## Defending Life at Its End

In 1985, after abortion became part of the American way of life, Surgeon General C. Everett Koop publicly stated his fear that as the right to life was taken away from our youngest, eventually it would be taken from our oldest. He predicted mandatory euthanasia would eventually result from the unwillingness of the younger generation to support the elderly. A Bloomington, Indiana baby with Down syndrome, widely called "Baby Doe," was denied routine lifesaving surgery by his parents, knowing it would result in the baby's death, which it did. Koop said, "My fear is that one day for every Baby Doe in America, there will be ten thousand Grandma Does."[6]

If we follow abortion to its inescapable conclusions, we'll have a society in which the powerful, for their own self-interest, determine which human beings will live and which will die. We're already seeing that with the "right to die" movement across the U.S., which opens the door for euthanizing those deemed undesirable. If the powerful can strip legal rights from the very young, should it surprise us to see them strip rights from the very old, sick, weak, and "useless?"

But as Creator and Sovereign, God alone has the prerogative of giving and taking human life. Active euthanasia usurps that prerogative. In its voluntary form it is suicide; in its involuntary form it is murder.

The Bible teaches us to honor and respect the elderly (Lev. 19:32, Prov. 20:29, 1 Tim. 5:1) and care for the weak and needy (Ps. 82:3-4, Isa. 1:17, Prov. 24:11-12). Therefore, God hates not only direct life-taking acts but neglect and withholding basic human care, such as food and water. (He holds us responsible not only for acts of commission, but omission.)

Certainly, there's a time to evaluate whether measures beyond basic care are wise in terminal cases. We are not morally obligated to use every possible means of medicine and technology to prolong indefinitely a life naturally nearing its end. That decision is ideally made in concert with the patient, family, doctors, and spiritual advisors. Allowing a death can be very different than taking a life.

In 1981, my mom was dying of a rapidly growing cancer. Eventually, she lost consciousness. The doctors said performing a difficult surgery

---

[6] C. Everett Koop, Action Line: Christian Action Council Newsletter 9, no. 5 (July 12, 1985), 3.

might add an extra month or two to her life, but it would certainly make her remaining life more miserable. It seemed clear it would be cruel to prolong her life, at the cost of unnecessary pain, when there was no hope of her survival. Especially considering the alternative was her going to be with Christ. I believe just as we can play God by taking a life prematurely, we can also play God by extending a life that has reached its end.

However, many people have succumbed to the temptation of prematurely withholding reasonable and possibly effective life-sustaining measures. They have withdrawn care from relatives because of the costs of time, energy, and money. When the patient can no longer participate in such decisions, the potential for abuse naturally increases. "The right to die" easily becomes the right for others to kill.

## Defending Life Is Our Main Business

What place do life issues have to Christians? Are they merely peripheral matters distracting the church from its main business? No. The defense of life is at the heart of the Great Commandment, which includes both loving God and loving our neighbors.

Loving God *cannot* be separated from loving our neighbor (Matt. 22:34–40). To a man who wished to define "neighbor" in a way to exclude certain groups of needy people, Christ presented the Good Samaritan, who went out of his way to help an injured man, as a model for our behavior (Luke 10:25–37). In contrast, the religious hypocrites looked the other way because they had more "spiritual" things to do.

In His Great Commission, Jesus didn't tell us only to evangelize. He told us to be "teaching them to observe all that I have commanded you" (Matt. 28:20). Jesus commanded us to be compassionate and to take sacrificial action for the weak and helpless. If we fail to do this—and if we fail by our words and example to teach others to do this—*then we fail to fulfill the Great Commission*. We show the world and the church our words about the gospel are only that—words.

Let me close with a personal story to illustrate the importance of Christians prioritizing the defense of life. In 1991, my eighty-four-year-old father, who was not yet a Christian, began contemplating suicide. He was resistant to the gospel and when I wrote him a letter detailing the biblical plan of salvation he was offended. A proud and independent man, he faced increasing mental and physical difficulties. Where once he found significance in hard work, he experienced the ravages and indignities of old age.

My father read with approval the accounts of Dr. Kevorkian and his suicide machine, which several sick or elderly people used to take their lives. Dad posted on his walls various newspaper clippings about death with dignity. I later discovered he actually approached several physicians, asking them if they would give him a lethal injection or some other means to painlessly take his life. A few were sympathetic but refused to violate the law.

As a resident of Washington State, Dad had high hopes that a November 1991 ballot measure legalizing physician-assisted euthanasia would succeed. It came very close but did not pass. Dad was disappointed because he was ready to take advantage of that law the moment it was put into effect.

Though I did not know the extent of his plans, on the one occasion my father spoke of suicide with me, I shared with him some of the same principles of Scripture I've shared here. I reaffirmed my love and my family's and offered to help him in any way that conformed to God's principles. Because he did not know Christ and was exposed to pro-euthanasia literature and movies, the biblical principles prohibiting active euthanasia didn't make sense to him.

One day my father called me to say "Goodbye." Two days earlier, he said, he'd been diagnosed with prostate cancer. That day he was unable to urinate and was convinced he was going to die a painful death. When he called me, he had a loaded gun ready to end his life. I begged him to wait while I made the thirty-minute drive. After running a few red lights, I pulled up to his house, jumped out, and knocked on the door. No answer. I opened it. On the floor were two guns. I called "Dad!" Still no answer. Holding my breath, I walked into the other room, and he bumped into me, disoriented but still alive.

I rushed dad to the hospital, where the doctor relieved his immediate problem with a catheter, and scheduled surgery for the next morning. Though Dad previously resisted me every time I'd shared the gospel with him over the years, in his desperation he now listened. I read Scripture and prayed.

The next morning before he went into surgery, I walked my Dad through the gospel one more time. Knowing full well the answer, I asked him, "Dad, have you ever confessed your sins to God and accepted Jesus Christ as your Lord and Savior?" He said, "No, I haven't," then after a pause added, "but I think it's about time I did." I had the joy of hearing my eighty-four-year-old father pray, confess his sins, and give his life to Christ. God then gave me five more precious years with my dad.

The issue of there coming a time to allow a loved one's death became personal when my mom was dying. The issue of helping take someone's life became just as personal because of my dad. Had one of those doctors "helped" my father in his desperation, or had voters in Washington passed that narrowly defeated law legalizing physician-assisted suicide, I have no doubt whatsoever my father would have ended his life and gone into a Christless eternity. So much for "mercy killing."

To this day I thank God for the Christians in the state of Washington who worked hard to defeat that ballot measure, realizing what was at stake—not just legislation but lives; not just politics, but *people*. People God created. People for whom Christ died. People God has a purpose for and over whose lives and deaths He alone has the prerogatives. (Unfortunately, in 2008 Washington voters joined Oregonians in legalizing physician-assisted euthanasia.)

When people are in pain, they need us to reach out, help, and remind them of their value. They don't need us to pass them a pill and wave goodbye. I have several friends who work as chaplains in care centers and have led many people to Christ in their final weeks. If they'd had a society-approved way to end their lives earlier, many of these people would have. Where would they be now?

The sanctity of life issue isn't just about unborn babies. It's about toddlers, teenagers, young adults, the middle aged, and the elderly. It's about the healthy and the unhealthy, the disabled, and Olympic athletes. It's about all of us. But first and foremost, it is about our Creator, who made all of us and granted us—and everyone else—the right to life.

# Why Life at All Stages Belongs
# to God, Not the State

*Russell Moore and Andrew Walker*

## Charlie Gard and Alfie Evans

These are names you might vaguely recall, but by now could have easily forgotten. In 2017 and 2018, respectively, these infant boys became the focus of worldwide attention. Their cases shocked a global audience and put focus on the clash between parental rights and the authority of the state to make life-saving or life-ending medical decisions on behalf of its citizens.

Gard was born with a rare genetic disorder known to attack the brain leading to incapacitation. Evans likewise suffered from a degenerative neurological condition. In both tragic cases, where survival seemed unlikely, the sentence of death was hastened by the power of the state.

Over days and weeks, the world looked on in dramatic tumult as news stories broke telling of the legal tussle between the parents of these infant boys and the state's determination that the quality of life and the prospect of suffering meant life-sustaining measures should be withdrawn.

In each of these cases, the state prohibited the parents from taking their infant boys to foreign countries for treatment voluntarily offered. And, in each of these cases, the state overrode the wishes of the parents who sought to prolong the boys' lives, deeming them better ended than prolonged. The state did not favor their death or look on with cruel disinterest. However, it did assume the role of arbiter in deciding a patient's fate.

13

The response and outcries by a watching world—drawing the attention even of Pope Francis—were, of course, correct. Even hardened secularists expressed doubt the state could so wantonly deny every measure to extend their young lives, especially against the wishes of the parents. The problem is the outcry did not go far enough. As tragic as the deaths of Charlie Gard and Alphie Evans were, they are but two vivid examples of the state's larger hostility and subversion of human life and human flourishing in other spheres as well. The cases of Charlie Gard and Alphie Evans serve as a reminder about the vigilance required when it comes to the state interfering in questions of life and human dignity.

In this chapter, we look at a few contemporary issues—abortion, euthanasia, In Vitro Fertilization, and conflicts over gender—highlighting the contemporary clash of orthodoxies between a Christian vision for human dignity and human flourishing and the state's undermining of said vision. It's important to note, however, that there are all sorts of challenges to human dignity in contemporary society. From issues of racial reconciliation, technology, immigration, family structure, opioid addiction, sex trafficking, bio-medical engineering, and other areas, a consistent human dignity ethic is facing tremendous challenge in our society. No society can hope to have a broad concept of human dignity and neglect these areas. We wish to draw readers' attention to these larger cultural issues as well, while focusing more intentionally in this chapter on those areas where *The Manhattan Declaration* originally focused, and those areas where the culture today, in conjunction with state, are threatening human dignity.

It's our conviction that ten years after its initial release, *The Manhattan Declaration*'s call for Christians to "proclaim the Gospel of costly grace, to protect the intrinsic dignity of the human person and to stand for the common good" remains just as urgent; and for the same reason ten years later, new controversies in the public domain require an ever-vigilant Christian response. This vigilance is done for the sake of our neighbor, for the proper stewardship of the common good, and for God's glory to redound upon the earth. As we'll argue, Christian discipleship in a secular age entails establishing guardrails and moral ecologies that help the state understand its obligation to protect and ennoble human personhood.

## A Christian View of Humanity

To begin, a Christian vision of the human person begins with the reality that all persons are made in God's image (Gen. 1:26-27) and personally and intimately known by the sovereign God who created them (Ps. 139:14-16). This oft-cited reference unlocks the mystery of human dignity. The idea that every person is made in God's image birthed the revolutionary idea that people possess intrinsic worth, value, and dignity. In the Christian paradigm, dignity cannot be added to or subtracted from the person because the quality of dignity is given by God. The concept of dignity revolutionized the status of the person before both law and the state.

Because God ordered this universe and endowed humanity with consciences, all persons have some working concept of human dignity, even if inconsistently applied and the foundation not explicitly acknowledged. For example, in the United Nation's Universal *Declaration* of Human Rights, "dignity" is mentioned five times without any explicit definition.[1] Moreover, if "human dignity" can be touted by the United Nations while at the same time it promotes unfettered abortion access as an extension of human rights, "human dignity" left exclusively to the provinces of international courts or liberal democracy is unstable. Whether one calls this dignity instinct "natural law" or "general revelation," it accords with reason and experience to treat fellow humans justly and humanely. It's obvious, though, that "dignity" serves as a starting point for human reason's attempt to ascribe significance to the human person. Christians should work with all people of goodwill to encourage this conversation in every arena available.

In contrast to the speculative debates of history's philosophers, Christianity's account of creation provides an anchor to dignity. According to the Christian tradition, the human person is endowed with moral agency, rationality, and freedom. In the void left by secular reason's attempt to provide a fixed, stable definition of dignity and personhood, Christianity—anchored in scriptural authority and witnessed to by both tradition and reason—offers a more robust ethic of human dignity and personhood, insisting the value of a person is not bestowed by the state, but by God. Because God retains ultimate authority over the human person,

---

[1] *Universal Declaration of Human Rights*, United Nations, available at: http://www.un.org/en/universal-declaration-human-rights/

who is a unique creation of God, any authority the state would claim for itself is a derived, penultimate authority.

Furthermore, image-bearing is not impersonal, but relational. All persons are made through and for God's divine *Logos*, Jesus Christ (Ps. 100:3; John 1:3; 1 Cor. 8:6; Col. 1: 16-17). In Christ, all persons find their ultimate foundation and ultimate apex. No greater reality faces the human person than being in intimate relationship with the Triune God who called them into being. As creator and sustainer, each person's existence and creative agency is owed to Jesus Christ. Ultimately, a Christ-centered view of the human person and their dignity means a person's worth and status is given to them by God and not meted out by the state.

## An Ethical Framework for Christian Anthropology

When asked whether it was lawful to pay taxes to Caesar, Jesus famously replied it was lawful to "render to Caesar the things that are Caesar's, and to God the things that are God's" (Matt. 22:21). This exchange has long been looked to by theologians and biblical scholars as a foundational passage for legitimizing and limiting certain demands the state can require of its citizens. The state does not own or control the human person. The state cannot tell you who to worship or who to marry, but because the state does possess authority to administer law and require its citizens to obey just laws, it can require you to pay taxes and honor contracts (Rom. 13:1-7). The key distinction is the state's jurisdiction is limited only to the areas involving social cooperation. The idea of a limited state means the freedom and dignity humans possess is not a subsidy given to him or her by the state. All of life is lived before God—*coram Deo*—"in the presence of God, under the authority of God, to the glory of God."[2] This means an ultimate foundation for legitimate state power begins with the state recognizing its limits.

Before getting to the specific issues, it's important to establish an ethical framework to guide our thinking about the relationship of the person to the state in the remaining chapter.[3] All the following axioms flow from the previous section and will be the matrix to evaluate contemporary

---

[2] R. C. Sproul, "What Does 'coram Deo' Mean?" *Ligonier*, November 13, 2017, available at: https://www.ligonier.org/blog/what-does-coram-deo-mean/

[3] We're grateful for Alex Ward's assistance in this chapter.

conflicts related to life and the state. *(1) Life belongs to God and not the state because God is the sovereign Creator of life, while the state's role in adjudicating and negotiating human affairs is derived.* This axiom simply re-states the truths mentioned above: The state does not write the metaphysical rules governing it; it looks to the law written on the heart and is duty-bound to craft laws that understand life is ordered toward God (Rom. 2:14-15). *(2) Because God is the creator of life, human rights precede the state's authority and are recognized by the state as it protects the God-given integrity and dignity of life at all stages.* Human rights originate when the state understands the human person possesses obligations preceding the state's authority. Any doctrine of human rights requires the state to understand its authority is limited. The right to life, speech, and conscience spring from the reality the state does not have unchecked authority over such spheres. *(3) The State has an obligation to protect life from the moment of conception to natural death.* Since life is ultimately a gift of God, the state has no authority to dictate its beginning or its unjust termination. *(4) The State should promote a view of human dignity oriented to human flourishing as evidenced in general and special revelation.* God has assigned to the conscience the ability to respond to general revelation such that the conscience, typically, can discern right from wrong. The state should therefore pass laws that materially cooperate toward humanity's flourishing. *(5) The state's authority over human life is circumscribed to the just use of the sword for punishing evildoers and ordering society for promoting justice for the sake of the common good.* The Christian ethical tradition has allowed for the use of retributive violence against persons only in circumstances where a threat to the common good is posed. *(6) When the State transgresses biblical anthropology and human dignity by wrongly eliminating life or advancing laws that unjustly tamper with human life, Christians have a moral duty to prophetically denounce such actions and in instances of last resort, to resist such laws.* Where the state passes laws tampering with, terminating, or subverting human life, Christian duty results in denouncing such laws as unjust and working to see justice restored.

Given the above axioms, let's now evaluate where contemporary issues relating to the sanctity and dignity of life conflict with laws passed by the state. In the topics below, it is worth noting that in each case, human dignity as a theoretical concept is tampered with or threatened resulting in bodily harm.

## Abortion

Ten years after the release of *The Manhattan Declaration*, tragically, America's abortion regime shows few signs of lessening its diabolical grip on America. The tragedy of abortion has had an outsized focus in American culture for nearly fifty years. Since 1973, sixty million lives have been sacrificed on the altar of personal convenience and sexual revolution. America's Holocaust enjoys the comfort of political correctness and highly-funded political campaigns jockeying for its continued legality.

From start to finish, abortion implicates and violates all the ethical axioms above. No issue more gravely highlights the conflict between state authority and God's authority than abortion. To put the issue in the starkest moral terms, in America, a positive legal right and legal infrastructure exists making possible the targeted extermination of a class of voiceless, vulnerable persons—the unborn. Innocent persons' blood is being shed in a heinous violation of human rights and insurrection against the Creator of the universe who decrees all life. The state's willingness to countenance abortion is a scourge on it, and no nation can pretend to stand for moral righteousness when injustice of this magnitude is not only sanctioned but celebrated. Hastening innocent death, the state is promoting the destruction of human life in furtherance of a culture whose faux-priority for human dignity is trumped by sexual autonomy.

If one of the state's obligations is to "punish those who do evil and to praise those who do good," (1 Peter 2:14) then the state's commitment to abortion completely inverts the purpose of true and proper government. Abortion violates not only biblical law, but it is an assault on the very nature of reason itself. A commitment to allowing the innocent to be killed soils the nation's character. In the case of abortion, the state finds itself committing the error of calling what is evil "good":

> *Woe to those who call evil good*
> *and good evil,*
> *who put darkness for light*
> *and light for darkness,*
> *who put bitter for sweet*
> *and sweet for bitter! (Isa. 5: 20)*

LIFE

Abortion is an unbiblical power grab. There is no greater usurpation of God's authority than the state putting itself in the role of making the death of the unborn a so-called "right." Christians must give no sanction or quarter to America's abortion regime. It is the greatest stain on America's history, and Christian civic duty requires a vigilant and proactive hastening of abortion's end through the democratic process. Recent actions in the states of New York and Virginia underscore this reality.

The reality that patently unjust laws exist around abortion demonstrates why there must be urgency in how we triage compared to other social evils.

While it is prudent to want to see abortion reduced, it is urgent it be abolished. At stake is the reality that the American legal regime has in place legal mechanisms allowing the targeted extermination of a class of vulnerable people. If another issue is substituted for abortion, the idea of merely "reducing" falls apart. No one talks about merely "reducing" sex trafficking, for example. People want it outlawed and criminalized. It is incoherent to say, "Let's not criminalize murder; let's just make it so people do not want to murder."

Our fear is we soft-peddle our language on abortion because we've grown accustomed to it and are content to "reduce" instead of abolish. However, this perspective ignores the crushing moral reality and injustice of abortion. Jim Crow laws should not have occurred, and they should have been eliminated, not "reduced." Laws subjugating and dehumanizing human beings need to be categorically overturned and put into the dustbin of history.

While Christians work on both fronts, there's greater moral urgency to repeal morally unjust laws than to ameliorate social evils that exist because of human wickedness and criminal behavior. The difference between abortion and sex trafficking (both abhorrent practices to be ended) is with the latter, no legal framework in America makes sex trafficking a positive right. There is no bad law to undo. There's simply injustice and criminal behavior needing to be policed. But with abortion, there is. In America, there is a positive right to terminate the life of a child. This is wicked, and the fact American law enables this grisly practice is a reproach on our country. Sex trafficking is an injustice without legal support. Abortion, on the other hand, is an injustice with legal sanction, and for that reason, is of primary urgency in combatting.

19

## Euthanasia

Physician-assisted suicide and euthanasia laws are slowly creeping across the American landscape. At present, six states and Washington, D.C. have some form of law on the books making possible what is euphemistically-labeled "medical-assistance-in-dying."

Framed as a compassionate alternative for those staring down the future of a terminable disease, the "rights" regime attending to American democracy is now offering a "right to die" as a solution to suffering.

Opponents of the practice warn that going down a path of state-sanctioned suicide will have unintended and inhumane consequences. Political communities permitting euthanasia tend toward ever-greater expansion of the practice. Indeed, states going down the path of euthanasia have a difficult time limiting its eligibility criteria over time. If autonomy and the elimination of suffering is the measure of its application, what is the limiting principle preventing some people's experiences from justifying euthanasia?

The introduction of euthanasia into public policy brings with it a new regime of calculations not previously considered. Why? Because the dignity and inviolability of life is no longer the assumed default. The presumption of life undergirding the philosophy of medicine is slowly being upended. This has enormous repercussions on questions related to human dignity, autonomy, and the purpose of medicine. It naturally follows that once euthanasia is permitted, insurance companies will take such legalities into consideration.

As potentially insensitive as it might sound, the implications of one person's suffering pales in comparison to how the morality of euthanasia impacts society's broader understanding of suffering and the response to it. We do not mean to overlook or disregard genuine human suffering when we point out the repercussions of legalizing and medicalizing the taking of human life. Slowly, the culture of death overtakes commitment to the sanctity and preservation of life. Such a culture promises pain and suffering can be eliminated by suicide, while overlooking the deeply human experience that comes with suffering. It makes a Faustian bargain on the assumption that one person's death by choice will not have implications for the weak and vulnerable across society. Death is thereby subtly invited, even encouraged. There are better ethical responses to suffering than suicide.

Less outrightly egregious than abortion, euthanasia and physician-assisted suicide still violate many of the above axioms by putting the positive right to end one's life within the purview of state law. The state is designed to protect the flourishing of life, not establish a legal infrastructure incentivizing individuals to take their own lives under the ghoulish pretense of autonomy. Moreover, by sanctioning suicide, the state cheapens the dignity of human life and the moral ecology of the surrounding culture. God is the author of life; humans are not self-sovereigns. Because we owe our life to God, we owe the entirety of our lives—even their end—to His sovereignty. Rather than promoting laws that dignify human life, euthanasia does the exact opposite.

## In Vitro Fertilization (IVF)

The practice of IVF is used often when prolonged infertility plagues married couples. The desire for children should be praised, and the corresponding childlessness should be grieved. All throughout Scripture, barrenness is a source of great grief and shame. The Scripture speaks to infertility with vivid reality, and Christians, of all people, should be the most compassionate in talking about this subject (Gen. 30:1; 1 Sam. 1:5-10). Christians should be sensitive to infertility, miscarriage, and children conceived through IVF without forgetting the importance of discussing the morality of IVF.

IVF is an enormously sensitive issue for Christians to discuss. Telling would-be parents they should not utilize IVF as a last resort to become parents can seem uncaring, unloving, and as depriving a husband and wife of something (children) God considers a blessing (Ps. 127:3). We should not minimize this longing. It is a primal desire given to us by a loving heavenly Father. While we offer thanks for all children generated through IVF, just like every child conceived in a womb, it is important for us to consider serious issues involved with IVF.

IVF is a complex issue, one that must be approached wisely, thoughtfully, and pastorally within a commitment to the sanctity of life. It is not like a flu shot or a hip replacement. The issue of conception—and where conceptions occurs—requires a certain context. The natural means of conception poses no ethical dilemma. With the use of IVF, however, at least two dilemmas immediately arise. There's an issue of the results and the means following IVF. There can be more embryos created than can be implanted, and the excess embryos are either destroyed, used for research, or frozen. How do we balance the good of wanting children with evaluating technology that can also lead to denying a whole class of persons—in this case, embryos—their right to exist?

Questions arise that capture the ethical difficulty of IVF: How many embryos (children) were created over multiple attempts? And how many remain frozen? How many were destroyed or used for medical research? Even where technology can allow the fertilization of only one embryo, preventing the death or destruction of other embryos, IVF still is problematic because it participates in the larger ecosystem of utilizing reproductive technologies that dispense with the one-flesh union of husband and wife. And moreover, there is no guarantee the use of IVF even to fertilize one embryo will lead to the successful implantation and development of the child.

But to a broader theological principle, children are an outflowing of the one-flesh union. The union sealing the marriage covenant, according to Scripture, is the same union designed to bring forth new life under the right conditions. As a part of our holistic human dignity ethic, Christians must understand the life of a frozen or destroyed embryo is just as precious as the enfleshed child. For us to minimize their humanity and personhood is to unwittingly fall prey to the pattern of thought that so dominates our culture's thinking about children being the product of choice and the will, rather than as a divine gift.

The reality, however, is IVF creates children conceived distinct from the one-flesh union of husband and wife (Gen. 1:28; 2:24). The medicalization of conception is an issue Christians must consider. They need to reflect deeply on these matters and ask hard questions. Good ethics involves not just answering questions but raising them. We must examine our desire for children with the pattern for how God designed children to be conceived. We must caution that the godly desire for children not become an idol allowing Christians to bypass the marital intercourse that brings children into this world and in the process, create a whole host of ethical dilemmas challenging human dignity.

Advanced technology that brings new questions to the experiences of life and the limits we are willing to impose on such technology is a serious challenge facing the Christian church. Pastors need to compassionately shepherd and disciple our churches to understand the availability of technology cannot mean its unquestioned use. Not all reproductive technologies must be rejected, but Christians will need discernment and wisdom, guided by faithful biblical understanding, to help us follow God's design for human life.[4]

## Gender

The transgender issue in America may not be as clearly connected to the question of the state's relationship to life. However, by examining the steps the state is taking to codify the concept of "gender identity" into law apart from biology, it is apparent the state is affirming a worldview which deludes individuals into invasive and often irreversible surgery which calls into question the existence of men and women altogether.

The subject of transgender identity is overturning the categories of male and female and attacking biblical anthropology too. From Hollywood to debates over non-discrimination statutes in public policy, proponents of transgenderism are making comprehensive claims. As a foundation of human existence and human society, the undoing of the male-female binary risks countless repercussions in society. We are left asking: How can the identity of male or female be established when reduced to psychology?

The Bible speaks of the male-female binary on both special revelation and general revelation grounds. As biblical scholar Richard Bauckham has written, "biblical commands are not arbitrary decrees but correspond to the way the world is and will be."[5] The Bible affirms the truth of an objective, enduring male-female binary; and second, the presence of this gender binary is made on creational and teleological grounds.

---

[4] Please see two perspectives on this subject: Stephen and Brianne Bell, "In Vitro Fertilization is Pro-Life" and Jennifer Lahl, "The Case Against In Vitro Fertilization," in the section on "Human Life and Reproduction Technology" in Joshua D. Chatraw and Karen Swallow Prior, *Cultural Engagement: A Crash Course in Contemporary Issues* (Grand Rapids: Zondervan, 2019).

[5] Richard Bauckham, *God and the Crisis of Freedom: Biblical and Contemporary Perspectives* (Louisville, KY: Westminster John Knox Press, 2002), 70.

The teleology of the male-female special revelation binary has three component parts. First, God made humanity in His image. This is the source of our dignity, and the image of God has relational, structural, and functional implications. Second, God designed humanity in the form of male and female counterparts. This binary is objective, universal, intelligible, and differentiated (e.g., primary and secondary sex characteristics). Third, God designed male and female for one another in a complementary, exclusive, and permanent relationship.

This means a biblical view of a man and a woman must be defined according to God's design in creation: A man and woman are image bearers of God whose biological design is oriented to fulfill a creational mandate of subduing creation by their covenantal marriage union with their sexual counterpart.

The Christian response to such a reality means Christian ethics have the postlapsarian responsibility to explain creation and nature to a world—and state—whose fallen natures refuse to believe the truth about itself and who fail to properly interpret the world's design in the fullness of God's revelation (John 1:3; 1 Cor. 8:6; Col 1:15-17).[6] It is a truth-telling act. Humanity is not elastic. Law ought to reflect the truth about human nature and not capitulate to the demands of what ethicist Oliver O'Donovan calls "psychological positivists"—those who would create reality based on psychological perception alone.[7]

The issue lurking beneath the surface of debates around gender and sexuality is whether we as human beings can redefine what it means to be human. Are we self-sovereigns capable of razing our bodies to the ground for the sake of self-supremacy? Are we the Creator? Or, are we creations? Are there limits imposed on us by genetic mapping overseen by a wise God?

Society may try to ignore, downplay, or subvert the male-female binary, but it will never overturn it. That's because our createdness as male and female is stamped onto human nature (Gen. 1:26-27). We may try, but individuals will never be able to transcend the limits of their

---

[6] Bernd Wannenwetsch, "Creation and Ethics: On the Legitimacy and Limitation of Appeals to 'Nature' in Christian Moral Reasoning," in *Within the Love of God: Essays on the Doctrine of God in Honour of Paul S. Fiddes*, ed. Anthony Clarke and Andrew Moore (Oxford: Oxford University Press, 2014), 212.

[7] Oliver O'Donovan, *Church in Crisis: The Gay Controversy and the Anglican Communion* (Eugene, OR: Cascade, 2008), 112.

embodiment. This is both a biblical and creational truth evidenced by scriptural witness and the recognition by cultures throughout history of the male-female binary.

The confusion that stems from blurring gender and denying the authority of biological sex is a grievous departure from God's authority over creation. Our design as men and women reveals God's will for creation. In this, Christians declare Christian and non-Christian alike can understand the difference between men and women. Our design reflects God's providential governance over the world. When culture and the state work to suppresses this truth, they deny God's lordship over creation and subvert human action in society.

## Conclusion: Taking a Risk on Life

Of the three pillars *The Manhattan Declaration* rests on, the focus on the sanctity of life stands at the forefront. According to the signatories, *The Manhattan Declaration* affirms the "profound, inherent, and equal dignity of every human being as a creature fashioned in the very image of God, possessing inherent rights of equal dignity and life." This is not merely an intellectual abstraction. The pro-life movement's language of "Abortion stops a beating heart" reminds us life and dignity are personal.

The value and dignity of life is not measured in its efficiency or utility by the state or the culture; it is measured by the immeasurable deposit of dignity given to it by its Creator.

# How the Church Can Defend Life at All Stages

*Trevin Wax*

"A culture of life." This phrase expresses a vision common among Christians who oppose the "culture of death," as described by Pope John Paul II. We recognize in our society a clash of competing visions, a war between irreconcilable cultures, most notably in our treatment of human beings at the beginning and end of life, where abortion or euthanasia creep along the edges of human existence with a quiet but lethal assault on human dignity. Therefore, we sense the need for Christians to defend and promote a culture of life.

Yet, too often we imagine Christians merely as individual agents doing their best to "stand for life" in the public square. We think of individual lights in a world of darkness. And while it is true Christians—as individuals—must promote the sanctity of human life in all our spheres of influence, we must not neglect the particular and powerful witness of the Church *as the Church* in defending life at all stages. We will not make significant progress in pushing back the darkness of the culture of death until our churches put on display what we mean by "the culture of life." The Church is not merely called to send out Christians to *engage* culture, but to *embody* a different culture all its own. *The Manhattan Declaration* offers wisdom and guidance in how we might strengthen churches in their defense of life.

Issuing statements and making declarations—no matter how true— do not constitute the totality of Christian faithfulness in our time. The authors and signers of *The Manhattan Declaration* recognize statements and slogans are not enough. The great need in every generation is for the Church to be the Church for the glory of God and for the good of the world. The Church in every era must answer the call to defend innocent life wherever it is assaulted—whether through the scourge of slavery in our day manifested in human trafficking, or through political movements dispensing with the elderly in the name of "dignity," or through societal blindness to the humanity of the unborn.

What is the best way for the Church to defend the vulnerable and helpless? In what ways can the Church today follow in the footsteps of our forefathers and mothers in the faith? When the sanctity of human life seems to be under attack from various vantage points, how can the Church marshal an effective defense? In what follows, I will offer several suggestions as to how we might better equip and empower the Church to defend human life at all stages.

## 1. The Church must recognize that our defense of life expresses enduring truth.

The most surprising response to *The Manhattan Declaration* was the number of people who seemed surprised by it. After all, none of the positions expressed in the *Declaration* were new or noteworthy. The Christians who came together across denominational lines to reaffirm basic and fundamental commitments to the dignity of all human life, the nature of marriage, and the importance of religious freedom did nothing innovative. They simply restated the historic truth claims of Christianity regarding these issues as opposed to the false and detrimental claims of many in our society and then they made clear their resistance to compromise and their willingness to experience cultural opprobrium for their stand.

*The Manhattan Declaration*'s writers made sure to emphasize their continuity with a long line of Christians stretching back through the ages. "We claim the heritage of those Christians who defended innocent life," the statement says, "by rescuing discarded babies from trash heaps in Roman cities and publicly denouncing the Empire's sanctioning of infanticide." *The Manhattan Declaration*, though issued by leaders with eyes wide open to their current moment as well as troubling signs on the horizon, grounded this call to action in a powerful appeal to history and a robust recommitment to an ancient heritage. Churches today must do the same. Our defense of life is an expression of ancient and enduring truth.

In the past two thousand years, the Church has frequently fallen short in her commitment to preserve and promote the dignity of all human beings. Churches claiming the name of Jesus Christ have not always defended human life at all stages. At times, communities of faith have been complicit in unjust systems or have promoted ideologies that cheapen human worth and value. Yet, the fact we can see so clearly when the Church has failed is a sign of the Church's ultimate success in passing down its legacy of standing for the sanctity of human life. Even when secular people judge the churches of the past for stumbling at times in defending life, they do so with a moral intuition formed by the Christian-influenced culture they've inherited.

The clarity and consistency of *The Manhattan Declaration*'s statement on human life reminds us of the need for churches to embody these ancient truths in our common life together. We need our works and our witness to back up our words, so that in a society that sees the bringing about of the death of one person as the inalienable right of another, the Church maintains its role as the defender of life at all stages—in what we think, say, and do. In this way, we take our place in a long line of faithful saints who witness to the enduring truth about God-given life.

## 2. The Church must promote and embody a counter-culture of life.

The old saying "the best defense is a good offense" is often applied in military or athletic endeavors and the point holds true for the Church that wants to defend life at all stages. Going "on offense" requires embodying and promoting a better vision of what is true, good, and beautiful. We must do more than win an argument; we must ignite the imagination. Whenever pro-life advocates say they long for "the day abortion is unthinkable," they give voice to a deep-rooted intuition that victory will come only when the cultural imagination is transformed.

### No and Yes

Ground zero for a Christian defense of human life should be the Church—a countercultural community radiating with the beauty of human dignity. The Church's firm *no* to euthanasia, even when marketed by society as "death with dignity," is issued from a community that celebrates and lifts the intrinsic worth of those whom society may consider only in economic terms ("a drain" or "unproductive"). The Church's *no* to elective abortion, even when refashioned by society as "reproductive rights," is issued from a community standing in awe of the miracle and mystery of God-given life, where the sanctity of the unborn child is so *felt*, any appeal to "choice" seems horrifically out of place. Whenever the Church forbids a practice or resists an ideology, our *no* must always issue forth from a counterculture embodying a greater and more glorious *yes*.

### A Contribution to the Public Good

Christians are not called merely to chastise the world for its evil, but to cultivate a counterculture of goodness. For this reason, *The Manhattan Declaration* links the Church's defense of human life to the promotion of the common good: "Like those who have gone before us in the faith, Christians today are called to proclaim the Gospel of costly grace, to protect the intrinsic dignity of the human person and to stand for the common good.... In being true to its own calling, the call to discipleship, the church through service to others can make a profound contribution to the public good."

The call to discipleship as envisioned here cannot be reduced to private and personal faith focused only on a heavenly afterlife. Costly grace leads to expansive discipleship. We are to follow Jesus in every sphere of life, trusting our obedience in community provides a foretaste of the world to come. In the Civil Rights movement, many faithful Christians embraced their role as the conscience of the culture by speaking prophetically against injustice while also cultivating a spiritual solidarity showing the world a glimpse of "the beloved community." Likewise, the cultivation of a counterculture of life contributes to the common good because the Church becomes a witness through word and deed to the existence of the Creator and the value of all who are made in His image.

### The Challenge Before Us

The biggest challenge standing in the way of our ability to defend life at all stages is the cultural captivity of our societal imagination, a vision of "the good life" influenced by philosophies of radical individualism and autonomy. We see this battle for the imagination when advocates for abortion rights, such as Katha Pollitt in her book *Pro,* claim abortion is a positive force for good in society.[1] Abortion rights activists realize it is not enough to claim abortion is "not bad." In order to maintain momentum and capture the commitment of the next generation, activists must recast abortion on demand as something good, something courageous that brings positive results to society, whether through the reduction of crime or poverty, or through the economic benefit of freeing women to enter the workplace unencumbered.

Those who market abortion as a social good take their place in a long line of people who throughout history have strained to make the case the social order is improved by trampling on the dignity of other human beings. Defenses of slavery appealed to the Southern imagination by arguing the "natural order" of racial hierarchy led to a more productive and peaceful society. A hundred years ago, "progressive" thinkers believed society would be bettered through the implementation of eugenics and forced sterilization. Sixty years ago, many leaders (including some in the Church, we must sadly admit) argued for the status quo of segregation in order to keep the peace and avoid racial strife.

Today, abortion rights activists have abandoned the notion that abortion should be "safe, legal, and rare" and instead encourage women to shout their abortion stories and celebrate them online to remove any stigma from the choice. Abortion is recast as a central element in a vision of the good life that demands individual rights and freedom and is willing to sacrifice something—anything—to maintain autonomy. In *Salon,* Mary Elizabeth Williams vents her frustration in "being bullied around by the vague idea that if you say we're talking about human life, then the jig is up, rights-wise." She recognizes the unborn child is human and yet concludes: "I would put the life of a mother over the life of a fetus every single time—even if I still need to acknowledge by conviction that the fetus is indeed a life. A life worth sacrificing."[2]

---

[1] Katha Pollitt, *Pro: Reclaiming Abortion Rights,* Picador, 2015.
[2] Mary Elizabeth Williams, "So what if abortion ends life?" https://www.salon.com/2013/01/23/so_what_if_abortion_ends_life/

## A Different Kind of Sacrifice

Every vision of "the good life" will require some sort of sacrifice. Our society is no exception. We are willing to sacrifice the elderly for our vision of efficiency and productivity; we are willing to sacrifice racial justice for our commitment to the status quo; we are willing to sacrifice the unborn for our right to self-determination and sexual freedom.

For the Church to defend life, we must display an alternative vision, a better way to live. We must recapture the imagination of our culture by showing heroism is not in shrugging off the sacrifice *of* the weak but in laying down one's comforts and conveniences *for* the weak. Heroes defend the good of all who bear God's image, and the Church defends life by forming and lifting ordinary heroes who resist the sacrifices acceptable to the world in favor of self-sacrifice in the footsteps of our Savior. The stories we tell, the people we celebrate, and the virtues we extol—these are ways in which the Church promotes a vibrant culture of life that forms disciples with righteous intuitions.

## 3. The Church must demonstrate a consistent and holistic commitment to the sanctity of human life.

Although *The Manhattan Declaration*'s section on human life focused primarily on abortion, the writers wisely recognized the sanctity of human life touches on a variety of other areas. The "whole scope of Christian moral concern" includes the "poor and vulnerable," even if the signers said they were most troubled by current threats against "the lives of the unborn, the disabled, and the elderly."

For the Church to truly be a counterculture, our efforts must be expansive, in line with our affirmation of "the profound, inherent, and equal dignity of every human being as a creature fashioned in the very image of God, possessing inherent rights of equal dignity and life." This kind of statement must be more than the main point of a sermon, but the foundational plank in an ecclesial structure that gives shape to this truth.

*The Manhattan Declaration* lists a number of cultural woes following from the denial of the intrinsic dignity of all human beings:

- "the abandonment of the aged"
- "genocide"

- "exploitation of vulnerable laborers"
- "the sexual trafficking of girls and young women"
- "racial oppression and discrimination"

These travesties flow "from the same loss of the sense of the dignity of the human person and the sanctity of human life that drives the abortion industry and the movements for assisted suicide, euthanasia, and human cloning for biomedical research."

The challenge for the Church in providing a counterculture of life is to remain consistent and committed in all these areas. It is impossible for every church to be equally focused on every one of these societal ills, but if we are lifting the sanctity of human life regularly in our teaching and preaching and counseling, and if we are celebrating regularly our congregants who make an impact in any of these areas, we should see across the country a consistent and committed witness to the value of human life, even if some churches may be more involved in particular causes than others. Pastors and church leaders should, with discernment, bless the particular gifts and callings of church members who may be involved in alleviating some of the suffering resulting from these travesties.

Likewise, for our witness to be truly holistic, pastors and church leaders will need to be aware of areas in which our congregations have compromised or become complicit in the same kind of ethical reasoning that leads to approval of assisted suicide, or the sanctioning of surrogacy. These practices are often driven by a strong sense of compassion, but they indicate just how easily our holistic approach to a culture of life can succumb to inconsistencies that lead to subtler assaults on human dignity at the beginning and end of life.

## 4. The Church must appeal to principles over partisanship.

If the Church is truly committed to the sanctity of human life in all the ways mentioned above, then we are driven in our social engagement by principles, not partisanship. A principled stand must always take precedence over partisan politics.

In a polarized society, it is easy for the Church to fall prey to our political parties' inconsistencies in defending life at all stages. Those on one side of the cultural divide may stand against abortion but be willing to minimize the dignity of the unborn in order to achieve results in other areas related to human flourishing. Those on the other side of the cultural divide may advocate for the unborn or the elderly and yet remain curiously quiet when it comes to legislative action related to racial discrimination or economic exploitation. Dan Darling writes: "If being pro-life is simply about unthinkingly voting for a political party who oppose legal abortion without considering other issues of justice, if it's about seizing a cudgel every election season, then we must ask ourselves if we are truly pro-life."[3] Yes, and likewise, if being "pro-life" means we expand our vision to the point we would minimize the reality of unborn slaughter or overlook the advocacy of such an atrocity in the people we campaign for, then we should do serious soul searching to see if we are driven more by partisanship than we realize. Churches seeking to adopt a holistic view on life (as mentioned above) must take care not to direct their enthusiasm solely to issues that elicit society's applause.

For the Church to defend life at all stages, we must offer a different path, a way of transcending the partisan alliances of the moment to offer a word from outside, a word from God not captive to the societal turbulence of the moment. *The Manhattan Declaration* calls the Church to rise above political allegiances in order to provide a clear and consistent witness to human life. "Our commitment to the sanctity of life is not a matter of partisan loyalty," it says, "for we recognize that in the thirty-six years since *Roe v. Wade*, elected officials and appointees of both major political parties have been complicit.... We call on officials in our country, elected and appointed, to protect and serve every member of our society, including the most marginalized, voiceless, and vulnerable among us."

To appeal to principles over partisanship on issues related to life does not mean we minimize the political ramifications or legislative importance of these concerns. The call to principled commitment that transcends partisanship is not a call to withdraw from political engagement. If we fall back on a transcendent "non-partisan approach" as an excuse for not defending life, we are merely relegating abortion or euthanasia to the

---

[3] Dan Darling, *The Dignity Revolution: Reclaiming God's Rich Vision for Humanity* (Epson, U.K.: The Good Book Company, 2018), 92.

category of "political issues" so we can cordon it off as "too controversial" for our churches to address. When debates over slavery were raging, too many Christians believed the best way to "transcend" polarization was to categorize slavery as a political squabble and then appeal to the spirituality of the church as a way of keeping slavery outside the realm of Christian concern. The Church must not make this mistake in her defense of human life.

The reason we must take a principled stand is because the Church is called to speak to political matters related to life without becoming coopted by the partisan allegiances of the moment. Only then will our message stand out above the endless roar of political rhetoric. The Church's fundamental call is to *witness* to human dignity at all times, not *win* a political battle at all costs.

## 5. The Church must speak *for* the voiceless and *to* the conscience.

The good news of Christ crucified and raised is the foundation of all Christian speech, especially in matters related to guilt and shame because of sin. In her defense of life at all stages, the Church must speak prophetically *for* the voiceless and pastorally *to* the repentant sinner who has been drawn into complicity with the culture of death. Creating a counterculture of life does not happen apart from life-giving words expressing truth about sin and grace. In this way, we follow in the footsteps of Jesus whose words were tough and unsparing regarding sin while rich and full of mercy toward sinners in need of forgiveness and healing.

### Speaking For

The Church must not be cowed into silence in matters related to the defense of human life. We speak up not in order to insert ourselves into other conversations, but to defend those who have no voice. *The Manhattan Declaration* says: "the Bible enjoins us to defend those who cannot defend themselves, to speak for those who cannot themselves speak. And so we defend and speak for the unborn, the disabled, and the dependent."

One of the ways in which we equip the next generation of believers to speak up prophetically and powerfully for the sanctity of human life is by giving church members clarity on just what it is we oppose and what we support. The Church must remain committed to telling the truth, and this will mean unmasking the euphemistic terminology of the culture of death and its false descriptors such as "reproductive health," "reproductive rights" and "reproductive justice."

"Christians must understand the gravity of framing abortion as an issue of women's 'reproductive rights,'" says Charmaine Yoest. "This label has far-reaching meaning related to a woman's worth as a person and human being, her self-fulfillment, career aspirations, and perception of equality, power, and opportunity. To engage requires us to understand. Our mandate is to speak the truth…about abortion, and about the significant and deeply flawed arguments advanced by abortion advocates."[4]

## Speaking To

Speaking out is one of the ways the Church defends life. We do so with boldness and grace—boldness in speaking *for* the voiceless, and grace in speaking *to* the conscience. Yoest continues: "Abortion is not a tonsillectomy; it is not an appendectomy. It is a real death—of a living human being. The church must fully realize this truth and engage with it because a real death of a living human being has moral weight and spiritual consequences. Christians must own and echo this truth. The church must bear witness to it and offer refuge to those suffering under its weight."[5]

It is here the Church does what only the Church can do—call to repentance those whose consciences are rightly plagued by their actions and offer the amazing absolution of forgiveness found in Christ. John Ensor imagines our speaking to the troubled conscience this way: "If I visited a hospital full of wounded soldiers—some missing eyes, others arms, others bound to wheelchairs the rest of their lives—would you not expect me to say something about how the gospel offers everlasting life that includes new bodies raised up that can see and hear and leap for joy?"[6] It is tempting for the Church to paper over guilty consciences with sentimental superficiality, but our call is to proclaim the need for the

---

[4] Charmaine Yoest, "How Should the Church Engage," in *The Gospel and Abortion* (Nashville: B&H, 2016), 78.

[5] Ibid., 69.

[6] John Ensor, *Innocent Blood: Challenging the Powers of Death with the Gospel of Life*, (Hudson, OH: Cruciform Press, 2011), 64.

Spirit to perform heart surgery through the gospel in order to transform and heal the sinful heart.

The Church must be a place where people are cared for, where the victims of our culture of death are welcomed and warmly reassured, not through the denial of their complicity in our cultural evils, but through the strong word of the cross that ends our shame through the sacrifice of God's Son to atone for the idolatrous sacrifices offered up by our nation.

## 6. The Church must serve and care for the vulnerable.

The Church defends life at all stages by caring for *all* the victims in a society committed to abortion. *The Manhattan Declaration* was right to focus on the ways in which we can stand in solidarity with the most vulnerable among us even while extending our arms in ministry to those who are in need. "We will work, as we have always worked, to bring assistance, comfort, and care to pregnant women in need and to those who have been victimized by abortion, even as we stand resolutely against the corrupt and degrading notion that it can somehow be in the best interests of women to submit to the deliberate killing of their unborn children. Our message is, and ever shall be, that the just, humane, and truly Christian answer to problem pregnancies is for all of us to love and care for mother and child alike."

It is the culture of death that pits the mother and child against one another, as if it is natural, normal, and even good for a woman to destroy her offspring if she so chooses. It is the culture of life that must lift both mother and child alike, standing against injustice and resisting complicity with the culture of death.

Unfortunately, our churches have not always cared well for women in distress. A recent survey from LifeWay Research in partnership with Care Net, shows widespread distrust among women toward the church. More than four in ten women who have had an abortion were churchgoers at the time. The survey showed 64 percent of these women believed "church members are more likely to gossip about a woman considering abortion than to help her understand options." The result? Women keep silent in church both before and after abortion.

The good news is regular churchgoers claimed their churches were more caring and helpful and loving. Thankfully, there are many Christians who are willing to help others along in this journey. The church is on the front lines of this battle, and has the opportunity to defend life through sermons, small group meetings, baby showers, support for pregnancy centers, and through offering housing and financial support.[7]

## Conclusion

Tracing the long line of those who have witnessed to the sanctity of human life takes us back to the first chapter of Exodus, where we encounter two women whose names are Shiphrah and Puah. These were the Hebrew midwives who decided to engage in creative civil disobedience and refused to carry out Pharaoh's evil order to throw all the Israelite boys into the Nile River. It is interesting to note the Bible gives us the names of these lowly midwives while never telling us the names of the great and mighty Pharaohs. In God's accounting of things, Shiphrah and Puah are more important than the men who commissioned the building of the pyramids in Egypt. God is on the side of life.

In the witness of these women, we see both prophetic resistance and care for others. We see resistance to the culture of death and cultivation of a culture of life. Let us learn from their example, and in line with *The Manhattan Declaration*, let us equip the Church to become a countercultural community that defends life at all stages, taking on the mantle of these and other believers through the ages.

---

[7] http://lifewayresearch.com/wp-content/uploads/2015/11/Care-Net-Final-Presentation-Report-Revised.pdf

# How the Church Can Protect
# the Dignity of the Most Vulnerable
# Among Us

*Joni Eareckson Tada*

Jillian is a shy, but happy twelve-year-old girl with Down syndrome. Her shyness did not bother Jillian's parents at first, but when they moved to a new town, they became concerned. Would their little girl fit in with children in their new neighborhood and school? After consulting with their doctor, the parents opted for cosmetic surgery on Jillian—they chose to alter the shape of their daughter's ears and eyes to make her appear more typical.

The surgery was labeled as cosmetic, but this procedure wasn't a matter of straightening crooked teeth or diminishing the size of one's nose. It was to hide a child's disability to make her more socially acceptable. These weren't surgeries to save a little girl's life; they were seriously invasive surgeries to satisfy the parents' concern about peer pressure.

When word spread, some people felt uneasy about it, but could not come up with a good reason why it was a bad idea. After all, Jillian wouldn't know, and the alterations *might* open the door to greater social acceptance. But others felt such surgeries revealed a dark fear and prejudice against disability and a dissatisfaction, even rejection of God's design. Many thought this action was an assault against Jillian's dignity.

"If it's a question of this child's dignity being violated," some might counter, "she has Down syndrome and lacks the cognitive capacity to experience any kind of dignity." Think of the logical outcome of such a statement. Why not then let the Alzheimer patient run around without clothes, or allow those with serious mental illnesses to eat off the ground, or permit the child with autism to flap his arms all day with no intervention?

God has called us to treat individuals like Jillian and her body with respect and to ascribe positive value to her disability. People deserve to be treated with human dignity even if a person like Jillian has no idea what human dignity looks or feels like.

## Human Dignity and Vulnerable Persons

Human dignity often feels distant when you are disabled, or unable to make your own medical choices. Human dignity could seem nonexistent to the elderly resident in an unlicensed nursing home, relegated to the back bedroom, and without family or friends to care. Or when you're a single mother and living in a car with your two small children. It can sound like a foreign word to the young man with cerebral palsy who languishes in front of a TV in a residential center. Human dignity can be obscured in a mesh of wires and tubes connected to a tiny preemie whose mother does drugs. And that same dignity is quietly swept aside when a twenty-three-week-old baby is aborted and discreetly disposed of in a trash bag.

Why do we default to the gifted, the morally upright, and healthy when we think about "human dignity?" The global "poor and wretched" have even less of a chance. The concept of human dignity is entirely acceptable to persons who are shrouded in entitlements, or to anyone above the fifth rung on the socio-economic ladder, but it's rarely ascribed to the homeless man in the alley. Could it be we have a shriveled sense of what dignity means, and are unable to understand its universality? What are we missing, and why is the idea of human dignity so important to the weak, poor, and vulnerable among us?

When I was first injured and became a quadriplegic; when others had to give me a bed bath, do my toileting routines, get me dressed, lift me into a wheelchair, brush my teeth, blow my nose, and feed me breakfast, I didn't feel human, let alone feel any dignity. Having someone wipe your backside? Wipe your spit, runny nose, or mop up your urine? Most people would say that's beneath their dignity. Trading your autonomy for a lifetime of dependence and inconvenience? "That's no quality of life; who wants *that?*" they would insist.

*This* is how human dignity has suffered. If comfort, convenience, and autonomy determine your life value, then one's dignity is up-for-grabs and shaped only by the whims of subjective opinion. But human dignity is not a feeling tied to someone's private assessment of himself or another. The concept is riveted in one powerful absolute, the God of the Bible, transcendent, immortal, and unchangeable. God created us as his image bearers.[1] We are God-reflectors, bearing the stamp of who He is. This makes every human being, no matter how old; how young or disabled; no matter how disadvantaged, sacred, precious, valued, and treasured. Human dignity is woven into our DNA.

But cut loose from the God of the Bible, an infant or an adult with a disability, even an elderly individual whose quality of life is judged as minimal, has no hope. They become trapped in a quality-of-life-net woven by the power and subjectivity of others. They assume their last chance for human dignity is to choose—with what little autonomy they have—to end their lives. Such an act is viewed by secular society as courageous and dignified. But if society agrees an elderly or disabled individual makes a reasonable, rational choice to end his life, then society has abandoned them. *Yes, you can attain human dignity by choosing to end your life, thereby fulfilling your duty to lighten the burden on your family, as well as society.*

Quality-of-life thinking, however, is double-minded. If a healthy person is, let's say, without a job or a home and becomes depressed and wants to end his life, he will be given mental health counseling, job-skills training, and placed in a homeless shelter. This scenario shows an even more sinister prejudice against old age and disability.

## God's Messengers of Human Dignity

God's people must intervene. If they do not, no one else will. When it comes to the weak and vulnerable, Christians must stand in the gap between a dehumanizing culture and its helpless citizens. It's a battle for

---

[1] Genesis 1:26

the glory of God and the preservation of the epitome of his creation. I am a Christian and a quadriplegic, and when I get up in the morning—as difficult as it is—it's a fight. I battle to remember in whose image I am made. I discipline myself to rehearse whose image I bear. My body may be broken, but I am a God-reflector. I mirror a God who was pleased to make me in His image. I did not discover this on my own. Christian friends taught me this principle from the Bible and put it into practice through their support and friendship.

They showed me *this* is the root of human dignity—not my ability to walk or use my hands or blow my own nose, cut my own food, or toilet myself. "And Joni," they said, "if you believe it's beneath your dignity to be weak and dependent, then you are operating out of pride. There is no room for pride when you bear the image of God. Only humility." Nothing fosters humility more than knowing you reflect the image of Almighty God. As Irenaeus said, "The glory of God is man fully alive." My body may be completely broken, but I am fully alive and my soul is worth more than all the wealth in the world (Matt. 16:26); I have purpose and meaning in my life (Isa. 43:7), all because I am the humble bearer of God's image (Gen. 1:26-28).

I am content in my wheelchair. But what if I weren't? What if I were still despairing? In a world that has twisted the definition of human dignity, I could get my death wish—I could qualify for physician-assisted suicide in Switzerland and Belgium. And the U.S. may not be far behind. Any one of the six states with assisted-suicide laws—and the District of Columbia—could expand the meaning of "terminal illness." All it would take would be a court decision modifying its definition, such as happened in Belgium, Switzerland, and the Netherlands. In Europe, multiple sclerosis or ALS is viewed as "terminal." Will one day the U.S. provide assisted suicide to people with severe spinal injuries, like mine?

How did we come to this? Why does our society, on one hand, celebrate the rights of the elderly and people with disabilities yet, on the other, imply "you are better off dead than disabled?"

America's broken and profit-driven healthcare system is already placing undue pressure on the medically fragile. There are constant calls to reduce "heroic" measures or late-life care in the name of cost-containment. Some leaders in government are coercing these people to consider it their "duty to die." In Oregon, Colorado, Montana, Vermont, Washington, and Hawaii—states where doctor-assisted death is legal—euthanasia is positioned as an end-of-life treatment option.

Why the push to legalize physician-assisted suicide? People—even Christ-followers—are afraid of suffering. We are afraid of being left alone or burdening others with our afflictions. These fears are reflected in a June 2017 Gallup poll[2] which shows 73 percent of Americans support euthanasia. When you couple these fears with an entitlement attitude, people are convinced they have a right to arrange the timing of their own deaths.

Do we want to help people die a good death? Then, followers of Jesus can do with others as they once did with me—define suffering from a Biblical perspective and provide hands-on help that draws people with disabilities out of isolation. If intractable pain is the issue, let's work to pour more research dollars into better pain management. If fear is the issue, Christians can surround hurting people with true spiritual community. Most of all, we can help terminally ill people understand what faces them on the other side of their tombstone. Jesus is the only One who conquered the grave and opened the path to life eternal. How awful if people choose three grams of phenobarbital in the veins, only to face a Christless eternity.

As I write, thirty states in the U.S. have either legalized assisted-suicide or are considering such laws in their state assemblies.[3] Find out if your state is numbered among them, then spread the word. Tell people there are good laws throughout the U.S. which already help people die with dignity—laws providing advanced pain management, as well as grant a patient the right to refuse treatment. And be alert if a right to die bill is introduced in your state assembly. The lives of thousands are at stake, so "speak up for…the rights of all who are destitute" (Prov. 31:8).

Christians must get engaged in this battle. First, by facing a disturbing fact: in that same Gallup poll, 42 percent of evangelicals agree doctors should be allowed to assist terminally ill people in suicide. In other words, followers of Christ are buying into the allure of assisted-suicide. *We* have fears of suffering!

God's Word helps us combat fear. When we are suffering, the Bible is filled with insights on the virtue of trusting the Man of Sorrows

---

[2] *Gallup Analytics*, June 2017 Report
[3] https://www.deathwithdignity.org/take-action/

acquainted with our grief. Besides, the sixth commandment in Exodus 20:13 says, "You shall not murder" (this logically includes self-murder). God knows our weak frame, and He states in Job 14:5, "Since his days are determined, and the number of his months is with you, and you have appointed his limits that he cannot pass." He will take care of us to the end, tenderly shepherding us beyond our tombstone into a life filled with joy, and no suffering.

So, for the sake of God's glory and human dignity, I get up in the morning and live for God *and* for other disadvantaged people who need to know whose image they bear. And you can too. I run a ministry called Joni and Friends that serves people with disabilities around the world, and when we deliver Bibles and wheelchairs in a village gripped by idol worship, we tell everyone Down syndrome is not a curse from the local witch doctor or a hex from animist spirits; we explain that child is a God-reflector and the village has a direct, moral obligation toward him. We *are* our brother's keeper, because we all bear the image of God.

You are your brother's keeper. The human stakes are high; the cosmic stakes are even higher—to waste or abuse a life; to forget about a nursing home resident, or the man with CP alone in his ward; to leave a child with Down syndrome on an African riverbank to die, or to flush a life down the toilet whether figuratively or literally is a direct assault against the glory of God (Ephesians 1:4-6). If others abuse people in catastrophic situations like mine, or take advantage of our physical weakness, or try to diminish our human dignity by perceiving us as somehow less than they, they are throwing dirty dishwater on the glory of God.

## A Global Issue

If human beings do not have intrinsic equal moral value, universal human rights become impossible to sustain. When nations deny intrinsic human dignity, the door is wide open to using human beings as objects and resources.

Consider the children with disabilities used in ritual sacrifice in Uganda, and many other countries where spiritism is the common religion. My missionary friend, Bob Goff, looked over Kampala and told me flatly there wasn't a high rise in that city that didn't have a disabled child encased in the concrete of its foundation—all to assure the animists spirits would look favorably upon that business venture. In the tanzanite mines of Tanzania, children with disabilities, especially albino ones, are tossed down mineshafts to ensure good fortune with mining efforts.

Don't think this only happens in less-developed nations. In Western industrialized nations, such as Belgium and Switzerland, unborn children with mild impairments are systematically aborted to spare the family the cost and inconvenience of raising that child. These same governments also sanction the lawful assisted suicides of people with simple impairments such as clinical depression. Iceland boasts in the success of achieving nearly a 0 percent birth rate of children with Down syndrome.

But there are many bright spots, internationally. Years ago, when I was in Africa with our Wheels for the World teams, we met an impoverished paraplegic who broke his back when he fell out of a tree. He lived with intractable pain in a little concrete hut with two walls and half a roof. He didn't wander far from his home, for he could only drag himself by his hands. Friends in his village gave him food and, occasionally, alcohol to deaden his pain. When we  learned of his story, we wanted to give him a wheelchair and take his photo. When my friend raised the camera, the African said, "Wait one moment." He then took great pains to lift the sleeve of his dirty T-shirt up on his shoulder. When he smoothed out its wrinkles with both hands, he looked up with a smile and announced, "*Now* I am ready." This crippled African was not about to have his picture taken with a T-shirt askew.

His words had the fragrance of human dignity, and his framed photo is still hanging on my desk wall. I look at it every day because his story—his words—illustrate how all of us simply want to be treated with human dignity. With respect. We want to be treated with esteem. God would have us treat each other with that kind of respect (Luke 6:31). To look into the eyes of the weak and vulnerable is to look squarely at the image of our Creator and Savior.

There are other abuses against the weak and vulnerable: The euthanasia of elderly people in unlicensed nursing homes where regulations are lax; the infanticide of newborns with GI issues; healthcare reform skewed against the medically fragile who consume scarce healthcare resources; the discarding of embryos during In Vitro Fertilization. And as we've seen, the growing trend to legalize doctor-assisted death in more states.

## What Can Christians Do?

In early 2018, the Oregon Health Authority (which studies and reports on Oregon's assisted suicide law) stated, "any chronic condition which, if left untreated, would result in death within six months could be considered a 'terminal disease.'" With that simple rewording, a terminal illness could mean muscular dystrophy, a disease which, left untreated, could take one's life in a short period of time. Most people would not consider MD as terminal, but a person with an "untreated" case of this disease *could* qualify under the law.

Thankfully, an outcry arose against this rewording. It was led by disability advocates, pro-life groups, and Christians. Against pressure, the Oregon Health Authority quickly backpedaled, abandoning the redefinition of terminal illness. Christians know the Bible calls Satan a murderer and our adversary likes to think the territory of disease and disability is his. The devil's last major battlefield is his assault on human dignity—and his most fierce battleground is played out upon the despair of people with terminal illnesses, significant disabilities, and old age.

And if the battle is confusing for Christians, they can find clarity in *The Manhattan Declaration*: "The Bible enjoins us to defend those who cannot defend themselves.... And so, we defend and speak for the unborn, the disabled, and the dependent. What the Bible and the light of reason make clear, we must make clear. We must be willing to defend, even at risk and cost to ourselves and our institutions, the lives of our brothers and sisters at every stage of development and in every condition."[4]

To hasten the premature death of a person, whether he is elderly, disabled, without cognitive abilities, or an unborn child or a newborn—is to rob them of dignity. Why? These people have become outcomes of

---

[4] https://www.manhattandeclaration.org/

scenarios other people devise, involving cost effectiveness, convenience, subjective opinions, and twisted ideas of mercy. There's no personal dignity in those scenarios. Persons who are euthanized are robbed of the right to life, their volition, of their independence, personhood, and individual liberty. Even worse, their untimely death is not in accordance with God's timing for that individual. God has been taken out of the picture.

Yes, it means the Church should become aware of pending legislation in Congress and in state assemblies which could jeopardize weak and vulnerable citizens. But it also means befriending the despairing people who could easily fall prey to physician-assisted suicide or other initiatives that erode life value. If marginalized persons are tempted to despair of their conditions, the Church can reach out to these individuals, ascribing virtue to their hardships and positive meaning in their situations. Christians can draw these people up out of social isolation and embrace them into spiritual community.

## Be an Advocate—Be a Friend

In short, the Church can be a friend to the weak and vulnerable. Whether or not we *welcome* the outcast, the homeless, those who are medically fragile, the elderly or persons with disabilities, or families with children who have disruptive disabling conditions into our fellowship is a test of our own bias or lack of awareness. Christians, do we recognize the human dignity inherent in each of these? Or do we ascribe them less respect due to their unfortunate situations? Do we treat them as "mission projects," or as friends? People in these fragile conditions should not be simply ushered into a segregated part of the congregation; they should be embraced into the church family.

For example, special-needs families don't want to be merely mainstreamed under a label of "inclusion;" they want to know they *belong*. They want to know they would be missed, if they failed to attend a worship service or church event. Kelly, who has an intellectual disability, lives in a residential facility. Her care center employs well-paid staff who organize picnics and community outings for the residents. Kelly very much enjoys these outings, but she once confessed, "Joni, I don't want people who are paid to be my friends. I want *real* friends who *want* to be with me."

There are many ways a church can embrace vulnerable and often lonely people into the church family. Many disability-aware churches hold respite programs for tired and weary parents of children with disabilities. These same churches organize one Saturday a month as a "Moms' Morning Out"—a pampering day where special-needs mothers can have their nails done, hair trimmed, or receive a massage from church volunteers. Such events say to families, "you are welcome here; we've prepared a place for you; we want to help."

If your church does not have an outreach to seniors or to persons with disabilities and their families, you can find resources and curriculum through Joni and Friends,[5] Friendship Ministries,[6] Nathaniel's Hope,[7] or perhaps through your denominational headquarters.

Jesus Christ gives a mandate to reach the weak and vulnerable when he states in Luke 14:13, 21, "But when you give a feast, invite the poor, the crippled, the lame, the blind,[14] and you will be blessed...[21] Go out quickly into the streets and lanes of the city, and bring in the poor, the crippled, the blind and the lame." God has a heart for people who are weak and vulnerable. He says in Psalm 10:17, "You, Lord, hear the desire of the afflicted; you will strengthen their heart; you will incline your ear." Almighty God smiles on his people when they remember the weak and vulnerable, for "...whoever is kind to the needy honors God."[8]

"Open your mouth, judge righteously, defend the rights of the poor and needy" says Proverbs 31:9. Christians must speak up and tell their neighbors and coworkers that as the moral fabric of our society wears thin, no one is more in jeopardy than those who are too weak, too depressed, or too small, or too elderly to grasp how dangerous the battle is.

Given the opportunity, society will move in the direction of convenience for the masses, at the expense of the weak and vulnerable, whether it's doctor-assisted death, euthanasia of the comatose, or the abortion of those with defects. Unless we confront our leaders with a Proverbs 31:9 perspective on the poor and needy, cost savings and the triaging of scarce healthcare dollars to benefit the mostly healthy will be the driving forces

---

[5] Joni and Friends, PO Box 3333, Agoura Hills CA, 91376; joniandfriends.org
[6] Friendship Ministries–US, 2215 29th St SE Ste B6, Grand Rapids, MI 49506, https://friendship.org/
[7] Nathaniel's Hope, 2300 Jetport Drive, Orlando, FL 32809, https://www.nathanielshope.org/
[8] Proverbs 14:31

behind how we treat the elderly, the medically fragile, and those with significant disabilities. Psalm 82 says, "Defend the cause of the weak… maintain the rights of the poor and oppressed. Rescue the weak and needy; deliver them from the hand of the wicked."

So Christians, take action…

- Volunteer with Joni and Friends at one of our Family Retreats for special-needs families. Sign up to serve as a mechanic on a Wheels for the World outreach, distributing wheelchairs, showing the love of Christ, and teaching a biblical worldview on disability to churches in developing nations. Serve as a Cause4Life intern with Joni and Friends and learn a biblical worldview on aging and disability.[9]

- Join the Colson Fellows program at the Colson Center for Christian Worldview and learn how to influence culture as you weave and work biblical principles into hot-bed cultural conversations. Colson Center Fellows speak up and speak out at Starbuck's and over their backyard fence, as well as demonstrate Christ-like love where God is needed most.[10]

- Be informed on issues. Follow the debate on healthcare reform and the future stability of Medicare and Medicaid. Even now, the removal of some regulations is drastically shortening the length of time Medicare will reimburse HMOs for much-needed rehabilitation. This is hurting countless numbers of people with disabilities and the elderly who lack other insurance.

- Follow up on bills seeking to help the vulnerable, such as The Disability Integration Act (DIA). Too many people with young wheelchair users are being forced into institutions—can we not come up with a compassionate solution so these young people with disabilities, as well as seniors, can live at home and have community-based services as an alternative to being warehoused in nursing homes?

---

[9] www.joniandfriends.org
[10] www.colsonfellows.org

- Do not tolerate irresponsibility in the media. When the media makes Iceland look progressive for eradicating Down syndrome, call them to task—write the station manager or newspaper editor.

- Showcase Christ-like love within community institutions, such as convalescent or residential facilities for the medically fragile, or in nursing homes, whether licensed or unlicensed. Start a Bible study, a Sunday afternoon worship service, or a weekly visitation program.

- In these same institutions followers of Jesus are needed to volunteer as ombudsmen—or a patient's rights advocates—on behalf of the elderly and disabled in these institutions. An ombudsman is a champion for vulnerable residents concerning the quality of their day-to-day care, health, safety, and personal preferences. Physical, verbal, mental, and even financial abuse *does* occur more frequently than you'd think, not to mention poor quality of care, and inappropriate use of drugs or physical restraints.

Sylvia Stein, a Christian friend, supervises our county's ombudsman program and this testimony appeared in the 2017 annual report: "My eighty-year-old friend was sexually abused in the nursing home where she was living. She was very afraid and would not tell anyone. Your Ombudsman visited her and noticed that she seemed fearful. The Ombudsman talked with her and my friend finally shared what had happened. She had not even told us. The Ombudsman gave her the encouragement she needed to call the police and file a formal complaint. As a result of your actions, the caregiver was arrested. I cannot begin to express my gratitude for what you did for her. She is her old self again."[11]

John Stonestreet describes our culture as contradictory: "Our society cries out for human dignity while actively working to eliminate both the elderly, those who are significantly disabled, and unborn children with disabilities—all because their quality-of-life is viewed as dismal, or their cost-of-care is too demanding or providing for their needs requires extraordinary manpower. So, remember how Jesus befriended widows, orphans, the elderly, people who were blind, deaf, lame, or mentally ill.

---

[11] 2017 Annual Report of Long-Term Care Ombudsman Services of Ventura County, California, page 5.

He loved them, spent time and energy relating to its them—and we must do the same."

*You* possess God's Good News and a message that uplifts the downtrodden and forgotten. Jesus was spot-on when he said, "In this world you will have trouble."[12] But you are charged with lightening the load for the last, the least, and the lost. And that is a most noble cause for Christ and his glory.

---

[12] John 16:33

# Why Being Pro-Life Is Also Pro-Woman

*Frederica Mathewes-Green*

Every year thousands of people gather in Washington, D.C., to commemorate the Supreme Court decision that made abortion legal—*Roe v. Wade*, handed down on January 22, 1973. On that day I was living in D.C., taking a break from college, and volunteering for the feminist underground newspaper *off our backs* [stet lowercase]. I wasn't a Christian then, but I was a feminist—the first feminist in my dorm, actually. I was loudly in favor of social revolution and women's rights, and took it for granted that abortion was necessary if women could ever compete fairly with men. (The bumper-sticker on my '66 Mustang read, "Don't labor under a misconception; legalize abortion.") The issue of *off our backs* covering the *Roe* decision opined that it didn't go far enough; why should a woman be denied her right to abortion in the third trimester?

But, at the time, we feminists didn't think the number of abortions would ever be very high. Surely, no woman would *want* an abortion; she would make this choice only under the most compelling circumstances.

Things didn't turn out that way. Since *Roe v. Wade*, the number of abortions has now topped sixty million. It's hard even to take in a number that high. I once heard a speaker say if there was a monument, like the Vietnam Memorial, listing the name of every child killed by abortion, it would have to stretch for fifty miles.

That was many years ago, and the wall would have to be much longer today; but such a wall cannot exist, because those children had no names.

51

We feminists didn't anticipate these high numbers of abortions because there was a factor we did not foresee: when abortion is available, it becomes the most attractive option for everyone *around* the pregnant woman. If she goes off and does this one thing, she won't cause any trouble for the father of the baby, or her boss, or the administrator of her scholarship; she won't embarrass her mom and dad. If she does this obviously sensible thing, everyone else can rest easy. *She* might not rest so easy, but since we've been led to expect abortion to be something women really want, everyone expects her to be grateful.

At that time, I didn't really know what an abortion *was*, how it worked, or what it did. At the time, we all said the unborn was just "a glob of tissue." People who protested abortion, I thought, were getting sentimental over mucous. But since the advent of ultrasound technology, we don't have that excuse. Today, everyone has seen a sonogram; we know an unborn baby looks like a baby within a few weeks, and its heart is beating at twenty-one days. Back then, we could be ignorant of things science has now made inescapable.

But even before sonography, I learned something about the unborn that shook up my pro-choice convictions. One Christmas I was home from college and picked up my dad's copy of *Esquire* magazine—January 1976. I came across a short essay titled "What I Saw at the Abortion," by a physician named Richard Selzer. He wrote he was pro-choice but had never seen an abortion and asked a colleague if he could be there the next time he had one on his schedule.

On the day of the procedure, Selzer says, he saw the patient lying on the procedure table, twenty-four weeks pregnant (most abortions are done much earlier). He watched as the doctor thrust a long needle into her belly, and through it delivered a dose of prostaglandin solution; this would bring on contractions and expel the premature fetus. (This prostaglandin procedure is no longer used, because too many babies were born alive.)

When the doctor released his hold on the needle, Selzer wrote, "*I see something!* ...It is the hub of the needle in the woman's belly that has jerked. First to one side. Then to the other side. Once more it wobbles, is *tugged*, like a fishing line nibbled by a sunfish."

Selzer realized he was seeing the fetus's fight for life. Whatever else a fetus does not have, it has this most basic human instinct, the will to live. Selzer concluded his essay, "Whatever else is said in abortion's defense, the vision of that other defense" (the child defending its life) "will not vanish from my eyes. And it has happened that you cannot reason with me now. For what can language do against the truth of what I saw?"

The "truth of what [he] saw" hit me hard. What he described was clearly an act of violence. If I saw someone do this to a *kitten* I would be horrified. I had a categorical opposition to violence; I was anti-war, anti-death penalty, and vegetarian. Yet, somehow I planted an act of violence at the very center of my feminism. I treated it as an essential freedom that women need to get ahead in a man-centered world. But I had to ask myself: When does a man ever have to choose between his career and the life of his child?

This was just one of the ways, I gradually saw, we feminists took the male condition as the universal human standard. Men never get pregnant, and therefore women have to be able to get un-pregnant. It was one more way of altering women's bodies to fit social expectations, like 19th century corsets laced so tightly they deformed the lower ribs.

The realization that abortion is an act of violence created an intolerable conflict within my own value system. How could I think it was wrong to execute homicidal criminals, but right to kill children? Not just any child, but our own children, as much our own as any child we ever bear. How can I think it wrong to kill an enemy soldier in wartime, but right to sacrifice our own sons and daughters? How had women been led to regard our own children as mortal enemies?

After this, none of the feminist arguments for abortion made sense. Like the idea the fetus is disposable because it is so small. Isn't that rather a dubious argument for feminists to make? Women are, in general, smaller than men. Does being small make you less a person? Babies are smaller than children, children smaller than teenagers. Do we really want to say big people are always allowed to kill smaller people?

Then there was the argument that it was all right to abort children who were "unwanted." A premise of my feminism was a woman has inherent value, without needing to please a man. Our rights and significance are not based on someone else's approval but are an inherent aspect of our humanity. So why were we now saying it was all right to dispose of a child if it is not wanted? Does a woman have the right to go on living only if someone else wants her? Men might find a woman desirable when she's young, but less so as she ages. Is it then okay to kill her?

(The criterion of whether a baby is "wanted" is false anyway, because there are thousands of couples waiting to adopt any baby, of any race or health condition. These couples wait because babies aren't often available for adoption; they usually get aborted instead. The children who have trouble finding adoptive parents are older, and perhaps have been in the foster system for some time. According to the "wantedness" argument, they deserve some kind of post-birth abortion.)

Overall, the idea that women want abortion became harder to defend, as the harrowing nature of the procedure became clear. Abortion is never something a woman wants in the positive sense; it is a painful, humiliating, heartbreaking thing to go through. No one comes out of an abortion clinic skipping. A woman "wants" an abortion only when all the other choices look worse.

In an essay many years ago, I wrote this line: "No woman wants an abortion like she wants an ice cream cone or a Porsche. She wants an abortion like an animal in a trap wants to gnaw off its own leg. Abortion is a tragic attempt to escape a desperate situation by an act of violence and self-loss."

It's surprising, when you're a writer, to see something you've written take on a life of its own, and this line was taken up and quoted frequently by pro-life sources. But the really surprising thing was it appeared in pro-choice publications as well. Though pro-life and pro-choice disagree about many things, there appears to be one thing both sides agree on: abortion is a miserable choice.

If that's the case, if no woman really *wants* to have an abortion, then why are they doing it 2,500 times a day? If women are doing something they don't want to do 2,500 times a day, it's not liberation we've won; we are colluding in a bizarre new category of oppression.

Favoring abortion rights is not consistent with feminism; in fact, the pro-life position is inherently pro-woman. That was obvious to the 19th century feminists, to Susan B. Anthony and Elizabeth Cady Stanton, who spoke against abortion in the pages of their journal, *The Revolution*. Even more recent feminists haven't always seen abortion as their most important cause. When the massive feminist anthology, *Sisterhood is Powerful*, was published in 1970, only one portion of one essay dealt with abortion. In 1967, when the National Organization of Women met for the first time, abortion and contraception were mentioned only briefly at the end of their "Bill of Rights;" abortion appears only as the last word in the document.

Abortion rose to the top of feminist concerns, I think, because it was concrete and measurable. How could you tell whether something as foggy as "respect for women" was increasing? But repealing a law, or passing a new one, was a tangible goal. You could make a plan to achieve it, then implement and correct the plan, and have something to assess at the end of the day. Legalizing abortion was a practical goal, and as a result it became important.

And two other ideas prevalent in '70s' feminism combined to create a situation in which abortion came to seem indispensable. Abortion is the solution, so to speak, of the problem of pregnancy. But when, and why, did pregnancy become a problem? Throughout most of human history, pregnancy has been a blessing. New children were welcomed, because they built the strength of a family and became the support of a couple's old age. New children mean new life; they mean both personal delight and growth of the tribe. But in the late 20th century pregnancy came to be seen as an unbearable burden, so much so that, a fifth of the time it occurs, women seek abortion to escape it.

No war or famine, no catastrophe, accounts for this desperation; America is the wealthiest, healthiest, most secure, and most comfortable nation in history. But pregnancy became unbearable due to a twofold change in expectations about women's behavior. One was the idea women should be promiscuous; the other was the idea women should place career above childrearing.

Both ideas were promoted by the feminist movement, yet in a profound irony, both ideas are contrary to the average woman's deepest inclinations. Both ideas, in fact, were borrowed from a perspective typically (or rather stereotypically) thought "male." Valuing career advancement over family, and seeking sexual encounters that entail no lasting ties, haven't traditionally been things women valued. But, at the time, anything that looked traditionally "feminine" made feminists uncomfortable, because men looked down on it and thought it weak. So, despite all the castigating of men, all the blaming and fault-finding, feminists still considered a man's life more worthwhile than the lives our mothers and grandmothers led. It certainly entailed greater power. So, if men were dismissive toward housewives, that was what housewives deserved. If men valued free sex and high-powered careers, that was what women should value.

Treating a career as the most important aspect of life is foolish, as reflected in the saying that no one wishes on their death bed they'd spent more time at the office. Oddly enough, in the period just preceding the rebirth of feminism, in the '50s and '60s, there was a lot of worry about the over-emphasis on getting ahead in a career. This was thought to be a "rat race," poisonous, and deadening to the soul. Hippies embraced this idea and famously advised "dropping out," washing one's hands of the world's power and money, and instead getting "back to the land." The early feminism that attracted me had a similar mother-earth flavor. But, within a few years, feminists began to long for worldly success, and the worries about over-investment in career evaporated. Now, rather than disdain the corporate world, feminists were banging on the glass ceiling and demanding to be let in.

The other pernicious idea was termed "free love," which more accurately could be called "free sex." It meant sex without any personal commitment, with no expectation of an emotional connection. This is another idea not historically associated with women's best interests. In the early days, feminists loudly denounced treating women like "sex objects," and *Playboy* magazine was a favorite target. But when *Playboy* took up the cause of abortion rights—it's no mystery why playboys find abortion useful—it was embraced as an ally. Feminists had once again adopted a viewpoint stereotypically associated with men.

Women have always competed against each other for male attention, but now the stakes were much higher. The precondition was not to care—to be sufficiently calloused that you don't need or want commitment or emotional security. But women have always understood that sex is inherently an act of risk and requires a willingness to be literally naked and vulnerable. This risk is manageable when both partners are pledged to love and honor each other; then, sex is indeed a coming-together, a union of whole persons and not just individual parts. But without such a commitment, there is always a risk of rejection, ridicule, or contempt.

So how did pregnancy, that eminently natural state, become unbearable? These two ideas, careerism and promiscuity, come together like two sides of a vise. If the modern woman is dutifully promiscuous, a high proportion of her sexual experiences are going to be with a partner who feels no responsibility for any resulting child. Indeed, a pregnancy is likely to seem like a failure on her part, a breaking of faith. Contraception fosters the illusion that sex has nothing to do with reproduction, but sometimes raw biology still wins out. When it does, though this woman may have far fewer pregnancies than her great-grandmother did, any one of them is more likely to be disastrous.

Likewise, if she thinks her career is more important than child-rearing, unexpected pregnancy can look like a disaster. Her great-grandmother, no doubt, lived in a way arranged to accommodate home and children; a surprise baby could be a complication, but not a logistical impossibility. But for a woman whose life is organized around her career, an unexpected pregnancy can dynamite years of carefully-laid plans. The trick of juggling motherhood and career is so intractable it's been front-page fodder for forty years. In all this time we've gotten no closer to solving the problem and another forty years won't help.

When these two ideas come together, abortion looks like the only escape. Feminism embraced, first, increased access to professional life and, secondly, increased sexual freedom. But participation in public life is greatly complicated by responsibility for children and uncommitted sexual activity is the most effective means of producing unwanted pregnancies. This dilemma—simultaneous pursuit of behaviors that cause children and are hampered by children—inevitably finds a resolution on the abortion table.

Feminists defend abortion with desperate passion because the whole shaky structure of their lives depends upon it. In the Webster decision (1989), Justice Blackmun wrote that women have "ordered their lives around" abortion; the Casey decision (1992) was based on the premise abortion has become a necessary part of the social machine. There's a sad accuracy in that; when abortion becomes available, surrounding expectations regarding reproduction and child care shift to accommodate it. Eventually, it seems indispensable.

That is why the fight against legal abortion cannot stand alone. If we could padlock all the abortion clinics tomorrow, we'd see the next morning a line 2,500 women long pounding on the doors. We wouldn't have solved the problems that make their pregnancies seem unbearable. We wouldn't have changed the context that normalizes promiscuity and undermines a woman's authority to say no. We wouldn't have restored respect for the profession of mothering, or respect for fathering for that matter, so men would be proud to love the moms and support the children whose lives they began.

These interlocking ideas present a complicated picture, and initially a depressing one. If you've ever played the game of pick-up sticks you know how impossible the task looks at the beginning, when you must gradually and carefully dislodge the first sticks one at a time.

Yet, pregnancy care centers across the country have been working on these problems for decades, ever since the first Birthright was founded in 1965. There are estimated to be three thousand pregnancy care centers across the nation, in comparison with only a few hundred abortion clinics. Over the years these centers have shifted and enlarged their focus, so the early years' emphasis on the baby grew to encompass the pregnant woman as well; then women who have already experienced abortion, and young people who can be encouraged to make better choices were included as well. Pregnancy care centers offer a wide range of goods and services: pregnancy tests, maternity clothes, medical referrals, practical advice, sonograms, help with housing, and in some cases, full pre- and post-natal care.

Yet, the most important thing pregnancy centers provide will always remain the individual support and friendship a pregnant woman needs. When I began research for my book, *Real Choices: Listening to Women, Looking for Alternatives to Abortion,* my goal was to discover the main reasons women had abortions. I thought if we could rank-order the problems women faced, material, practical, and financial, we'd be able to address them more effectively.

To my great surprise, I found these practical forms of support were only secondarily important. Over and over, women told me the reason they had the abortion was someone she cared about told her she should. The people she needed to lean on for support in a crisis pregnancy, like her boyfriend or mother, instead encouraged her—sometimes, sadly, coerced her—to have an abortion instead.

While pro-choice advocates present abortion as an act of autonomy, it can feel to the pregnant women like a response to abandonment. All those first-person-singulars—my body, my life, my choice—reveal how alone the woman feels. Pregnancy is the icon of human connectedness, binding a woman to her child and the father of the child. Abortion shatters those connections and leaves her alone.

When I asked women, "What would you have needed in order to finish the pregnancy?" over and over they told me, "I needed just one person to stand by me." Of all the things pregnancy centers can provide, what women told me they needed most was a friend.

We need to reach young men too. In our culture men are almost continually insulted and conservatives and pro-lifers are not immune to the temptation. Pregnancy care workers can find it easier to send a woman to the welfare office than to explore whether the father of the child might be called on instead. We expect these men to be "bums," and they live down to our expectations.

Pro-lifers speak readily of God creating new life, saying he knit together the woman and her unborn child, but they should also recognize God has appointed a third person in the situation. I wince when I hear pro-lifers say "She found herself pregnant;" it sounds like Victorian euphemism, as if the woman just discovered the baby in a parking lot. No, she had help with that project. For every "unwanted" pregnancy there is a dad who needs to be challenged to do the right thing, for his own sake as much as his new family's.

Restoring young men to the role of husband and provider is a very long-term strategy for reducing the need for abortion, and at present it's hard to even imagine how it might be done. But even apart from an unexpected pregnancy, men need a reason to respect themselves, to see themselves as strong. The increasing numbers of "deaths of despair" and suicides have something to do with seeing oneself only as a consumer, a black hole of need. Self-respect derives from self-control and both men and women need to recover the way to that destination.

The tide of culture pushes so hard against the pro-life cause that it's easy to feel overwhelmed. There are plenty of reasons *not* to speak out against abortion; the pro-life position is despised, and if you take a stand, you will be attacked. It looks pointless to take such a stand, when the deck is stacked so high against you. But every generation faces an issue that draws a line between those who will stand up for what is right and those who just go along. It's only the bravest who take a stand and continue to bear witness even when others mock them and misrepresent them; only the bravest keep standing when, from a worldly perspective, the cause looks lost. Only the most dedicated people are willing to keep working for change, when the struggle is all uphill and they reap nothing but rejection.

That is your calling. And you are not alone. The struggle is *not* lost. Heroes are made in hard times, and this is one of those times, for those who oppose abortion; this is our time to stand up for the truth, for the protection of both women and children. This time will pass, as the great wheel of history turns and our whole era will be a footnote in the past. Then we will take our places among the "great cloud of witnesses" (Hebrews 12:1) who have borne witness to the truth in all generations. The challenging times we live in provide everything we need to become heroes too.

# PART TWO

# Marriage

# Why Marriage Matters Most:
# Sharing the Gospel in Matrimony

*Timothy Cardinal Dolan*

*Vast human experience confirms marriage is the original and most important institution for sustaining the health, education, and welfare of all persons in society. Where marriage is honored, and where there is a flourishing marriage culture, everyone benefits—the spouses themselves, their children, the communities and societies in which they live. Where the marriage culture begins to erode, social pathologies of every sort quickly manifest themselves.*

It is a scene replayed on many occasions for people of faith, but many years ago it ranked as one of the more uncomfortable moments of my life: on an otherwise beautiful autumn day, a crowd of protestors shouted vicious taunts as we ended Sunday Mass at St. John the Evangelist Cathedral in Milwaukee, where I was then serving as archbishop. As people left the church they were met with hatred and vitriol by those who detested our beliefs. In this case, it was our belief, and the teaching of the *Catechism of the Catholic Church*, that men and women who experience same-sex attraction are worthy of dignity and respect, and that any unjust hatred or discrimination against them is wrong.

Afterward, a reporter asked me for a comment on the protest, to which I replied, "They're right: we do love and respect those with a homosexual attraction. These protestors understand Church teaching very well." Fringe groups like this are still around today, but thankfully they seem to be fewer in number. Yet, the issue of homosexual relationships continues to be a major flashpoint in our culture, notably from those who think biblical teaching amounts to discrimination and oppression. More than ever today, it is our belief that marriage is the lifelong union of love and fidelity between one man and one woman that has drawn, and continues to draw, protests from those who object.

This traditional Christian teaching, which is also confirmed by nearly all world religions, history, and Natural Law, has seemingly been jettisoned by contemporary society. If ten years ago, when *The Manhattan Declaration* was issued, we were aware there was a "serious erosion of the marriage culture" that contributed to the "impulse to redefine marriage," how much greater is that erosion today, especially now when the redefinition of marriage is a legal reality? In addition, the troubling sociological trends identified in *The Manhattan Declaration*, such as out-of-wedlock births, cohabitation, single parent families, and divorce, continue to demonstrate troubling trends.

The protestors I encountered years ago understood what the Church believed and rejected it. Yet, I strongly suspect they failed to understand *why* we believe the way we do. Did they grasp the rationale for this teaching: that all people, regardless of sexual attraction, are made in the image and likeness of God and therefore worthy of dignity and respect? It is doubtful.

Similarly, I wonder whether those who today reject Christian teaching on marriage have more than a superficial understanding of the underlying reasons for our belief. One piece of evidence suggesting they do not is the constant characterization of our belief as "anti-gay" or homophobic. Christians are not *anti*-anybody; we are, however, *pro-marriage*.

Ten years ago, *The Manhattan Declaration* urgently expressed the need to rebuild a healthy and thriving marriage culture. Undoubtedly, there are many outstanding efforts to achieve this worthy goal, but we can always do more. A critical part of this effort to rebuild a healthy marriage culture must be an ongoing educational effort. It is not enough for people to merely know *what* we believe about marriage, they must also know *why* we believe it. Yes, most people have heard traditional Christian teaching upholds the historic definition of marriage as the lifelong, faithful union of one man and one woman, but do those who disagree with this view hear from us in a clear and compelling way *why* we are so committed?

There are a number of approaches one can take to answering this question, but allow me to lay out a case for why marriage matters by reflecting on the Gospel of Marriage, a phrase used by both Pope Francis and Pope Emeritus Benedict XVI. In recent years, a lot of attention was given to the two synods on marriage and the family held in Rome (2014 and 2015). These gatherings of Catholic bishops from around the world demonstrated the recognition that marriage and the family are in special need of support by the Church. However, the previous synod of the Catholic Church, held in 2012, was devoted to the theme of evangelization. In his message to the bishops gathered to celebrate Mass before the meeting began, Pope Benedict XVI noted the following:

> *The theme of marriage…deserves special attention. The message of the word of God may be summed up in the expression found in the Book of Genesis and taken up by Jesus himself: "Therefore a man shall leave his father and his mother and hold fast to his wife, and they become one flesh" (Gen 2:24; Mk 10:7-8). What does this word say to us today? It seems to me that it invites us to be more aware of a reality, already well known but not fully appreciated: that matrimony is a Gospel in itself, Good News for the world of today, especially the dechristianized world. The union of a man and a woman, their becoming "one flesh" in charity, in fruitful and indissoluble love, is a sign that speaks of God with a force and an eloquence which in our days has become greater because… marriage, in precisely the oldest regions evangelized, is going through a profound crisis. And it is not by chance. Marriage is linked to faith, but not in a general way. Marriage, as a union of faithful and indissoluble love, is based upon the grace that comes from the Triune God, who in Christ loved us with a faithful love, even to the Cross. Today we ought to grasp the full truth of this statement, in contrast to the painful reality of many marriages which, unhappily, end badly. There is a clear link between the crisis in faith and the crisis in marriage.*[1]

This profound insight can also serve as a challenge to us as we continue striving to rebuild a healthy marriage culture: how do we express the Gospel of Marriage? In what ways can we demonstrate and share that

---

[1] Pope Benedict XVI, Homily for the Mass for the Opening of the Synod of Bishops, October 7, 2012.

Scripture and the tradition of the Christian church both bear witness to the reality that marriage is, in fact, good news?

The Gospel of Marriage is good news in a similar way to the Gospel of Jesus Christ: it has natural and supernatural consequences. The life, death, and resurrection of Jesus quite literally changed the world. His followers, of whom we are all descendants, heard Him proclaim the Kingdom of God and the need for repentance and baptism. From the first disciples to today, Christians have tried to live by Jesus's teachings in the Sermon on the Mount, and this love of God and neighbor has influenced the "natural" world in innumerable ways. But God did not send His only Son simply to make the world a better place, even though that is certainly a result of the Incarnation. Jesus, our Savior, came because our souls were stained by sin and in need of a salvation only He could provide. It is only the saving work of Jesus Christ that provides the opportunity for us to spend eternity with God. This supernatural consequence of the Gospel far exceeds anything of this world and is why faith in Christ remains such a potent source of hope for the poor and suffering. Likewise, marriage has important, tangible consequences in this life, as well as possessing supernatural significance. Let us briefly consider each of these in turn.

One of the better sources for understanding the impact of marriage on society today is *Why Marriage Matters: Thirty Conclusions from the Social Sciences*. This project, led by W. Bradford Wilcox at the University of Virginia, brings together a diverse group of eighteen distinguished family scholars from across the country to consider the latest social science research on marriage and family issues. What they found, over several years and multiple updated editions of the project, is that marriage is quite clearly linked to a number of benefits. The thirty conclusions they present demonstrate the wide-ranging positive impact accompanying marriage and they group these findings under the following categories: family, economy, physical health and longevity, mental health and emotional well-being, crime and domestic violence. A sampling of these conclusions is sufficient to illustrate the importance of marriage:

- Children born into a married family are more likely to enjoy family stability, thrive, and have good relationships with their mother and father.

- Married couples on average build more wealth and enjoy greater economic stability than singles or cohabiting couples and marriage appears to reduce poverty for disadvantaged women and minorities.

- Children who live with their own married parents experience better physical health on average than those children in other family arrangements, and in general marriage tends to be correlated with a host of positive health outcomes for both men and women.

- Divorce is associated with higher rates of psychological distress and mental illness for children, and family breakdown appears to significantly increase the risk of suicide.

- Marriage is a safer family arrangement than alternatives in terms of the likelihood of women and children experiencing violence or abuse.

Social science continues to show the good news about marriage is that it produces better overall well-being for both the married couple and, importantly, children. The positive social benefits alone are not why Christians believe marriage is important, but they also matter and deserve to be part of how we advance our position.

Further evidence that the natural consequences of marriage are significant was evident to me during the discussion at the synods on the family in Rome. Bishops from around the world shared how obstacles to marriage in their own countries were creating societal problems. *Amoris Laetitia,* the document written by Pope Francis after the two synods, gave ample consideration to the material circumstances of the family today, devoting the entire second chapter to "the experiences and challenges of families," and began by utilizing the insight of his predecessor, Pope Saint John Paul II:

> *The welfare of the family is decisive for the future of the world and that of the Church. Countless studies have been made of marriage and the family, their current problems and challenges. We do well to focus on concrete realities, since "the call and the demands of the Spirit resound in the events of history," and through these "the Church can also be*

*guided to a more profound understanding of the inexhaustible mystery of marriage and the family.*"[2]

Cultural trends, economic challenges, migration, and gender ideology are just some of the issues highlighted by Pope Francis as areas of concern and obstacles to a healthy marriage culture. Christians must account for the experience of married couples today, as well as those men and women who might otherwise fear or delay marriage due to socioeconomic circumstances.

Yet, the natural consequences of marriage are only part of the story. For Christians, marriage matters because of what it reveals about God's love for us. When *Amoris Laetitia* was released, it generated some controversy within Catholic circles over how to understand its teaching on sacramental practice for those who are divorced and remarried. Unfortunately, this issue, which was only a very small portion of our synod discussion and which received rather brief treatment in the document, distracted attention away from the beautiful and positive vision of marriage presented by Pope Francis. In the fourth chapter, Pope Francis offers a lengthy reflection on 1 Corinthians 13, which he introduces by reminding us of the link between the natural and supernatural elements of marriage is love:

> *All that has been said so far would be insufficient to express the Gospel of marriage and the family, were we not also to speak of love. For we cannot encourage a path of fidelity and mutual self-giving without encouraging the growth, strengthening and deepening of conjugal and family love.*[3]

The characteristics of love that Saint Paul exhorts us to demonstrate are, of course, attributes of God's love for us. For example, in his reflection on the characteristic that love is not resentful (v. 5), Pope Francis writes that the power of forgiveness in relationships must have a divine origin:

> *All this assumes that we ourselves have had the experience of being forgiven by God, justified by his grace and not by our own merits. We have known a love that is prior to any of our own efforts, a love that constantly opens doors, promotes and encourages. If we accept that God's love is unconditional, that the Father's love cannot be bought or sold,*

---

[2] Amoris Laetitia, 31, with the quotations from John Paul II's *Familiaris consortio,* 84.
[3] Amoris Laetitia, 89.

*then we will become capable of showing boundless love and forgiving others even if they have wronged us.*[4]

Grace is the link between the natural and supernatural significance of marriage, and marriage fundamentally matters because to Christians "it is an institution ordained by God, and blessed by Christ in his participation at a wedding in Cana of Galilee. In the Bible, God Himself blesses and holds marriage in the highest esteem."[5]

The synods on the family and *Amoris Laetitia* were perhaps the most significant global conversation about marriage held within the Catholic Church in the past decade, but they were not the only collective effort of Catholic leadership to address this crucial issue. In fact, in that same autumn of 2009 when *The Manhattan Declaration* was issued, the United States Conference of Catholic Bishops approved and released a pastoral letter, *Marriage: Love and Life in the Divine Plan*. The overlap, both in timing and in content, between this pastoral letter and *The Manhattan Declaration* is striking.

In the pastoral letter we see many of the same themes already mentioned in this discussion of the significance of marriage. The first part focuses on understanding *what* is marriage according to God's plan, as well as some threats to its flourishing. Part two of the letter considers marriage in the order of the new creation and explains why Catholics consider it a sacrament. There are many noble insights in this section, but I would like to focus in particular on two that illustrate the Gospel of Marriage: marriage as a reflection of the life of the Trinity; and marriage as a means of growth in virtue, which the letter calls a "school of love and gratitude."

One of my great privileges as Archbishop of New York is that I preside over various celebrations in St. Patrick's Cathedral. I always look forward to the annual Jubilee Mass, where we recognize and honor couples who have been married for fifty years. A few years ago, this Mass also coincided with Trinity Sunday, which Catholics celebrate on the first Sunday after Pentecost. It struck me as particularly appropriate, because marriage is a mirror of the love we find in the Blessed Trinity.

---

[4] Amoris Laetitia, 108.
[5] *Manhattan Declaration*

As I preached to the wonderful couples seated in front of me, I realized they might not all make an immediate connection between their fiftieth wedding anniversary and the Trinity. But marriage and the Trinity have *everything* to do with each other, and we would do well to fully understand and share this aspect of our Christian faith with others. First of all, the Most Blessed Trinity is the origin and goal of all reality. All creation—the world, humanity—did not arise by chance, but rather by the action of God the Father, God the Son, and God the Holy Spirit, three persons, an infinite, eternal Trinity of love and life. And if the Trinity is our origin, it is also our destiny, as all creation makes its way back to the Triune God. This creation and journey to an eternal destiny with God is reflected in the experience of a married couple who goes through life together, ending ultimately in the everlasting embrace of Father, Son, and Spirit.

Another way in which marriage reflects the life of the Trinity is that both are a *communion* of life and love. When we talk about men and women being made in the image and likeness of God, one of the implications is we were made not for solitary lives, but rather to be in communion with God and with one another. We are created for relationships, for friendships, for bonds of solidarity. Marriage is a shining example of this communion of life and love, when man and woman, two individuals, become *one*:

> *Therefore, just as the Father, the Son, and the Holy Spirit are distinctly who they are only in relation to one another, so a man and a woman are distinctly who they are as husband and wife only in relation to one another. At the same time, in a way analogous to the relations among Father, Son, and Holy Spirit, which unites the three persons as one God, the inter-relationship of the husband and wife make them one as a married couple.[6]*

Moreover, just as the communion of persons in the Trinity is life-giving, so also is the married couple when they bring children into the world.

Marriage provides both the opportunity and challenge for growth between husband and wife. The "real work" of marriage begins after the

---

[6] *Marriage: Love and Life in the Divine Plan*, 37.

wedding and here again I am reminded of the summons of John Paul II: "family, become what you are!"[7] This *becoming* suggests a transformation over time and one that will only reach its fulfillment with the assistance of grace. All disciples of Jesus Christ are called to grow in holiness and married couples can never forget their gaze must first be fixed on God, then on each other. Another way to think about this process of growing in holiness is that couples must increase in virtue.

Of course, all the virtues are important, and we have already spoken of the most important one: love. But another virtue central to a healthy marriage, and one we must continue to emphasize as we look to recreate a healthy marriage culture, is gratitude. It is not controversial to say a major problem affecting society at all levels and layers is a troubling lack of gratitude. A selfish and narcissistic mentality has taken hold across our culture which is fundamentally at odds with this virtue. Even our Thanksgiving and Christmas holidays are encroached upon by an individualist consumer mentality with little patience for the giving and receiving of thanks. However, I believe if married couples dedicated themselves to intentionally living in a spirit of gratitude, it could have a profound impact.

Gratitude is a virtue we should all strive to embody, of course, but gratitude between spouses can be especially potent. Why? Because it is precisely in the mundane regimen of daily life, especially as years of marriage add up and the monotony of routine can seem unbearable, gratitude is most difficult to practice. We often exalt the practice of a given virtue under extremely difficult conditions. Think of the brave soldier during battle or the firefighter rushing into a burning building as exemplars of fortitude. But when is it most difficult to be grateful? Certainly, it is hard to be grateful in the face of tragedy and suffering, but perhaps it can be just as challenging to be grateful to those people we count on so much we lose sight of the fact we are receiving anything at all from them. The *ordinary* can be the enemy of gratitude. Over the years I have counseled many couples who were struggling in their marriage and a common refrain was the feeling of *taking for granted* one's husband or wife. Or in our spiritual lives, how easy is it to assume God's love for us, instead of praising and thanking Him for it?

---

[7] *Familiaris Consortio*, 17.

These are the times when gratitude is most essential, and it is because we experience so much of life as routine it can be difficult to practice this virtue. Yet, it is possible and we should never forget that gratitude and grace have the same origin. Our lives and all we have are fundamentally gifts from God; when we recognize this and thank God, we are better able to express gratitude to others for the gifts they give us. Few things are as touching as the elderly couple, married for decades, who quietly sit together in gratitude for their presence in each other's lives.

Finally, the impact of gratitude between husband and wife is not restricted to them alone, or even to their family. As the bishops' letter states, "the virtue of gratitude overflows from the marriage and family to embrace the Church and the world."[8] This overflowing of gratitude leads men and women to lives of service, hospitality, and love of neighbor. The powerful witness of a joyfully married couple is likely to do far more to persuade than any argument alone.

Marriage matters because it is a sign. It is an image of God's love for the Church and a sign of the coming Kingdom. Jesus describes the Kingdom of Heaven as a wedding feast, and the Book of Revelation says, "Blessed are those who are invited to the marriage supper of the Lamb" (Rev. 19:9). We must continue to give witness to the biblical and historical Christian understanding of marriage because it is an integral part of God's plan and what matters to God must also matter to us. The hope we share for the rebuilding of a healthy marriage culture must never be extinguished by the challenges we face. God's design for marriage has both natural and supernatural consequences. When met by protestors, we must share with them this good news.

---

[8] *Marriage: Love and Life in the Divine Plan*, 52.

# What Must We Do?
# An Evangelical Perspective[9]

## Rick Warren

*Our culture has accepted two lies: if you disagree with someone's lifestyle you must hate them or are afraid of them, and to love someone means you must agree with everything they believe or do. Both are nonsense.*

In Hebrews 13:4 we are given this clear command: "Let marriage be held in honor among all." Sadly, today, marriage is dishonored by many. It is dismissed as an archaic, manmade tradition, denounced as an enemy of women, discouraged as a career-limiting choice, demeaned in movies and television, and delayed out of fear it will limit one's personal freedom.

Today, marriage is ridiculed, resented, rejected, and redefined. What are we going to do about this? The church cannot cower in silence! What, then, must we do?

## A. Affirm the authority of God's Word.

We do not base our worldview on fads or feelings or opinions or political correctness. We build our lives on the unchanging truth of God's Word. Jesus affirmed, "Heaven and earth will pass away, but my words will never pass away." Isaiah affirmed, "the grass withers, and the flowers

---

[9] This chapter has been adapted *from Not Just Good, but Beautiful: The Complementary Relationship between Man and Woman* (Walden, NY: Plough Publishing House, 2015), and is used herein with permission.

fade, but the word of God stands forever." David affirmed, "Your word, O Lord, is eternal. It stands firm in the heavens" (Ps. 119:89). Truth is still truth no matter who doubts it. I may deny the law of gravity but that doesn't change gravity. And just because we break God's laws, that does not invalidate them.

## B. Believe what Jesus taught about marriage.

In Mark 10:6-9, Jesus quotes the Old Testament and gives us the Owner's Manual on Marriage. Many speakers have referred to this.

> *But from the beginning of creation, "God made them male and female. Therefore, a man shall leave his father and mother and hold fast to his wife, and the two shall become one flesh." So they are no longer two but one flesh. What therefore God has joined together, let not man separate.*

In this one passage, Jesus gives us five convictions we must believe. First, gender is God's idea. God chose to make us either male or female. Our identity as either a man or woman is far deeper than a sociological construct, a psychological condition, or a personal preference. God created us male and female. Second, marriage is God's idea. He defines it, not us. It's not a manmade idea we can toss away. Third, sex was created for marriage. God created male and female body parts to naturally fit together. That's obvious. And they fit together for a purpose—they create life. Even if you disbelieve the Bible, every human body and every living person is a witness and testimony to God's intended purpose for sex. Sex was not created for recreation, but for the connection of a husband and wife and procreation of life. If sex was only physical, unfaithfulness would not hurt so much; there is no "safe" sex because no condom can prevent a broken heart. Fourth, marriage is the union of a man and a woman. There are many other kinds of relationships, but those aren't marriage. Definitions matter. Fifth, marriage is to be permanent. Jesus repeats Genesis, adding, "What God joins together, no human being should separate." Marriage is meant to last a lifetime.

Today, all five of these truths are dismissed and ridiculed. But a lie doesn't become truth, and wrong doesn't become right, and evil doesn't become good just because they become popular.

## C. Celebrate healthy marriages.

Be a proponent of what's right, rather than just being an opponent of what's wrong. We must offer an appealing alternative to the empty promises of the world. Celebrating and highlighting great marriages is the best defense of marriage. We will convert more opponents by being winsome and positive about the beauty and joy of marriage than by being negative about immorality. How? I have four suggestions for local churches:

1. *Use testimonies of happy marriages in your church services.* Both single adults and married couples are inspired more by example than by exhortation. They need to see the sermon in action. Having couples regularly share their journey with the whole congregation will create a culture of marriage in the church. Remember, a marriage does not have to be perfect to be healthy.

2. *Do an annual "Renewal of Wedding Vows" service for your entire congregation.* We invite couples to dress up and do a processional. It is a very tender service; people weep for joy. It's a great model. For unmarried couples living together we announce it two months in advance so they can repent and take our required eight pre-marriage counseling courses.

3. *Publicly recognize and reward long-term marriages in your parishes.* Whatever gets rewarded gets repeated! If we want people to value marriage, we must reward it. Celebrate the sweetness and beauty of love that lasts a lifetime; we're wired to crave this.

4. *Continually point out the benefits of marriage.* When a culture claims to care about children, we must point out children who grow up with both a mother and a father grow up healthier, happier, and stronger. They are less likely to fail in school, less likely to abuse drugs and alcohol, less likely to do jail time, and less likely to experience distress, depression, and thoughts of suicide. They are also less likely to perpetuate these problems to the next generation.

When a culture claims to champion women, we must point out women who marry and stay married have lower rates of depression, have a lower risk of being a victim of crime or violence, and have a higher net worth than those living with an unmarried man.

When a culture claims to care for the poor, we must point out that the dissolution of marriages disproportionately hurts the poor. A single mother with children has never been a viable economic unit and poor children get hurt the most by the economic consequences of divorce. Children who grow up without both mother and father are more likely to live their entire lives in poverty.

And what about men? Men who marry and stay married have fewer illnesses, fewer injuries, and live longer than single men. They earn more money and amass more net worth than single men with similar education and job histories, including men who live with unmarried women.

## D. Develop small group courses to support marriages.

We've developed several of these at Saddleback and small groups are one of the keys to our growth. We teach that as a couple, you should choose as your best friends other couples who are as committed to their marriages as you are to yours. Otherwise, you set up for failure.

## E. Engage every media to promote marriage.

Right now, the church is being out-marketed by opponents of marriage. The minority view is getting the majority of media attention. Right now, Christians are known more for what we are against than what we are for. Whichever side tells the best stories wins.

We need more television shows and movies portraying joyful, committed married love.

We also must use media to question the cultural lies. For example, the media has conditioned our culture to believe the lie that sex is only exciting outside marriage. We need tasteful movies and television shows celebrating sex in marriage. Sex is not dirty. It is holy, and it is a gift to married couples. We need movies that teach the difference between love and lust. Love can always wait to give; lust can never wait to get.

As Christians, we need a cooperative media strategy for producing television shows, films, and YouTube videos that portray the joys and benefits of a healthy marriage, and the hard work it takes to maintain a great marriage.

## F. Face attackers with joy and winsomeness.

Yes, there is a raging cultural battle. But the Bible says, "The weapons we fight with are not the weapons of the world." The Bible tells us to overcome evil with good and to bless those who curse you. Attackers are not the enemy; they are the mission field. Jesus died for them.

Our culture has accepted two lies: if you disagree with someone's lifestyle you must hate them or are afraid of them, and to love someone means you must agree with everything they believe or do. Both are nonsense.

Over the past thirty-five years, I've trained over 400,000 pastors in 164 countries. Every church leader needs training in how to represent Christ when attacked. But it's a fact: if you stand courageously for the truth, you will be attacked. How do you stay winsome under attack?

First, remember your reward: "Blessed are you when people insult you, persecute you and falsely say all kinds of evil against you because of me. Rejoice and be glad, because great is your reward in heaven…" We must be willing to be ridiculed, and even to suffer, for the truth. Courage by its very nature often requires taking an unpopular stand.

Second, live for an audience of One. Remember who we answer to at the end of the day.

On CNN I was asked, "Can you imagine ever changing your mind about gay marriage?" I said "No." "Why?" I said, "Because I fear God's disapproval more than I fear your disapproval or society's." As Saint Peter has said, "We must obey God rather than men."

The only way to always be relevant is to be eternal. What is in style goes out of style; no revolution lasts. Every lie eventually crumbles under its own deception. Cultures rise and fall, cultures come and go, but the Word of God and the Church of God continues. It isn't necessary to be on the right side of culture or the right side of history. It is just necessary to be on the right side!

In many ways, the debate over the definition of life, of sex, and of marriage is, in reality, a question of leadership. Who is going to lead? Will the church follow the crowd, or will the church lead the crowd? In Exodus 23:2 God says "You shall not fall in with the many to do evil…"

Why? Because history shows the majority is often wrong. The dustbins of history are stuffed with the conventional wisdom of cultures that proved false. Truth is not decided by a popularity contest.

## G. Give people confidence.

Two Catholic leaders I respect have talked about this. Archbishop Kurtz told me, "We must restore confidence that even in a broken world a biblical marriage is attainable." And Cardinal Chaput has said, "Believers don't have the luxury of pessimism."

We must preach the good news about marriage with hope and faith, not doom and gloom. Instead of merely telling it like it is, pastors must tell it like it can be. We must show them how they can beat the odds. We must help couples imagine how good their marriages could be if they will make the effort to improve it. This is preaching for faith! Jesus said, "According to your faith it will be done to you."

We must help people see their primary identity is found in Christ and not in their sins or any other distinction. For example, Saddleback's Celebrate Recovery program differs from Alcoholics Anonymous. At AA meetings a person identifies himself as "I am an alcoholic," but in Celebrate Recovery, which we base on the Beatitudes of Jesus, a person says "I am a disciple of Christ who struggles with alcohol." That makes a huge difference in both theology and practice.

## T. Teach the purposes of marriage.

You cannot value something until you understand its purpose. Anytime we forget God's intended purpose for any of his gifts, that gift will be misused, confused, abused, wasted, perverted, and even destroyed. This is true of your time, your money, your health, your freedom, your sexuality, and even marriage.

The Bible, primarily in Genesis, tells us God created marriage for six purposes:

1. *For the elimination of loneliness.* In Genesis 2:18 God tells Adam, "It is not good that man should be alone. I will make him a helper fit for him."

2. *For the expression of sex.* In Genesis 2:24 God says, "Therefore a man shall leave his father and his mother and hold fast to his wife, and they shall become one flesh."

3. *For the multiplication of the human race.* In Genesis 1:28 God says, "Be fruitful and multiply and fill the earth." This is the only command humans have obeyed successfully. Seven billion of us prove it.

4. *For the protection and education of children.* In Ephesians 6:4 God says, "Fathers, do not provoke your children to anger, but bring them up in the discipline and instruction of the Lord." Many speakers have already pointed out that children are hurt the most in a culture that devalues and dissolves marriage. I love The Message paraphrase of Malachi 2:15: "God, not you, made marriage. His Spirit inhabits even the smallest details of marriage. And what does he want from marriage? Children of God, that's what. So guard the spirit of marriage within you."

5. *For the perfection of our character.* 1 Corinthians 7:14 tells us, "For the unbelieving husband is made holy because of his wife, and the unbelieving wife is made holy because of her husband..." A purpose of marriage is to make us holy, not merely happy. It is the laboratory for learning to love. It's the school for learning sacrifice. It's the university for learning unselfishness. It's the lifelong course for becoming like Christ. If you are married, the number one tool God uses to shape you is your spouse!

6. *For the reflection of our union with Christ.* Ephesians 5:25–33 explains that marriage is a metaphor, a model of the mystery of Christ's love for his bride and body:

*Husbands, love your wives, as Christ loved the church and gave himself up for her, that he might sanctify her, having cleansed her by the washing of water with the word, so that he might present the church to himself in splendor, without spot or wrinkle or any such thing, that she might be holy and without blemish. In the same way husbands should love their wives as their own bodies. He who loves his wife loves himself. For no one ever hated his own flesh, but nourishes and cherishes it, just as Christ does the church, because we are members of his body. "Therefore a man shall leave his father and mother and hold fast to his wife, and the two shall become one flesh." This mystery is profound, and I am saying that it refers to Christ and the church. However, let each one of you love his wife as himself, and let the wife see that she respects her husband.*

This is the deepest meaning of marriage. This is the most profound purpose of marriage. This is the strongest reason marriage can only be between a man and a woman. No other relationship, including the parent-child relationship, can portray this intimate union. To redefine marriage would destroy the picture God intends for marriage to portray. We cannot cave on this issue.

Jesus said there is no marriage in heaven. Why? Because in heaven we won't need any of the six purposes of marriage. In a perfect place, we won't need protection of children, or the perfection of character, or even the reflection of our union with Christ because we will experience the reality.

In closing, I want to encourage you to never give up and never give in. The Church cannot be salt and light in a crumbling culture if it caves to the sexual revolution and fails to provide a countercultural witness. It is a myth we must give up biblical truth on sexuality and marriage in order to evangelize.

Twenty years ago, I wrote *The Purpose Driven Church*. The subtitle of that book was "Growth without Compromising Your Message and Mission." I think we've proved that is possible. Last month our local congregation baptized our 40,000th adult convert. Compromising truth has never grown anything. It only leads to decline and death and I warn those flirting with this myth that it would be a terrible mistake for the Church.

In the end we must be merciful to the fallen, show grace to the struggling, and be patient with the doubting. But when God's word is clear we must not and we cannot back up, back off, back down, or backslide from the truth.

The Church must never be captivated by culture, manipulated by critics, motivated by applause, frustrated by problems, debilitated by distractions, or intimidated by evil. We must keep running the race with our eyes on the goal, not on those shouting from the sideline. We must be Spirit-led, purpose-driven, and mission-focused so we cannot be bought, will not be compromised, and shall not quit until we finish the race.

# The Vindication of *The Manhattan Declaration*, Then and Now

*Mary Eberstadt*

Ten years ago, a countercultural declaration did what almost no generation before us could imagine doing: defending marriage, and taking flak for that defense. Seen one way, the *Declaration*'s position was, and is, "controversial." Seen otherwise—through the lens of empirical evidence—it stated truths social science had been documenting for decades and it documents still. Consider one towering example.

Over ten years before the *Declaration* appeared, James Q. Wilson, one of the most eminent social scientists of the 20th century, identified the root of America's fracturing in the dissolution of the family—put differently, the implosion of marriage. Wilson, professor emeritus of Harvard and UCLA and a former head of the American Political Science Association, received the American Enterprise Institute's 1997 Francis P. Boyer award at the think tank's annual gala. He used the opportunity to introduce a new line of sociological argument: what he called "the two nations" of America.

The image of "two nations," Wilson explained, harked back to a famous speech given a hundred years earlier by Benjamin Disraeli, Prime Minister of Great Britain. These were the separate, non-intersecting worlds of rich and poor. Disraeli said between these two nations, there was "no understanding and no sympathy"—they were "as ignorant of each other's habits, thoughts, and feelings as if they were inhabitants of different planets."

A century later, the great researcher argued, the United States had also become "two nations," but the dividing line was no longer one of income or social class. Instead, it became all about the family—specifically, whether one hailed from a broken or intact home. "It is not money," he observed, "but the family that is the foundation of public life. As it has become weaker, every structure built upon that foundation has become weaker."

Wilson called attention to what he saw as a national catastrophe in the making: the creation of generations of young men unhabituated to responsibility and protection of others. His argument harnessed decades of the kind of social science once channeled into the pages of *The Public Interest* and related venues. His speech was also, of course, part of the continuing commentary on the problems famously (and infamously) identified in 1965, in Daniel Patrick Moynihan's *Report on the Negro Family*. By 1997, as Wilson explained, family breakdown in America was no longer a phenomenon of the ghetto, but a fact of everyday life for more and more of the country.

Wilson pointed above all to the library that social science built over decades, filled with books and studies about the correlations between family particulars and behavioral probabilities. Family structure, he demonstrated, became more important to positive outcomes than race, income, or one's station at birth.

Children in one-parent families, compared to those in two-parent ones, are twice as likely to drop out of school. Boys in one-parent families are much more likely than those in two-parent ones to be both out of school and out of work. Girls in one-parent families are twice as likely as those in two-parent ones to have an out-of-wedlock birth. These differences are not explained by income. Children raised in single-parent homes [are] more likely to be suspended from school, to have emotional problems, and to behave badly.

So much of this social-science evidence now exists, Wilson joked, that as of 1997 "even some sociologists had come to believe it." The comment was made in jest, but it presaged our current puzzling situation. Over twenty years ago, evidence from all over the social sciences *already* indicated the sexual revolution was leaving a legacy of destruction. Two decades, and many more books and scholars and research studies later, a whole new wing has been added to that same library, all demonstrating the same point Wilson emphasized throughout his speech: The new wealth in America is familial wealth, and the new poverty, familial poverty.

Twenty years later, it is past time to ask: What has been the effect of all this social science? Has it helped to make two nations into one again? Has it ameliorated the problems Wilson and other bold thinkers have been elucidating since the 1960s? The answer to the latter two questions is *no*. To acknowledge this reality isn't to fault sociology itself, let alone the theoreticians brave enough to keep pursuing such unwelcome truths. To the contrary, their work, like Wilson's, remains vital. The monks of the Dark Ages toiled to preserve truths for the sake of truth, keeping faith that the time might come when the record would be better understood. The brave academics today who keep adding to that library of familial social science share more than a little in common with the truth-keepers of times past.

To reflect on Wilson's two nations from this moment in time is to understand that the sexual revolution remains apparently immune to his "library" of social-science fact. This is all the more reason to bring new "lenses" to understanding the continuing, largely unseen, transformative power of the revolution itself—including those transformations that could not possibly have been foreseen twenty years ago, by even the most towering diagnosticians.

## No Ties that Bind

We live in a moment of fantastic paradox. For even as the foundering of marriage has been regarded by many in Western society as a liberation, empiricism has delivered proof after proof the revolution has rendered terrible consequences. Some of that evidence can be found in places like Wilson's "two nations" speech, as well as throughout his other work. It has also been analyzed in conservative magazines and journals stretching back to the 1960s; in the books of writers like Midge Decter, George Gilder, and other intellectual pioneers; and in the ongoing works of contemporary sociologists like Brad Wilcox and Mark Regnerus. (Several years ago, I worked similar ground in my own book, *Adam and Eve after the Pill*, examining many examples of what social science was documenting about the damage to individuals of sexuality unbound.) These and other entries in the modern library take what might be called a "microscopic" lens to the revolution.

Yet, these are not the only proofs religious traditionalism may have gotten something right that most of the rest of the world keeps getting wrong. There are what might be called some "macroscopic" proofs—new evidence that the turn away from marriage not only continues to disfigure individual lives but is also widening its effects into society and politics in ways now amounting to signature problems of our times.

Begin with an example that dominated and transformed conversation from 2017 onward: widespread sexual harassment and the #MeToo movement. The most salient point to be made about these scandals hasn't made the rounds yet. It's not about one man or another newly fallen from worldly grace. It's rather about what, exactly, has made these multidimensional scandals possible in the first place. Men behaving badly, as some skeptics have shrugged, isn't exactly viral news. But a great many men taking for granted the sexual availability of any given woman, in one arena after another—that *is* new. That is something only the Pill and related technologies could have made possible.

Only in a world where sex is allegedly free of consequences would any man dare to proposition women on the spot, over and over, as appears to be the case among the repeat offenders accused in the harassment revelations of 2017. Put differently: No Pill, no sexual-harassment scandal, at least not *on the scale seen today*.

The revolution also appears connected to today's scandals in another, more subtle way. The shrinkage of the family brought on by contraception has deprived many men of sisters and daughters. It has deprived many women of brothers and sons. And, of course, divorce and cohabitation have also deprived boys and girls of biological parents, particularly fathers.

And what might be the net effect of all that deprivation? At a numerical minimum, it's a world in which the sexes know less about one another than they used to—in which many women no longer know any men as protectors, only as predators. It's a world in which many men who lack sisters, cousins, and the rest know women mainly through the lies absorbed in watching pornography.

Reading some of the grislier details of the ongoing scandals, many have been asking themselves: "What's wrong with these guys? Don't they have mothers, sisters, and other women to protect? How could they act this way, if that were the case?" The answer may well be in part that, after the sexual revolution, many men don't have much familial experience of the opposite sex—just as many women don't, either.

Just as formative, we also live at a moment when more and more people have no experience of organized religion. As Pew Research and other sources have been documenting for years, rising numbers of Americans, especially under the age of forty, are falling away from religious practice and religious literacy. This trend has many implications for society, of course—as the work of Arthur Brooks, president of the American Enterprise Institute, has shown, one is that charitable giving will likely decline—but it also has fallout we haven't yet begun to map.[1] It means many people no longer experience the opposite sex as those with a religious background are instructed to—as figurative sisters and brothers, united in fellowship. Once more, people have been deprived a familial, non-sexual knowledge of the opposite sex.

Again, behold the irony: The revolution has made sex more ubiquitous than ever before. But it has also estranged men and women as never before, both by shrinking the family and by increasing the mistrust between men and women thanks to widespread sexual consumerism. That includes not only dating apps like Tinder, but also the consumption of pornography, whose false accounts of relations between the sexes are poisoning romance on a macrocosmic scale. To offer just one indicator also unthinkable twenty years ago, internet pornography use is now a major factor cited in divorces.

Pornography's lies not only make the rounds—they are believed, and they affect personal behavior. When one prominent newsman fell from grace following multiple accusations of what just about any woman would call predatory conduct, he offered in his farewell tweet "I always felt I was pursuing shared feelings." Awful though his conduct allegedly was, those words bear the mark of authenticity. It seems safe to bet many modern men, especially those without religious attachments, believe similarly in the untruths spreading across the human race for half a century now—beginning with the untruth that both sexes take the same view

---

[1] Arthur C. Brooks, "Why Giving Makes You Happy," New York Sun (December 28, 2007); Brooks, *Gross National Happiness* (New York: Basic Brooks, 2008).

of supposedly consequence-free recreational sex. To observe the potency of this lie, particularly over certain male imaginations, isn't to exonerate offenders. It is merely to acknowledge the mass confusion plaguing interactions between the sexes.

To employ an image, think of sculptor Frederick Hart's magnificent and often-photographed work *Ex Nihilo*, on the front of Washington National Cathedral. It depicts beautiful human bodies emerging from chaos as God creates the world. Post-revolution romance for many seems the opposite of what Hart so famously rendered. Today, beautiful human beings do not so much arise from chaos fully formed, but instead plummet into it like Dante's Paolo and Francesca—endlessly circling and never really touching.

## After the Revolution

Consider another area in which post-revolutionary sexual habits are having profound and pernicious effects not seen twenty years ago: politics. Here I would like to focus on two ways in which the revolution now shapes, indeed disfigures, today's political order.

The first of these concerns the modern welfare state as we know it and its sustainability in the coming decades. It doesn't take an economist to see welfare schemes premised on family sizes of yesteryear cannot be sustained by demographic shrinkage.

It also doesn't take a Ph.D. to grasp that the fractured family is a major engine of the increased welfare state. Why? Because in many cases, the state is the financial backer making single motherhood—and absent fatherhood—possible. In effect, the state has become the angel investor of family dysfunction. The fracturing of the family has rendered the modern state a flush but controlling super-daddy. The state moves in to pick up the pieces of the shattered family—but, by bankrolling it, the custodial government ensures more of the same.

Economists are fond of saying that if we want more of something, we should subsidize it. And, though it's been done with the best intentions, that is exactly what the welfare state has been doing across the free societies of the West: subsidizing family breakdown.

This dynamic has profound political implications, including for those people who regard themselves as conservatives and constitutionalists first.

Unless and until there is family and religious revival, arguments on behalf of limited government are futile. Over 40 percent of children born in the United States today are born to unmarried parents. Twenty years ago, that number was around one third. Absent meaningful backlash against the revolution in the form of *some* kind of moral or religious revival, the state will continue to play the role of super-daddy.

Put differently: Without a rollback of the sexual revolution, there can be no rollback of the federal government. Another way in which the revolution is having macrocosmic political effects is more prosaic, though no less compelling for its obviousness. Even more than two decades ago, evidence today abounds that, whether of their own accord or that of others, a great many people out there are suffering. Something about the way we live now is manifestly making many fellow human beings miserable.

The national election of 2016 was widely held to be one of the most rancorous in history—a signal new low for politics. But it surely reflected even greater social discontent roiling underneath the surface. From the United States to Western Europe and beyond, many people in the world's most advanced societies are feeling angry, ignored, and disenfranchised. And today, as was the case ten years ago or twenty, it seems an incontestable truth that politics alone won't heal their wounds.

Millions are looking to government and to their political-cultural tribes to replace what they have lost—connections to family and transcendent communities. Vital books about the opioid epidemic, like J.D. Vance's *Hillbilly Elegy* and Sam Quinones's *Dreamland*, wrestle some of this pain into prose. Even so, beneath visible crises like unemployment in the Rust Belt and the heroin explosion, the fault line remains the same one identified by Wilson: the family, as the manifold dysfunctions in the pages of both books go to show.

Globalization is part of this same crisis, of course. So is the immediacy of the internet, which shows the have-nots what the haves enjoy up close and more personal than ever before, and also provides the angry and discontented with a power never available until now. Even so, what most ails great swaths of the country today is something more elemental than income disparity or a Gini coefficient, and more natural than any digital act of bonding.

Anthropological evidence from every culture and era verifies that human beings by their nature live in families—just as coyotes and elephants and many other mammals live in families rather than in random collections of individuals of the same species. The same evidence shows human beings across history have been pulled into transcendent communities of some kind. Both are elemental human demands. And since the revolution, a great many people can no longer figure out how to supply them.

## The Case for Hope

Given this current state of dysfunction, the inevitable question arises: What is to be done?

Wilson's proposed answer was ameliorative—and essentially, political. He advocated early, massive, extensive, and expensive intervention for the youngest children at risk, based on the fact social science has also shown those early years to be critical. Of course, nothing like that experiment has been run, at least not as ambitiously as he imagined.

On the other hand, with twenty more years' experience, seasoned observers today would cast a colder eye on the possibility of relief from the political quarter. Though some of the rip tides of 2018 are obviously political—arguments over immigration, tax reform, and the Supreme Court—others, like those already discussed, are springing from a more primordial place. Politics *per se* cannot account for the passion now attached to identitarianism, nor to the despair incarnate in today's rates of substance addiction, nor to the related fact psychiatrists and psychologists have been reporting for many years that a real rise in mental health trouble is underway, especially among women and the young. Politics did not create these problems. The revolution did. That's why politics alone will not solve them either.

The case for hope lies elsewhere, and it begins, paradoxically, in the very debasement in which we find ourselves. There is something unnatural and inhuman about the way many human beings pass their days. The same has also been true during other eras in history—often when society was on the verge of great renewal and reform movements.

The gin alleys of London gave rise to Victorian moral renewal. The rough mayhem of an earlier America spawned a Great Awakening that continues to echo through the sturdier corridors of American

Protestantism. Earlier waves of American drug addiction—cocaine, crack cocaine, crystal meth, even nicotine—are no longer focuses of great public concern because the crises passed.

If the examples of history offer one kind of ground for hope, up-to-the-minute reality holds out another. The recent scandals, by their very inescapability, have made it harder to mock the arguments made on behalf of marriage and embodied in *The Manhattan Declaration* and elsewhere. Up until now, to question any aspect of the fallout around us has been to consign oneself to the public dunce chair—the one sitting in the religious corner, where secular people expect to see zealots wearing medieval hoods. #MeToo just might reverse that course. After the scandals rolled out for weeks, in November 2017, the *Washington Post* published a piece that would have been unthinkable in that secular standard-bearer pre-Weinstein. "Let's Rethink Sex," by writer Christine Emba, criticized what she called "America's prevailing and problematic sexual ethic—one that is in no small part responsible for getting us into this sexual misconduct mess in the first place." This is surely only one example of other revisionism to come, and from outside religious orbits. Put differently, the perpetrators in the #MeToo stories may yet succeed in doing what generations of clergy have not: getting a new hearing for religious traditionalism.

Whatever else it has wrought, the revolution has divided and scattered ineradicably familial beings—human beings—like no other force in our time. Twenty years after Wilson's "two nations" speech, ten years after *The Manhattan Declaration*, there is more evidence than ever for the charge. There's a reason why "loneliness studies" are now the hottest academic stock in sociology. There's a reason why "happiness studies" document over and over what most people could have asserted without embarrassment the day before yesterday—people who live in families and practice religion tend to be happier and more productive than those who don't.

Occam's razor bends toward truth. Traditionalists and other contrarians have been right to argue that the revolution would lead to rising trouble between the sexes and a decline in respect for women. Future decades will show whether the secular sex scandals of 2017 amount to a passing drama soon to be replaced by some other, or an actual turning point in secular society's understanding of the sexual revolution. But the empirical record remains even clearer now than it was ten or twenty years ago—and it will still be clear ten, or twenty, or for that matter 200 years from now, whether a world mired in denial acknowledges as much, or not.[2]

---

[2] This chapter is adapted from Mary Eberstadt, "Two Nations, Revisited," *National Affairs* (Winter 2019).

# Why Marriage Belongs to God, Not to the State

*Jennifer Roback Morse*

Does marriage belong to God or the State? I will craft two contrasting portraits. What would our world look like if we organized society around the principle that marriage belongs to the State? What would our world be like if we took seriously the idea that marriage belongs to God?

In this portraiture, I will not use a generic "religion" or an abstract "state." I will instead refer to the modern State, based on the early modern philosophers, as we live in it today. The United States in principle, is limited by the Constitution. But in actual practice, the Administrative State in today's United States has vast powers not easily limited, predictable or even understood.

I do not propose some generic formless "religion" proposed by religious studies departments. Likewise, I reject the watered-down versions of Christianity so often presented in modern churches across many denominations. Their positions are nearly indistinguishable from the modern secular world. Instead, I refer to the God of the Christians, as revealed in Sacred Scripture and the best Christian tradition.

## If Marriage Belongs to the State

Let us begin with Thomas Hobbes and the image on the frontispiece of *Leviathan*. Hobbes' Sovereign towers over the countryside, including the Church. In an idolatrous inversion of the Mystical Body of Christ, all the people face inward toward the Sovereign. The whole society is ordered toward the Sovereign instead of toward Jesus Christ, whose divinity entitles Him to adoration. Hobbes' State takes on the role once reserved for God.

Every person *gets to become an individual* in Hobbes' structure, by surrendering his or her will to the State. 20th century political theorist Robert Nisbet interprets Hobbes in this way. Hobbes wanted to concentrate power within the State and suppress the power of all possible competing powers, such as the Church, guilds, and family:

> *Despite the…limitations put upon religion and all other autonomous systems of morality, it is the individual whom Hobbes has in his mind as the embodiment of virtue. Hobbes did not seek the extermination of individual rights but their fulfillment. This could be accomplished only by removing social barriers to individual autonomy. In his eyes the greatest claim of the absolute State lay in its power to create an environment for the individual's pursuit of his natural ends.*[1]

Nisbet argues further that Jean-Jacques Rousseau completes what Hobbes began. The powerful unitary State makes citizens truly free, by releasing them from the oppression of social convention and society.

---

[1] Robert Nisbet, *The Quest for Community: A Study in the Ethics of Order and Freedom,* (Wilmington, DE: ISI Books, Background Edition, 2010, reprinted in 2014), 127-8.

Rousseau sees the State as the most exalted of all forms of moral community: "…The State and the people are basically one. Only the State can provide the environment of equality, freedom, and tranquility for which man's nature calls."[2]

The early modern theorists like Hobbes and Rousseau were reacting against the social world of multiple competing authority structures. Institutions like the family, the Church, the guild, and the towns were more powerful than the centralized State. Hobbes' and Rousseau created an intellectual structure that removes these competitors. Their Sovereign is answerable to no one but himself. They regarded this as an advance in freedom for the individual.

We can characterize their position this way: An individual might very well experience the constraints of his parents and teachers and neighbors to be more pressing than the commands of a distant, impersonal State. Generations of young people have fled small towns for the "bright lights" of the city, because urban anonymity creates the sensation of freedom. In a small town, a person is accountable to his parents, his next-door neighbors, his pastor, and his Great Aunt Susie.

A person is only accountable to the impersonal forces of the law, for transgressions serious enough to come to the attention of the authorities. In theory, everyone willingly subordinates themselves to the General Will. In practice, some people are more powerful than others, thus the interests of the powerful dominate the State. Their power is not checked by any competing system of authority or legitimacy standing above or outside the State.

To some extent of course, the powerful dominate policy-making in any society. That is what it means to be powerful, whether power is defined in terms of material wealth, the prestige of an aristocracy or meritocracy, or simply physical strength. The modern difference is the Leviathan faces no competitors. The modern theory of sovereignty de-legitimates other social institutions and even reason. The power of the powerful is unlimited. Truth is whatever the State says it is. In other words, the law of the strongest prevails.

---

[2] Robert Nisbet, *The Quest for Community: A Study in the Ethics of Order and Freedom*, (Wilmington, DE: ISI Books, Background Edition, 2010, reprinted in 2014), 130.

In our time, this applies with particular force with respect to marriage and family. Marriage has been redefined to be whatever the State says it is. Individuals are free from any moral system other than the State's. Individuals can marry a person of the opposite sex, their own sex, more than one person, or even themselves. The State will not interfere with these lifestyle choices.

But the State most certainly will interfere with anyone who proposes a system of morality that competes with its own. One might think in a society that so values "choice," individuals should have a choice between marrying "until death do us part," or "for as long as love shall last." In practice, though, a lifelong marriage agreement is not legally enforceable. Through unilateral, no-fault divorce, the State has made marriage neither permanent or sexually exclusive. The State takes sides with the person who wants the marriage the least. Marriage is arguably no longer a social institution at all, but a mere collection of individuals.

When marriage belongs exclusively to the State, it guards its privileges jealously. The State favors a form of marriage that poses no threat to its power. The deepest foundations for attachments and loyalties are those flowing from the body: the relationship between parents and children, between mothers and fathers, between brothers and sisters. Some regard these relationships as the building blocks of the social order. But one must admit: these attachments provide individuals with possible sources of support, identity, and meaning, apart from the State. Hence, the kind of unitary State envisioned by Hobbes or Rousseau may very well conclude these family bonds threaten its unique position of power.

We might imagine Rousseau would approve our modern mores of behavior toward our sex partners and toward children. Here is his description of sexual pairings in the "state of nature:"

> As males and females united fortuitously according to encounters, opportunities, and desires, they required no speech to express the things they had to say to each other, and they separated with the same ease.

Rousseau could be describing our modern hook-up culture, down to and including the reluctance of hook-up partners to even talk to each other. He has no clue there may be some psychological and spiritual downsides to impersonal sexual couplings. Rousseau continues:

*The mother nursed her children at first to satisfy her own needs, then when habit had made them dear to her, she fed them to satisfy their needs; as soon as they had the strength to find their own food, they did not hesitate to leave their mother herself; and as there was virtually no way of finding one another again once they had lost sight of each other, they were soon at the stage of not even recognizing one another.*[3]

His description of the relationship between mother and child overlooks the significance of that most basic human attachment between mother and infant. He seems to think mothers do nothing more than deliver calories to the baby. The modern sciences of attachment and failure to thrive and child development put Rousseau's stripped-down theory of human relationship completely to shame. The vulnerability of the pregnant or nursing mother, the vulnerability of the infant, these patently obvious facts are assumed away in Rousseau's state of nature. Mothers and their infants could scarcely have survived the environment he imagines for them. But Rousseau's construct does remove competitors to the State's position as provider of material resources, personal identity, and social authority.

Perhaps incidentally, Rousseau's intellectual system does not require him to concern himself with the impact of his sexual activity on others, including the woman and any of the children she may bear. Indeed, Rousseau's personal irresponsibility is one of the best-known facts of philosophical history. He lived with a woman for years without burdening himself with the social convention of marriage. When she became pregnant, he insisted she take the children to the foundling hospital, an institution of civil society of which he no doubt disapproved. When she resisted this, he persuaded her mother to intervene and take her own grandchildren to the foundling hospital, where they very likely perished. I cannot forgive Rousseau for this, no matter how brilliant his philosophy may be.

The man of today is no longer accountable to his parents, his next-door neighbors, his pastor, and his Great Aunt Susie. His parents are divorced and preoccupied with their latest love interests. His neighbors open their garage doors from their cars, drive into their garages and go

---

[3] Jean-Jacques Rousseau, *A Discourse on Inequality* part one, translated by Maurice Cranston (1750; New York: Penguin, 1985).

into their houses, without ever seeing another person. He no longer has a local pastor, because the clergy has been relegated to the margins of society and are considered irrelevant or ridiculous. And Great Aunt Susie is in a nursing home in Dubuque.

But Jean-Jacques and his descendants are entitled to do what they want, without any interference or even any input from anyone else. Right up until the moment they bump into the Almighty State and its functionaries. And the rest of us are indescribably lonely.

Whether Rousseau or Hobbes could have predicted it, or would have approved, there can be no doubt of this. Today, the State shapes and regulates family life in a myriad of ways:

- The State promotes the idea that sexual activity has no procreative consequences. People can act as if sex produces neither children nor attachments to the child's other parent.

- The State promotes its own view of sex in its tax-supported schools, against the wishes and sometimes even the knowledge of the children's parents.

- The State provides material support to children, thus inserting itself into the most primal natural duties of parenthood, namely the parental responsibility to provide for their own young.

- Mothers can kill their own children prior to birth.

- No-fault divorce undermines lifelong marriage contracts: The State will not enforce them.

These policies, and many others, are consistent with the hypothesis that the State views the family and its system of natural attachments as a threat.

Finally, the concept of "love," so basic to the life of a family, plays no significant role in today's understanding of the State or society. Generations of Sexual Revolutionaries have reduced "love" to mere sentimentality. The slogan "Love is all you need," was really mostly about sex. And so was the thinly veiled invitation to promiscuity: "If you can't be with the one you love, love the one you're with." Most recently, "Love makes the family," begs the question of what happens to the family if the feelings of love go away.

The State has no place for love. This ideological system favors the powerful. Why then should we be surprised about "Patriarchy" becoming toxic? Men are physically more powerful than women. According to the law of the strongest, with love stripped out, men have license to boss women around. On what principle can anyone object to this? Patriarchy in the home is a special case of the loveless law of the strongest implemented at the top of society.

The form of feminism that arose with the promise of addressing patriarchal excesses had some very special properties. The ideology we now call "feminism" also has no place for love. Feminism solves problems inside the family by empowering the State to enter the family and supplant it.

Not all women approve of or desire this form of "feminism." Some women strenuously and conscientiously object to this ideology's claim to speak in their name. These women and their protestations have not slowed the advance of "feminism" in the least. Empowering women was not the point. Empowering the State was the point, of what we can now safely call Establishment Feminism.

To summarize, when the State takes possession of marriage and society, here is what we get:

- Marriage is whatever the State says it is.

- The law of the strongest prevails: there is no objective standard of right and wrong. The strongest take control of the State and bend it toward their own purposes.

- "Patriarchy" is a special case of the law of the strongest. There is no philosophical reason why the physically strongest should not prevail.

- The concept of "love" is barely recognizable and is most definitely not at the center of the social order. "Love" is a catchphrase, not a reality.

- The desire for attachment to other people has no significance or meaning. Attachments can, and perhaps should be, broken at will.

- The State inserts itself into "natural" relationships in the sense they are relationships based on the human body.

- The State and its allies have continuing incentives to diminish the importance of the human body, and the relationships built around it.

## If Marriage Belongs to God

By contrast, let us imagine a society formed around the idea marriage belongs to God. Law and social custom are decisively influenced by the ancient Christian beliefs about marriage, family, human sexuality, and the human body. What would such a social universe look like?

Let's start with some basics:

1. The Judeo-Christian God created the universe, and we didn't.

2. The transcendent God is totally Other.

3. God reveals Himself as "He."

4. The life and teachings of Jesus reveal God is love and a communion of three persons.

These points taken together have great significance for marriage.

Christians believe God created the universe out of nothing, as an act of pure love. He did not need to create: He is completely sufficient in Himself. But the Divine love among the three persons of the Trinity, Father, Son, and Holy Spirit overflowed into the series of creative acts recorded in Genesis. God declared everything He created to be "good" (Gen 1:10). After the creation of man, God declared His creation to be "very good" (Gen 1:31). "Let us make man in our image, according to our likeness.... So God created man in His own image; in the image of God He created him; male and female He created them" (Gen 1:26). Christians believe "God is love," (1 John 4:8) and God is a communion of persons, the Father, Son, and Holy Spirit. To be created in the image of a Trinitarian God, is to be created for love and for communion with others. Because "it is not good for man to be alone," God created woman. Upon seeing her, Adam exclaimed, "this one at last is bone of my bone and flesh of my flesh" (Gen 2:23). Eve is not a clone of Adam, nor is she so different she is another species. She is like him but not identical with him. Genesis continues, "Therefore, a man shall leave his father and mother and be joined to his wife, and they shall become one flesh" (Gen 2:24). With these words, God created marriage, the first human social institution. He told Adam and Eve to be fruitful and multiply, the first of His commands (Gen 1:28).

God created Adam and Eve out of love, and for love. God intended them to love Him and to love one another. Love cannot be coerced. Love must be freely given. Therefore, God created us with the capacity to choose to love or not love. All other choices pale before this basic choice: to love or not to love. It is the unbroken teaching of the Catholic Church, (though not all Protestant traditions) that God created us with freedom. With that great gift of freedom comes the possibility of choosing wrongly, of choosing against the love of God. And that is exactly what our first parents did. The serpent convinced them "You shall be as gods," if they chose against God's one simple rule not to eat of the Tree of Knowledge of Good and Evil (Gen 3:5). Of course, they became no such things as gods. We men and women are not gods, but creatures of God.

God reveals Himself as masculine. Some modern scholars wish to dismiss this as a mere bowing to misogynistic cultural values contemporaneous with the writing of Scripture. This claim is unpersuasive.

God created the very concept of sexual reproduction, which includes gendered bodies. Surely this was not some kind of divine accession to human weakness, for God created those very humans with all those very weaknesses. It is much more reasonable to suppose God knew exactly what He was doing when He created us in His image, both male and female. If Scripture is to be believed at all, God was trying to tell us something, which he baked into the nature of creation.

In his letter to the Ephesians, Paul shows us a parallelism between man and woman and Christ and the Church. The marriage between Christ and His Church is the deep reality; the marriage between men and women is the image. Our experience of marriage is meant to provide us with an icon pointing to Christ and the Church. Christ is always faithful and loving. Christ is masculine. The Church, the bride, is feminine. The significance of this is so deep we can hardly comprehend it. Wives must submit to their husbands, as to Christ. This passage drives feminists crazy-angry. This same passage makes some men power-crazy. Both groups fail to read the next sentence. The husband must love his wife, as

Christ loves the Church. This is supposed to point men toward a self-sacrificing love unto death.

Paul no doubt expected his listeners to look back to the tremendous Hebrew scripture imagery of Israel as a prostitute. God always took her back. Yes, God punished Israel and Judah for "playing the harlot," by running after other gods. But He was not arbitrarily bossing them around. They deserved the Babylonian Exile and all the rest. And He always took them back. Some feminist theologians invented a new religion. The product of their speculations was certainly not historic Christianity. The confusion they created continues to do harm.

## Human Love in the Divine Plan

Human love is part of the divine plan. God, the author of all life, could have arranged human reproduction differently than He did. He could have created the world so He performed an act of special creation with every new person, without requiring any human participation at all. But in the world as He created it, the sexual act between a man and a woman can bring forth new life. Human participation in procreation flows from an act of love between man and woman. The love of human parents for each other overflows into the creation of a new life, just as the divine love within the Trinity sprang forth into the creation of the world.

Our participation in the creation of new life is emphatically not "control" or "making" or "creating" on our part. The creation of a new human being requires the cooperation between man, woman, *and God*. Even artificial reproductive technology, which seems to be the ultimate in human control over procreation, has a large random element to it. It has been said "random" acts are God's way of remaining anonymous. But I don't think that description does justice to God's participation in the creation of new life.

God's part in the creation of new life is always love, even if our part falls greatly short of love. A man and woman may conceive a child by accident, or through rape. They may conceive a child in a drunken stupor or in the back seat of a car. They may conceive a child without having any relationship with each other at all, using artificial means.

But God's participation is always love. No matter what our motives or behavior, no matter how careless or violent or unjust or unprepared we may be, God's participation in the process is always love. God loves every child conceived, no matter how they were conceived. Therefore, no matter what wrong we may have done, we must never regret the child. God loves the child and wills his or her existence.

This is why God wants our participation in the sexual act to take place inside marriage. By making a lifelong commitment to each other before even having sex, the couple prepares themselves for parenthood. Their relationship will be the foundation for their child's life, for the rest of the child's life. Traditional Christian sexual morality safeguards the relationship between children and their parents. Children need their parents. We could even say children are entitled to care from, and relationship with, both of their parents.

These entitlements of children impose responsibilities on adults. Sometimes people regard traditional Christian sexual morality as a series of prohibitions:

- No sex before or outside marriage (And no, abortion and contraception do not excuse us from this requirement).

- No divorce without cause.

- No petty criticism of your spouse.

We often chafe at these obligations. Yet in the civilizations shaped by Christianity, people have come to see that living up to these responsibilities is a great adventure and worth the effort. God wants us to love our children into existence, as a by-product of loving our spouses.

To summarize, when *society organizes itself around God's view of marriage*, here is what we get:

- Love is a meaningful and central concept.

- Children have the lifelong commitment of their parents.

- People are loved into existence by God and by their natural parents.

- Everyone, at least in principle, is accountable to God, who stands outside the created order.

- The objective moral order exists independently of the will of the strongest, including the State.

- God created men and women, equally in his image and likeness.

- Marriage is an icon of the relationship between Jesus Christ and His bride, the Church.

- Patriarchy requires men to sacrifice themselves for their wives and children.

## Conclusion: Comparing the State's Marriage with God's Marriage

This is what Christians believe: God loves each of us into existence and wants us to participate in His creative process through love. At the center of the universe is a deep abiding love. We are called to be part of it. We are not ashamed to believe this.

We invite each reader to consider: are you really satisfied with the alternative the modern secular world has created? We invite everyone to accept the challenge to live as if we are loved into existence.

# Marriage Equality, Marriage Reality

*Ryan T. Anderson*[1]

Most everyone in America was and is in favor of marriage equality. Most everyone was and is in favor of marriage equality because most everyone wants the law to treat all marriages equally. The debate in the United States in the decade and a half before *Obergefell* wasn't about equality. It was about marriage. We disagreed about *what marriage is*.

Of course, "marriage equality" was a great slogan. It fit on a bumper sticker. You could make a red equal sign your Facebook profile picture. It was a wonderful piece of advertising. And yet, it's completely vacuous. It doesn't say a thing about *what marriage is*. Only if you know what marriage is can you then decide whether any given marriage *policy* violates marriage *equality*. Before you can get to considerations of equal protection of the law, you have to know what it is the law is trying to protect equally.

Sloganeering aside, appeals to "marriage equality" betray sloppy reasoning. Every law makes distinctions. Equality before the law protects citizens from *arbitrary* distinctions, from laws that treat them differently *for no good reason*. To know whether a law makes the right distinctions, whether the lines it draws are justified, one has to know the public purpose of the law and the nature of the good it advances or protects.

After all, even those who want to redefine marriage to include same-sex couples will draw lines defining what sorts of relationships are a

---

[1] This essay is drawn from Ryan T. Anderson, *Truth Overruled: The Future of Marriage and Religious Freedom* (Washington, D.C.: Regnery, 2015).

marriage and what sorts are not. If we are going to draw lines based on principle, if we are going to draw lines reflecting the truth, we have to know what sort of relationship marriage is. That's why Sherif Girgis, Robert P. George, and I wrote a book a few years ago titled *What Is Marriage?*[2] You have to answer *that* question before you talk about recognizing marriage equally.

And yet implicit throughout the Court's opinion redefining marriage in *Obergefell* is the assumption marriage is a genderless institution. But as Justice Samuel Alito pointed out two years earlier in his dissenting opinion in the Defense of Marriage Act case, the United States Constitution is silent about what marriage is. Justice Alito framed the debate as a contest between two visions of marriage—what he calls the "conjugal" and "consent-based" views.[3]

Justice Alito cited the book I coauthored as an example of the conjugal view of marriage: a "comprehensive, exclusive, permanent union that is intrinsically ordered to producing new life."[4] On the other side, he cited Jonathan Rauch as a proponent of the consent-based idea that marriage is a commitment marked by emotional union.[5] The Constitution, he explained, is silent on which of these substantive visions of marriage is correct.[6] Justice Alito, of course, was right about the Constitution.

But were there ever any reasonable grounds for this debate in the first place? The consent-based view of marriage is primarily about an intense emotional union: a romantic, caregiving union of consenting adults. It is what the philosopher John Corvino describes as the relationship that establishes your "number one person."[7] What sets marriage apart from other relationships is the priority of the relationship. It's your most important relationship; the most intense emotional, romantic union; the caregiving relationship that takes priority over all others. Andrew Sullivan says marriage has become "primarily a way in which two adults affirm

---

[2] See generally Sherif Girgis, Ryan T. Anderson, & Robert P. George, *What Is Marriage? Man and Woman: A Defense* (New York: Encounter Books, 2012); Sherif Girgis, Robert P. George, & Ryan T. Anderson, What is Marriage?, 34 Harvard Journal of Law and Public Policy, 245 (2011).

[3] *See United States v. Windsor*, 133 S. Ct. 2675, 2711 (2013) (Alito, J., dissenting).

[4] *Id.* at 2718 (citing Girgis, Anderson & George, *supra* note 3).

[5] *Id.* at 2716 (citing Jonathan Rauch, *Gay Marriage: Why It Is Good for Gays, Good for Straights, and Good for America* (New York: Times Books, 2004) 94.

[6] *Id.*

[7] John Corvino & Maggie Gallagher, *Debating Same-Sex Marriage* (New York: Oxford University Books, 2012).

their emotional commitment to one another."[8] *This* vision of what marriage is does all the work in Justice Anthony Kennedy's majority opinion in *Obergefell.*

In *What Is Marriage?*, my coauthors and I argue this view collapses marriage into companionship in general.[9] Rather than understanding marriage correctly as *different in kind* from other relationships, the consent-based view sees in it only a *difference of degree*: marriage has what all other relationships have, but more of it. This, we argue, gets marriage wrong. It cannot explain or justify any of the distinctive commitments that marriage requires: monogamy, exclusivity, and permanence, nor can it explain what interest the government has in it.

If marriage is simply about consenting adult romance and caregiving, why should it be permanent? Emotions come and go; love waxes and wanes. Why would such a bond require a pledge of permanency? Might not someone find the romance and caregiving of marriage enhanced by a temporary commitment, in which no one is under a life sentence?

In fact, if marriage is simply about consenting adult romance and caregiving, why should it be a sexually exclusive union? Sure, some people might prefer to sleep only with their spouse, but others might think agreeing to have extramarital sexual outlets would *enhance* their marriage. Why impose the expectation of sexual fidelity?

Lastly, if marriage is simply about consenting adult romance and caregiving, why can't three, four, or more people form a marriage? There is nothing about intense emotional unions limiting them to two and only two people. Threesomes and foursomes can form an intense, emotional, romantic, caregiving relationship as easily as a couple. Nothing in principle requires monogamy. Polyamory (group love) seems perfectly compatible with the consent-based view of marriage.

The consent-based view of *what marriage is* simply fails as a theory of marriage because it cannot explain any of the historical marital norms. A couple informed by the consent-based view might live out these norms if temperament or taste so moved them, but there would be no reason of principle for them to do so and no basis for the law to encourage them to do so. Marriage can come in as many different sizes

---

[8] Andrew Sullivan, *Introduction*, in *Same-Sex Marriage: Pro and Con: A Reader* (New York: Vintage, 2004), xvii, xix.

[9] Girgis, Anderson & George, *supra* note 3.

and shapes as consenting adults can dream up. Love equals love, after all. And why, in any case, should the government have any involvement in this kind of marriage? If marriage is just about the love lives of consenting adults, let's get the state out of their bedrooms. And yet those who supported the redefinition of marriage wanted to put the government into more bedrooms.

There is nothing "homosexual" or "gay" or "lesbian," of course, about the consent-based view of marriage. Many heterosexuals have bought into it over the past fifty years. This is the vision of marriage from the sexual revolution. Long before there was a debate about same-sex anything, heterosexuals bought into a liberal ideology about sexuality that makes a mess of marriage: cohabitation, no-fault divorce, extramarital sex, non-marital childbearing, pornography, and the hook-up culture all contributed to the breakdown of the marriage culture. The push for the legal redefinition of marriage didn't cause any of these problems. It is, rather, their logical conclusion. The problem is it's the logical conclusion of a bad train of logic.

If the sexual habits of the past fifty years have been good for society, good for women, good for children, then by all means it's reasonable to enshrine the consent-based view of marriage in law. But, if the past fifty years have not been so good for society, for women, for children, indeed, if they have been, for many people, a disaster, why would we lock in a view of marriage that will make it more difficult to recover a more humane vision of human sexuality and family life?

The law cannot be neutral between the consent-based and conjugal views of marriage. It will enshrine one view or the other. It will either teach marriage as consenting adult love of whatever size or shape the adults choose, or it will teach marriage as a comprehensive union of sexually complementary spouses who live by the norms of monogamy, exclusivity, and permanency, so children can be raised by their mom and dad. There is no third option. There is no neutral position. The law will embrace one or the other.

## The Conjugal View of Marriage

Here I utilize an Aristotelian methodology that can be used to analyze any type of community. Aristotle suggests we can understand any community by analyzing three factors: the actions the community engages in, the goods the community seeks, and the norms of commitment that shape the community's common life. To illustrate how this method of analysis works, consider an uncontroversial example: the academic community of a university.

## An Academic Community

What makes a university an *academic* community rather than a big business or a sports franchise, even though most universities engage in both business and athletics on a large scale? Following the Aristotelian methodology, I argue a university is an academic community because of the academic actions it engages in, the academic goods it seeks, and the academic norms it lives by.

Members of an academic community engage in academic action. What sorts of things are academic actions? Professors research and write academic articles and books and assign students to read them. They deliver lectures, which students attend and take notes on. Students take exams and write papers, and professors grade and discuss them with students. These are the sorts of activities constituting an academic community *as* an academic community. Annual giving campaigns and football games are nice additions, but they don't go to the heart of what makes a university a university. These academic activities are the heart of a university (or at least they should be).

Now what are these academic activities ultimately seeking? What are the goods toward which they are oriented? They're oriented toward the goods of the truth and of knowledge. All the exercises professors make students perform, the homework, the term papers, the research projects, and all the work they do, writing those books and papers and delivering those lectures, are all about eliminating ignorance from our lives and coming to a better appropriation of the truth. Academic actions aren't supposed to be exercises in propaganda or defenses of prejudices. They are about discovering the truth so we don't live in ignorance or as slaves to prejudice. Academic actions are oriented toward academic goods, the goods of knowledge and of the truth.

So what norms do such actions in pursuit of such goods require of an academic community? This is where all the commitment to academic integrity, academic freedom, and academic honor codes come into play. Students shouldn't plagiarize, researchers should cite all their sources, scientists should assess all the data, not just those supporting their hypothesis. If one researcher finds weaknesses in another's study, the latter shouldn't view it as an attack but as assistance in the common pursuit of truth. When a professor critiques a student's paper, the student shouldn't view it as an insult but as help in his understanding the truth.

There are three easy steps. Academic actions (research, reading, writing, discussion) are ordered toward academic goods (knowledge of the truth and elimination of ignorance) and thus demand academic norms (academic honesty, academic freedom, academic honor codes) so the community can fulfill its purpose: the discovery of truth.

## The Marital Community

We can understand the marital relationship in the same way. What makes marriage different from other forms of community, like a football team, say, or a university? In every aspect, marriage is a *comprehensive* relationship. It is comprehensive in the act that uniquely unites the spouses, in the goods the spouses are ordered toward, and in the norms of commitment it requires from them.

Marriage unites spouses in a comprehensive act: marital sexual intercourse is a union of hearts, minds, and bodies. Marriage, like the marital act seals it, is inherently ordered toward a comprehensive good: the creation and rearing of entirely new human organisms, who are to be raised to participate in every kind of human good. And finally, marriage demands comprehensive norms: spouses make the comprehensive commitments of permanency and exclusivity, comprehensive throughout time (permanent) and at every moment in time (exclusive).

If that sounds abstract, let us move in for a closer look. First, the comprehensive act. How can two persons unite comprehensively? To unite comprehensively, they must unite at all levels of their personhood. But what is a person? Human beings are mind-body unities. We are not ghosts in machines or souls somehow inhabiting flesh and bones. Rather, we are enfleshed souls or ensouled bodies: a mind-body unity.[10] Thus, to

---

[10] See, for example, Patrick Lee and Robert P. George, *Body-Self Dualism in Contemporary Ethics and Politics* (Cambridge: Cambridge University Press, 2009).

unite with someone in a comprehensive way, one must unite with him at all levels of his personhood: a union of hearts, minds, and bodies.

Ordinary friendships are unions of hearts and minds. Uniting bodily is not a part of the typical understanding of friendship. But bodily union is part of what it means to be in a spousal relationship. This, of course, raises the question: How can two human beings unite bodily? To answer this, we need to understand what makes any *individual* one body.

What is it that makes each one of us a unified organism? Why aren't we just clumps of cells? The answer is all our various bodily systems and parts work together for the common good of our biological lives. Your heart, lungs, kidneys, muscles, and all the other organs and tissues coordinate to keep you alive. Coordination toward a common end explains unity, in this case bodily unity of an individual.

And in most respects, you are complete as an individual. With respect to locomotion, you can set this book down, get up, and walk into the kitchen for a bite to eat. With respect to digestion, you can digest that bite all by yourself. With respect to circulation and respiration, you can breathe and pump oxygenated blood throughout your body as an individual. In all these functions, you're complete.

Yet, with respect to one biological function, you are radically incomplete. In the marital act, a man's body and a woman's body do not just make contact as in a kiss or interlock as when holding hands. The Hebrew Bible reveals something true about our humanity when it says a man and a woman in the marital act become "one flesh." This is not merely a figure of speech. The Bible does not say the husband and wife are so much in love it's *as if* the two become one. The Scriptures rightly suggest that at the physical and metaphysical level, a man and a woman truly become two in one *flesh*. The sexual complementarity of a man and a woman allows them to unite in this comprehensive way.

In the marital act, the husband and wife engage in a single act with a single function: coordination toward a common end unites them. They form a single organism as a mated pair with a single biological purpose, which the couple performs together as a unity. Note the parallel. The muscles, heart, lungs, stomach, and intestines of an individual human body coordinate with each other toward a single biological end: the continued life of that body. In the same way, a man and a woman, when they unite in the marital act, coordinate toward a single biological end:

procreation. This is true regardless whether any particular marital act results in the fusion of a sperm with an egg. What matters is the voluntary behavior in which the spouses engage. That is what unites them.

And the union this act brings about is so complete that frequently, nine months later, it requires a name. The lovemaking act is also the life-giving act. The act uniting a man and a woman as husband and wife is the same act that can make them mother and father. This begins to tell us something about what the marital relationship is ordered toward.

In the same way academic communities engage in academic actions ordered toward the academic goods of the pursuit of truth and knowledge, the marital relationship is (like the act that embodies it) ordered toward the marital good of procreation and rearing and education of children. The good toward which the marital act is ordered is not a one-time good like winning the next football game or passing the next test. The marital act is comprehensive. It unites the spouses in heart, mind, and body, and is thus oriented toward a comprehensive good, the procreation and education of new persons who can appreciate human goodness in all its dimensions. Marriage is unlike any other community in being comprehensive.

Now it should be clear why marriage requires the comprehensive commitments of both exclusivity and permanency. Let us start with exclusivity. What sort of exclusivity does marriage call for? *Sexual* exclusivity. You do not cheat on your spouse by attending a lecture with someone else. You do not cheat on your spouse by playing football with someone else. But you do cheat on your spouse if you have sex with someone else. It is the sexual act that transforms an ordinary friendship, a union of hearts and minds, into the comprehensive community of marriage, so the marital norm of exclusivity focuses on sexual fidelity. The act distinctive to marriage, which we therefore call the "marital act," must be reserved exclusively for the spouses. To unite comprehensively with your spouse requires you to pledge not to unite sexually with others. It requires you, in the words of the traditional marriage vow, to forsake all others.

Something similar is true for the other comprehensive commitment of marriage. Because marriage is a comprehensive union, it requires the comprehensive commitment of permanency. To unite comprehensively, spouses cannot hold anything back. If they have a sunset clause, if they have an escape date, if they have a way out, they are not really uniting comprehensively.

Comprehensive union requires an open-ended commitment. So, marriage requires "forsaking all others" not only for the time being but also into the future: "till death do us part." Ordered toward the comprehensive good of procreation, marriage must be permanent. The families that marriage produces—not only parents and children but also grandparents, nieces and nephews, aunts, uncles, and cousins—will be stable only if the marital union is stable. Again, the comprehensive nature of marriage explains its comprehensive act, good, and norms.

## Human Nature, Not Anti-Gay Animosity

Many diverse political, philosophical, and theological traditions, each with its own vocabulary and with differences around the margins, have articulated something like the conjugal, comprehensive view of marriage. They have arrived at this truth by grappling with basic human realities, not out of animosity toward same-sex relationships. Indeed, cultures with no concept of "sexual orientation" and cultures taking homoeroticism for granted have understood the union of husband and wife is a distinct and uniquely important relationship. Citing the historical consensus, Justice Alito asked during oral arguments:

> [H]ow do you account for the fact that, as far as I'm aware, until the end of the twentieth century, there never was a nation or a culture that recognized marriage between two people of the same sex? Now, can we infer from that that those nations and those cultures all thought that there was some rational, practical purpose for defining marriage in that way, or is it your argument that they were all operating independently based solely on irrational stereotypes and prejudice?[11]

Support for marriage as the union of a man and a woman can't simply be the result of anti-gay animus, Justice Alito pointed out, because "there have been cultures that did not frown on homosexuality.... Ancient Greece is an example. It was well accepted within certain bounds."[12] The Justice added that "people like Plato wrote in favor of that."[13] And yet, the

---

[11] Obergefell Argument Transcript, *supra* note 9, at 9.
[12] *Id.* at 14.
[13] *Id.*

ancient Greeks, including Plato, never thought a same-sex relationship was a marriage.

As Chief Justice John Roberts explained in his dissenting opinion in *Obergefell*, marriage as the union of husband and wife is about serving the common good, not excluding anyone:

> *This universal definition of marriage as the union of a man and a woman is no historical coincidence. Marriage did not come about as a result of a political movement, discovery, disease, war, religious doctrine, or any other moving force of world history—and certainly not as a result of a prehistoric decision to exclude gays and lesbians. It arose in the nature of things to meet a vital need: ensuring that children are conceived by a mother and father committed to raising them in the stable conditions of a lifelong relationship.*[14]

Defying the universal consensus about marriage requires breathtaking presumption. Whatever arguments there may be in favor of doing so, that consensus cannot be dismissed as a relic of irrational animus against men and women attracted to members of their own sex.

## Threatening Religious Liberty

The redefinition of marriage will lead to the further erosion of monogamy, exclusivity, and permanence. It will lead to the further denial that children deserve both a mother and a father. It will lead to the further abuse of assisted reproductive technologies, to further the trend to prioritize the desires of adults not the needs—or rights—of children. And so too will it lead to further threats to religious liberty.[15]

With marriage now redefined, we can expect to see the marginalization of those with traditional views and the erosion of religious liberty. The law and culture will seek to eradicate such views through economic, social, and legal pressure. With marriage redefined, believing what virtually every human society once believed about marriage will increasingly be deemed a malicious prejudice to be driven to the margins of culture. The consequences for religious believers are becoming apparent.

---

[14] Obergefell v. Hodges, 135 S. Ct. 2584, 2613 (2015) (Roberts, C.J., dissenting).

[15] On all of these consequences see Ryan T. Anderson, *Truth Overruled: The Future of Marriage and Religious Freedom*.

Here is what we can expect: The administrative state may require those who contract with the government receive governmental money, or work directly for the state to embrace and promote same-sex marriage even if doing so violates their religious beliefs. Nondiscrimination laws may make even private actors with no legal or financial ties to the government—including businesses and religious organizations—liable to civil suits for refusing to treat same-sex relationships as marriages. Finally, private actors in a culture that is now hostile to traditional views of marriage may discipline, fire, or deny professional certification to those who express support for traditional marriage.

The attack on religious liberty has in fact already begun, as I describe in more detail in *Truth Overruled*.[16] Now is the time for all Americans to work to ensure citizens who believe we are created male and female—and male and female are created for each other in marriage—are not penalized by the government.

Protecting this freedom takes several forms. Charities, schools, and other organizations interacting with the government should be held to the same standards of competence as everyone else, but their view of marriage as the union of a man and a woman should never disqualify them from government programs.

Educational institutions, for example, should be eligible for government contracts, student loans, and other forms of support as long as they meet the relevant educational criteria. Adoption and foster care organizations that meet the substantive requirements of child welfare agencies should be eligible for government contracts without having to abandon the religious values that led them to help orphaned children in the first place. Protecting the diversity of private providers, each serving families sharing its values, will increase the number of children who are connected with permanent, loving families.

Government rightly withholds taxpayer dollars from certain organizations—those that perform abortions, for example, or those with racist policies—but upholding marriage as the union of a man and a woman is nothing like killing or racism. Government policy should not trample the consciences of citizens who dissent from political correctness on sexuality. Government policy discriminating against social service providers that

---

[16] Anderson, *supra* note 93, at 85–104.

believe marriage is a male–female union undermines our nation's commitment to pluralism and diversity.

The court has redefined marriage, and beliefs about human sexuality are changing. America is in a time of transition. During this time, it is critical to protect the right to dissent and the civil liberties of those who speak and act in accord with what Americans had always believed about marriage—it is the union of husband and wife. Good public policy is needed at the local, state, and federal levels to protect cherished American values. We must work to achieve civil peace amid disagreement and protect pluralism and the rights of all Americans, regardless what faith they may practice.

# PART THREE

# Religious Liberty

# Why Religious Freedom Matters:
# A Brief History

*Michael Farris*

The First Amendment protects six particular freedoms: free exercise of religion, freedom from state-established religion, free speech, free press, freedom of assembly, and the right to petition for redress of grievances.

When Americans claimed these freedoms in the revolution and codified them in the following years, they often referred to their collective liberties as "the rights of Englishmen." But broad religious and expressive freedoms were not always protected in England. And it is the history of the struggle for religious liberty in particular that explains the development of constitutional liberty in the United States.

In the 16th through 18th centuries in England, none of these ideals were recognized as innate human freedoms; all were curtailed in the wake of coerced religious uniformity. Bible translators, like William Tyndale, played a unique role in the battle for these liberties. It was the demand to publish, own, discuss, teach, and believe the Bible in English that collided with the forces of religious coercion. That collision created the demand for freedom among people who wanted to think, speak, and believe for themselves as informed by their own reading of the Word of God.

The conflict did not merely involve the freedom to believe, nor a narrowly-defined free exercise of religion. In order to believe, teach, publish, meet, and evangelize for their Bible-inspired faith, a robust set of freedoms were demanded.

The fact the freedoms eventually enumerated in the First Amendment are ultimately interdependent is evident in the history of their development in England. A few snapshots demonstrate the comprehensive freedoms necessary to truly achieve religious freedom. Tyndale attempted but failed to get official permission to translate and publish the Scriptures into English. Freedom of the press was non-existent in a nation practicing prior restraints. Those found in possession of his unsanctioned portions of Scripture were jailed or burned at the stake. Free exercise of religion was viewed as damnable heresy. Members of small dissident religious groups seeking to meet secretly in homes, like the Kent Conventiclers, were arrested. Freedom of association was punished for creating schisms. An illiterate farmer named John Maundrel (who owned a New Testament read to him by any willing literate person) was arrested, convicted, and eventually burned at the stake for speaking up about what he thought were theological errors in a prayer by a vicar. Freedom of speech was not an accepted ideal. And when about a thousand reformed pastors sent a petition to King James urging a variety of changes to the Church of England, he railed that they would conform to his edicts or be run out of their jobs or worse. Petitioning for redress of grievances was not a protected right.

Despite an oft-repeated claim that these freedoms arose from the Enlightenment, historians specializing in the history of religious liberty have long recognized these freedoms were not attained by secular philosophers who were indifferent to religious belief.

Historian Perez Zagorin thoroughly examined the claim that the Enlightenment was the catalyst for the development of religious liberty. He found little evidence of a direct influence. Rather, Zagorin looked to those like the Kent Conventiclers and Baptist pastors like Thomas Helwys who risked and, in many cases, lost their lives for religious liberty. He concluded, "[T]he intellectual changes…since they occurred only gradually, cannot possibly account for the theories and defenses of toleration that appeared in the second half of the sixteenth century." Rather, religious freedom was wrought "not of minds inclined to religious indifference or unbelief" among "nearly all the major theorists of toleration in the seventeenth century."

The fabled Harvard historian, W. K. Jordan, said much the same in the opening pages of his four-volume work on the history of religious toleration in England: "It cannot be denied that skepticism and indifference have been powerful agents in weakening the theory and practice of persecution. But is an error to say that the indifferent man can be tolerant of a religious belief; he is simply indifferent to it." Writing in the 1930s, Jordan continued, "There can be little doubt that the modern tolerance towards religious diversity has a large content of indifference, but religious toleration, was achieved, at least in England, before public indifference to theological questions had attained a place of dominant influence."

Any suggestion that advocacy for secular free expression rights (speech, press, assembly, petition) paved the way for all freedoms including religious freedom has little historical support. In fact, religious dissenters who wanted to practice their faith were the ones who opened the doors for every component of what we now call First Amendment liberties.

It is important to distinguish those who wanted religious sanctuary only for themselves from advocates for true religious liberty, which treats all faiths evenhandedly. W.K. Jordan explained the theoretical framework for those who believed in liberty for all:

> *It is true that every persecuted sect which holds that it teaches divine truth and follows the divine will maintains that the State cannot justly punish its members for beliefs which are held in conscience. But such groups, unless their underlying philosophy rests upon the assertion of the religious necessity of freedom for every Christian man, will not be likely to argue for the toleration of groups which differ both from them and from the established order...*

Those who believed true faith was necessary for salvation refused to believe the King should attempt to force anyone to confess a particular faith. This would only result in hypocrisy, not true faith. Moreover, they believed personal faith was a matter falling solely within the jurisdiction of God and not any King. In this way, it was commitment to these religious truths that ultimately motivated the conviction that the state must refrain from enforcing those truths.

England's first Baptist pastor, Thomas Helwys, pointedly made this argument in a handwritten inscription penned to King James—who was no friend of religious liberty. In 1612, Helwys published a 212-page treatise entitled *A Short Declaration of the Mystery of Iniquity* that was pointedly written to King James. The remaining copy in Oxford's Bodleian Library contains a handwritten message from Helwys to the King on the inside cover:

> Hear, O King, and despise not the counsel of the poor, and let their complaints come before thee. The king is a mortal man and not God: therefore hath no power over the immortal souls of his subjects, to make laws and ordinances for them, and to set spiritual Lords over them. If the king have any authority to make spiritual Lords and laws, then he is an immortal God, and not a mortal man. O King, be not seduced by deceivers to sin against God whom thou oughtest to obey, nor against thy poor subjects who ought and will obey thee in all things with body, life and goods, or else let their lives be taken from the earth. God save the King. Spittlefield, near London. Tho. Helwys.

Just as the rationale for religious freedom requires that it must extend to all beliefs, so too it requires the preservation of other practical freedoms, like the liberty to speak, publish, and assemble with those who share one's beliefs. And the need for this full range of liberty was not lost on Helwys. King James did not arrest Helwys for what he believed. It was the publication and dissemination of this book that landed him in the King's Bench prison where he ultimately died from mistreatment. Freedoms travel together—for better or worse.

Many who have practiced repression in the last century have claimed to be protecting liberty in some fashion. But in the days of Helwys and Tyndale, it was not fashionable to give even lip-service to the idea of religious liberty. The very idea was denounced.

Opponents of religious liberty, like George Gillespie, a Scottish member of the Westminster Assembly of Divines, forthrightly denounced religious liberty as a "pernicious, God-provoking, Truth-defacing, Church-ruinating, & State-shaking" idea.

Despite our tradition of saying those who left England coming to the American colonies to find religious liberty, a great deal of persecution still followed. In Massachusetts, the Puritans wanted liberty for themselves but vigorously persecuted those with doctrinal differences. Many were banished. A small number were executed. Virginia, controlled by high church Anglicans, persecuted dissenters including New Light Presbyterians and Baptists. Baptists who demanded the right to preach, believe, speak, and meet without government interference or the necessity for prior government approval were being jailed up until the early 1770s in Virginia.

In the United States, such demands for freedom coincided with a new understanding of government's function. Because men are "endowed by their Creator with certain unalienable rights" and "that to secure these rights, governments are instituted among men," the ability of government to fulfil its purpose depends on its protection of rights preceding its own existence. And, for the high-order rights of "life, liberty, and the pursuit of happiness" of *The Declaration of Independence* to be practically enjoyed, the concrete protections of religious exercise and expression were ultimately codified in the First Amendment.

Freedom ultimately prevailed and for nearly two centuries, the vast majority of Americans agreed with the central premise that religious freedom should be protected for everyone. The same was true of freedom of speech—which was readily accepted in broad terms. This conviction withstood many challenges throughout the 20th century. And even though some grumbled when the ACLU successfully defended the free speech rights of Nazis to march in Skokie, Illinois, most Americans ultimately agreed defending free speech for all was in fact our constitutional duty. We affirmed our commitment to freedom itself was so strong we would defend even the most distasteful expressions of hostility to that very freedom.

It was this same spirit that animated the label-defying coalition that drafted and successfully lobbied for the passage of the Religious Freedom Restoration Act in 1993—at a time when the Democrats controlled both houses of Congress and Bill Clinton was president. As the co-chairman of the drafting committee for RFRA, I witnessed the unwavering stance of the ACLU, People for the American Way, and every stripe of countless religious faiths behind the principle that the free exercise of religion was fundamental and should be protected for everyone. In 1993, it passed the House unanimously and the Senate 97-3.

The unfortunate truth is RFRA would not pass today. Much of the original RFRA coalition has retreated from defending religious liberty for all and the culture has followed. For example, the state version of RFRA in Indiana in 2015, which was legally indistinguishable from the 1993 federal version, was labeled a "hate" bill because of a potential conflict between religious freedom and LGBT anti-discrimination ordinances. After passing the state RFRA, Indiana was bludgeoned by a partnership between big corporations and the LGBT community forcing the legislature to amend the measure, dramatically reducing its protections.

This episode might suggest that some favor reduced protections solely for religious freedom while continuing to support the rest of the freedoms protected by the First Amendment. Closer examination suggests otherwise.

The forces arrayed in the political, legal, and social conflicts of the early 21st century in the United States have a clear and dangerous parallel to the 16th through 18th century in England. Freedom for all is no longer a universally celebrated ideal. Coercion of belief and repression of expression in service of the greater good is now being openly advocated in high and important places.

A popular reaction to three Supreme Court cases decided in June of 2018 revealed the clear willingness by important components of the progressive left to jettison the very concept of liberty for all. *Janus v. AFSCME* and *NIFLA v. Becerra* were both decided using classical free speech principles. The *Masterpiece Cakeshop case*, was argued on both free speech and free exercise of religion grounds. The Court invoked religious freedom in *Masterpiece* to the same end as its speech decisions in the other two cases: freedom is for all.

In *Janus*, the Court held that the government cannot force public employees, via compulsory union dues, to financially support speech on matters of public concern contradicting their own views. In *NIFLA*, which I argued, the Court held the government cannot force pro-life clinics to advertise California's free abortion services. The key similarity is the Court said in both cases the state's goals were legitimate, but the way they coerced individuals to support those goals through compelled speech was improper. And in *Masterpiece,* the Court embraced the idea that laws against discrimination were a legitimate goal, but the state cannot use such laws to punish a religious believer, like Jack Phillips, for little more than sincerely applying his faith to his work. Tolerance is supposed to be a two-way street.

These cases set off a wave of charges that conservatives are "weaponizing" the First Amendment. A *New York Times* article published after *Janus* quoted several law professors playing variations on this theme. Catharine

MacKinnon of the University of Michigan, complaining that free speech now serves to reinforce and amplify injustice, said:

> *Once a defense of the powerless, the First Amendment over the last hundred years has mainly become a weapon of the powerful. Legally, what was, toward the beginning of the 20th century, a shield for radicals, artists and activists, socialists and pacifists, the excluded and the dispossessed, has become a sword for authoritarians, racists and misogynists, Nazis and Klansmen, pornographers and corporations buying elections.*

Louis Michael Seidman, a professor at Georgetown, said, "When I was younger, I had more of the standard liberal view of civil liberties. And I've gradually changed my mind about it. What I have come to see is that it's a mistake to think of free speech as an effective means to accomplish a more just society."

Professor Seidman expanded on this position in a law review article entitled, *Can Free Speech Be Progressive?* His answer is *no*, and the reason is critical: progressivism includes an understanding of freedom that cannot support the principle that constitutional liberties like free speech should be protected equally for all. For progressives, government exists to correct "unjust distributions produced by the market" and to dismantle "power hierarchies based on traits like race, nationality, gender, class, and sexual orientation." But, a government that protects individual liberties for all is antagonistic to the goals of redistribution and identity politics. If the government protects every person's speech, the wealthy enjoy a natural advantage. If the government protects all viewpoints, minority messages will be protected but must compete directly with the views of the powerful. So, Seidman admits, "At its core, free speech law entrenches a social view at war with key progressive objectives." He continues:

> *Instead of providing a shield for the powerless, the first amendment [has become] a sword used by people at the apex of the American hierarchy of power. Among its victims: proponents of campaign finance reform, opponents of cigarette addiction, the LBGTQ community, labor unions, animal rights advocates, environmentalists, targets of hate speech, and abortion providers.*

Other legal academics have voiced a similar antagonism to liberty, aimed this time at the Christian homeschooling movement. Catherine

Ross, law professor at George Washington University, makes a breathtaking and logically incoherent claim on the limits of religious tolerance:

> *In order for the norm of tolerance to survive across generations, society need not and should not tolerate the inculcation of absolutist views that undermine toleration of difference. Respect for difference should not be confused with approval for approaches that would splinter us into countless warring groups. Hence an argument that tolerance for diverse views and values is a foundational principle does not conflict with the notion that the state can and should limit the ability of intolerant homeschoolers to inculcate hostility to difference in their children—at least during the portion of the day they claim to devote to satisfying the compulsory schooling requirement.*

The Dean of Northwestern University School of Law, Kimberly Yuracko, also criticizes religious and parental liberty and, like Ross, refuses to extend tolerance to those she finds intolerant:

> *Virtually absent from the debate has been any discussion of the extent to which a liberal society should condone or constrain homeschooling, particularly as practiced by religious fundamentalist families explicitly seeking to shield their children from liberal values of sex equality, gender role fluidity and critical rationality.*

Yuracko contends her progressive values (which she creatively describes as "constitutional norms" for education) are of sufficient import to justify the use of state power to deny First Amendment liberties to those with whom she disagrees.

Martha Albert Fineman, professor of law at Emory, says explicitly what Ross implies. She wants to ban all private education. "Perhaps the more appropriate suggestion for our current educational dilemma is that public education should be mandatory and universal." Why does she advocate for such an extreme measure? While she questions the academic achievement of home education, despite the overwhelming proof of its success, her real objection is rooted in her distaste for the views many homeschools hold and teach without state supervision. Because homeschoolers, in her mind, "unfairly impose hierarchical or oppressive beliefs on their children" it must be banned, along with all private education.

These three professors are training many of the future leaders of the legal profession and, quite possibly, not a few future elected officials. Taken in combination with Seidman at Georgetown and McKinnon at Michigan, these progressive academics are forthrightly and publicly denouncing treasured American principles of liberty. It is impossible to square their views with those of the Supreme Court in the seminal case of *West Virginia v. Barnette.*

If there is any fixed star in our constitutional constellation, it is that no official, high or petty, can prescribe what shall be orthodox in politics, nationalism, religion, or other matters of opinion, or force citizens to confess by word or act their faith therein. If there are any circumstances which permit an exception, they do not now occur to us.

A fair-minded Christian conservative, as I aspire to be, must admit it is not just progressives whose views threaten our national commitment to liberty. Some within our own religious and political ranks occasionally advocate positions that sound dangerously close to being the mirror image of the left's—freedom is only for those who agree with us. And some who profess Christianity have openly questioned the wisdom of insisting on protections for our freedoms, when it makes us appear to be unkind. This theme has been raised with troubling frequency in connection with Jack Phillips and Masterpiece Cakeshop. Despite the fact Jack willingly serves all people, including those who identify as LGBT, his unwillingness to express all messages or celebrate all events has drawn their condemnation. Jack believes faithfulness to God requires him to decline to create messages celebrating an event the Bible clearly opposes. Those who profess faith while condemning Jack for following his own understanding of his duties to God, basically contend that unless Jack follows their views of religious faith, his freedom should not be protected.

There is nothing wrong with wanting to appear kind or believing all Christians should do so. But believing the extent of another's religious liberty ends when it crosses the line you have drawn according to your own religious convictions undermines religious liberty in all cases—even the ones you approve. Whoever rejects liberty for those with whom they disagree, rejects liberty.

For these and other reasons, it is important for us to develop a philosophical framework to reaffirm and defend our commitment to a robust version of religious freedom for all.

Consider the following propositions:

**1. *We should not judge other people's convictions by our own.***

There are three famous religious freedom incidents in the Book of Daniel. The first involved Daniel being asked to eat the King's meat and drink the King's wine. The second was the command to bow down to the massive gold image of Nebuchadnezzar. The third was Daniel's prayers to God during the period where no one was supposed to pray to anyone other than Nebuchadnezzar.

It is easy to conclude that no one would criticize Daniel and his friends for refusing to worship the image of gold or for continuing prayer to God instead of praying to the King. But the question of eating and drinking appears to be a lot closer call.

If it happened today, some professing believers might say, "Daniel, what's the big deal? Your refusing to accept the King's hospitality is both ungracious and impractical. You should just eat and drink."

The obvious answer is Daniel gets to decide and no one else. But why? For believers, Romans 14:4 gives the controlling answer: "Who are you to judge someone else's servant? To their own master, servants stand or fall." Daniel and Jack Phillips each serve God. They answer to their Master alone. This approach is fully consistent with the controlling decision from the Supreme Court. In *Thomas v. Review Board*, the Court considered the case of a Jehovah's Witness who refused to make parts used in tanks. All Jehovah's Witnesses believe they cannot participate in war. One member believed his faith allowed him to make parts at the factory. Thomas believed otherwise and refused to do so. Which Jehovah's Witness correctly understood the requirements of their faith? The Court answered:

> [T]he guarantee of free exercise is not limited to beliefs which are shared by all of the members of a religious sect. Particularly in this sensitive area, it is not within the judicial function and judicial competence to inquire whether the petitioner or his fellow worker more correctly perceived the commands of their common faith. Courts are not arbiters of scriptural interpretation.

Religious freedom protects both groups and individuals. The First Amendment protects shared beliefs and individual beliefs. Religious freedom is for all. The fact religious freedom extends to all people does not mean it protects all practices. As with all constitutional liberties, free exercise of religion is not an absolute right. Even when one is motivated by a sincere faith, there is no protection when "interests of the highest order" are implicated. Stopping homicide, for example, will always qualify. No one, from any religion, can commit human sacrifice. The key is all religious claims must be evaluated under the same standard, not just the standard we prefer. That is the legal rule.

It is also the moral rule. While protecting freedom to worship and follow God arises from the moral law of God, one cannot legitimately claim to be exercising the moral law of God concerning freedom in a way that violates the moral law of God concerning murder, rape, theft, or other such crimes.

### 2. *Treating religious freedom as a second-class right will inherently erode other First Amendment freedoms.*

The freedom of speech will be the first victim if religious speech is treated as a second-class right.

Here's why.

There is a fundamental rule in free speech cases that the government may not choose to regulate one's speech based solely on the content of that speech. This is called "content discrimination." By the same token, the government can never regulate speech based on the viewpoint of that speech. This is called "viewpoint discrimination." The seminal Supreme Court case on this point arose from a dispute about a school janitor who picketed on a sidewalk outside the school that employed him: *Chicago Police Department v. Mosely.*

The Illinois law in question prohibited all picketing on sidewalks outside a school, except for picketing involving labor disputes. Mosely's picket sign was aimed at demanding racial equality rather than any form of a labor dispute and was banned solely because of its message.

The Court's cases have been consistent. When speech is regulated because of its content (racial issues banned, labor issues permitted) or because of its viewpoint (pro-life messages banned, pro-abortion messages permitted), the First Amendment has been violated.

Religious speech can face either content bans or viewpoint bans depending on the circumstances. But the outcome has never been different in any Supreme Court case simply because of the religious nature of the speech. For example, in *Widmar v. Vincent*, the Supreme Court addressed a university policy prohibiting the use of university facilities "for purposes of religious worship or religious teaching." The Court, following *Mosely*, found this was content discrimination and, because the state cannot claim a legitimate interest in trying to achieve more religious separation than the Establishment Clause would require, the policy was unconstitutional. Current protections for religious speech and activity, then, rely on many of the same principles that protect speech and expression more generally. Therefore, if our courts allow religious speech to be undermined, other disfavored speakers or viewpoints are sure to follow.

In fact, this is obvious from the previously-quoted statements by Professors Seidman and McKinnon. They deny the legitimacy of protecting the speech of anyone who could threaten the advance of the progressive agenda.

Ultimately, the same thing is true for freedom of the press, freedom of assembly, or any other First Amendment freedom. If religious speakers, groups, or publishers are afforded only diminished protections, the rule that no one may be disfavored on the basis of their viewpoint or content is severely undermined. And ultimately, the only viewpoint allowed is the one favored by today's dominant political force. Anything less than freedom for all is not freedom at all.

The history of the freedoms now protected by the First Amendment reveals it was the battle for religious freedom that ultimately established the necessity of protecting speech, press, assembly, and the right to petition. And the history of these liberties in the United States shows they continue to share a common foundation. If we undermine religious freedom, the whole First Amendment is in jeopardy.

# Why Our Conscience Belongs
# to God, Not the State

*Chad Hatfield*

*In those days, John the Baptist came preaching in the wilderness of Judea, and saying, "Repent, for the kingdom of heaven is at hand!" For this is he who was spoken of by the prophet Isaiah, saying: "The voice of one crying in the wilderness: Prepare the way of the Lord; Make His paths straight"* (Lk. 3:1-3).

The Synaxarion of the Orthodox Church notes six feast days for the Glorious Prophet and Forerunner, John the Baptist. Three of these are focused on his beheading.[1] Often called the last of the Old Testament Prophets, John is the living fulfillment of Hebrews 11:33 as a suffering prophet: "Who through faith subdued kingdoms, worked righteousness, obtained promises, stopped the mouth of lions." He is counted among those who: "...had trial of mockings and scourgings, yes, and of chains and imprisonment" (Heb. 11:36). In his martyrdom we know him to be: "Of whom the world was not worthy" (Heb. 11:38).

A type of *Nazarite*[2] he came in from the desert tested and spiritually formed to lay aside all earthly cares not counting the cost of using a prophetic voice to call sinners to repentance in preparing to receive the

---

[1] Hieromonk Makarios of Simonos Petra, ed. *The Synaxarion: The Lives of the Saints of the Orthodox Church*, Vol. 6 (Ormylia, Greece: Holy Convent of the Annunciation of Our Lady, 2008).

[2] See definition of Nazirite, *The Interpreter's Dictionary of the Bible*, Vol 3, (New York, Abingdon, 1962).

Messiah. This call to repentance and amendment of life included Herod Antipas, the Tetrarch of Galilee who violated the law when he married Herodias, the wife of his brother Phillip, while Phillip was still alive. The civil authority, the Tetrarch, was living in sin with Herodias and the voice of the Prophet, John the Baptist, called him out for the sake of his salvation. The perfidious Herodias would have her way when Salome danced and made the request for John's head to be brought to her on a platter. Jerome records that Herodias desecrated the head even further and she pierced his tongue with a small knife as part of her revenge.

Such is the life of those who speak with a prophetic voice. Christian hagiography overflows with the stories of saints and martyrs who dared to speak and challenge the accepted status quo when it stands in violation of God's law and brings destruction to souls. Although this may seem as something from a distant past we, in fact, are living in a time when the beheading of righteous believers is an almost daily occurrence. Violence against Christians is on the rise.[3] The 20th Century produced more martyrs than any other in Christian History. This was especially true in the former Soviet Union and the Eastern Bloc Countries.[4]

Closer to home we recognize the prophetic voice is struggling to be heard in the so-called "free-world" of Western Europe and North America. In our time we have clearly moved from being a "Post-Christian" society to an aggressively "Anti-Christian" society. Basic social values and moral teachings are being eroded at a rapid pace. Social Media plays an active role where there is little accountability and much influence on a younger generation filled with "Nones" and "Dones."[5]

An anemic Christian voice has also contributed to the rapid pace of decline. As noted in their book *Resident Aliens*, published in 1989, Stanley Hauerwas and William H. Willimon wrote: "An accommodationist church has little to offer the world."[6] Churches have failed to teach and preach the faithful who now seem to have their worldview formed from

---

[3] A UK Report by *The National* says 215 million Christians worldwide faced "high" levels of persecution in 2018.

[4] For further reading see Metropolitan Hilarion Alfyev. *Orthodox Christianity I* (Yonkers: SVS Press, 2011), 257-279.

[5] For a response to the 2015 Pew Research Survey noting the rise in Nones and Dones see Rodney Stark. *The Triumph of Faith* (Wilmington: ISI Books, 2015).

[6] Stanley Hauerwas and William H. Willimon. *Resident Aliens: Life in the Christian Colony* (Nashville: Abingdon Press, 1989).

the entertainment industry rather than from the theology or teachings of Christ and His Church. John Chrysostom lamented the people were not in church but in the Hippodrome.[7] Are we not living with a modern variation of the same scenario?

Prof. Robert P. George has written regarding the attacks on religion and pro-family values as follows:

> ...attacks on the family, and particularly on the institution of marriage on which the family is built, are common in the academy. The line here is that the family, at least as traditionally constituted and understood, is a patriarchal and exploitative institution that oppresses women and imposes on people forms of sexual restraint that are psychologically damaging and that inhibit the free expression of their personality. As has become clear in recent decades, there is a profound threat to the family, one against which we must fight with all our energy and will. It is difficult to think of any items on the domestic agenda that is more critical today than the defense of marriage as the union of husband and wife and the effort to renew and rebuild the marriage culture.
>
> What has also become clear is that the threats to the family (and to the sanctity of human life) are necessarily threats to religious freedom and to religion itself—least where the religions in question stand up and speak out for conjugal marriage and the rights of the child in the womb. From the point of view of those seeking to redefine marriage and to protect and advance what they regard as the right to abortion, the taming of religion (and the stigmatization and marginalization of religions that refuse to be tamed) is a moral imperative.[8]

This "taming" of religion has now become an attack from the inside. The drift and decline of Mainline Protestant churches is well documented. The dance with the *zeitgeist* has left these once influential Churches in deep numerical decline.[9] Prof. Rodney Stark in reflection on this fact has noted:

> The wreckage of the former Mainline denominations is strewn upon the shoal of a modernist theology that began to dominate the Mainline

---

[7] *See, Homily of St. John Chrysostom: "Against Those Who Have Abandoned the Church and Deserted it for Hippodromes and Theatres"* http://www.tertullian.org/fathers/chrysostom_against_theatres_and_circuses.htm [accessed on 1/28/2019].

[8] Robert P. George, *Conscience and its Enemies: Confronting the Dogmas of Liberal Secularism*, (Wilmington: ISI Books, 2013), 9.

[9] Rodney Stark. *The Triumph of Faith*, 193.

*seminaries early in the nineteenth century. This theology presumed
that advances in human knowledge had made faith outmoded. If religion were to survive, it must become 'modern and progressive and...
the meaning of Christianity should be interpreted from the standpoint
of modern knowledge and experience' (as the theologian Gary Dorrien
puts it). From this starting point, science soon took precedence over
revelation, and the spiritual realm faded into psychology. Eventually,
Mainline theologians discarded nearly every doctrinal aspect of traditional Christianity.*[10]

As the proverbial camel's nose crept further into the tent, so-called
"conscience clauses" were created to alleviate the fears of the small "o"
orthodox faithful in these denominations.[11] Always, in due course,
these safe guards are abandoned as the numbers of traditional membership fades.

An example is the last of the bishops in the Episcopal Church, USA,
who refused to permit same-sex "marriages" in his Diocese of Albany,
New York. Bishop William Love, though he holds the 2,000-year-old
Christian view of marriage was inhibited and will be tried as a violator of
his oath to uphold the doctrine and discipline of the Episcopal Church,
USA. His informed conscience and traditional theological views cannot
be tolerated.[12] The "taming" is coming from the inside.

The understanding of an informed or educated Christian conscience
has become quite muddled, again, from inside the ecclesiastical bodies.
"Who am I to judge?" is often heard from Christian leaders. "I am spiritual but not religious" is cover for people who reject the Gospel teachings
but find their own "feelings" and opinions are the driving force that
passes as the rule for following your conscience above all else. Experience,
my "personal experience," allows even members of pro-life churches and
pro-family churches to find no moral problem with abortion on demand
(including late-term abortions) and same-sex marriage.

I was present at the 2014 Erasmus Lecture, sponsored by *First Things*,
when Archbishop Charles J. Chaput declared in his address:

---

[10] Idem, 196.

[11] For the history of the Port St. Lucy Conscience Clause see *An Episcopal Dictionary of the Church*, www.episcopalchurch.org/library/glossary/consciene clause [accessed on 1/28/2019].

[12] As reported on www.virtueonline.org

*On October 6, 2014, the Supreme Court declined to hear a variety of state appeals on the nature of marriage. In effect, the court has affirmed the validity of gay marriage, and I believe this creates a tipping point in American public discourse. The silencing of any privileged voice that biblical belief once had in our public square is just about complete.*[13]

He went on to say:

*The most disturbing thing about the debate around gay marriage is the destruction of public reason that it accomplished. Emotion and slogan-eering drove the argument, and the hatred that infected the conversation come less from so-called 'homophobes' than from any gay-issue activist themselves. People who uphold traditional moral architecture for sexuality, marriage, and family have gone, in the space of just twenty years, from mainstream convictions to the equivalent of racists and bigots.*[14]

When Archbishop Chaput made these remarks it was as if the reality of "we have lost" suddenly struck the audience. Those words were a marker on the timeline when the question became "how shall we survive" as traditional Christians and how will the next generations be nurtured and formed for what is surely a type of persecution known to the martyrs on whose blood the Church of Christ stands today?

Justice Samuel Alito, writing in his dissent, in *Obergefell v. Hodges* was a prophet in his own right when he saw the Supreme Court's decision as a way to eventually silence, "…those who cling to old beliefs will be able to whisper their thoughts in the recesses of their home but if they repeat those views in public, they will risk being labeled as bigots and treated as such by governments, employers, and schools."[15] I might add, many of "their churches" and "their pastors" will label them as such. A pathway to the future is needed as we were now clearly past the tipping point.

In 2017, one pathway was put forward when Rod Dreher published *The Benedict Option: A Strategy for Christians in a Post-Christian Nation.* It caught the attention of a multitude but it also seems many missed the point of the message. Some, even those who had not read the book, claimed Dreher was calling for a retreat into a world of ghetto Christian Communities cut off from the "real world." I would, argue these critics

---

[13] Charles J. Chaput, "Strangers in a Strange Land," *First Things*, (January 2015).
[14] *Ibidem.*
[15] Justice Samuel, Alito, "Dissent in Obergefell v. Hodges".

need to look closer at what is being proposed. There is an admission of defeat in battle but not the war itself. What is being called for is a recognition that a tsunami-like hit on traditional Christians and their teachings, values, and morals is about to hit hard. The small "o" orthodox need to be like Noah and prepare an Ark to see us through the storm so we may come out on the other side ready to start anew when shambles of a cultural collapse comes looking for Truth once again.[16]

At the end of his chapter on "Education as Christian Formation" he paints the reality of our current situation and what we must do next when he writes:

> *Because of florists, bakers, and photographers having been dragged through the courts by gay plaintiffs, we know that some Orthodox Christians will lose their businesses and their livelihoods if they refuse to recognize the new secular orthodoxies. We can expect that many more Christians will either be denied employment opportunities by licensing or other professional requirements, because they have been driven out of certain workplaces by outright bigotry or by dint of the fact that they cannot in good conscience work in certain fields. What will they do?*
>
> *As you about to learn, it is not too early for Christians to start asking that question and making plans.*[17]

A realignment of traditional Christians, across denominational lines, seems to be called for. It is an idea reflecting the "New Ecumenism" that Pope Benedict XVI referenced in his pontificate. This idea has caught the attention of groups making formal statements such as *The Manhattan Declaration* in 2009.[18] The revival of Orthodox Christianity in Russia has also seen an interest in finding common traditional Christian values as a platform for a united witness. Speaking in 2010 Patriarch Kirill of Moscow said:

> *Christians have to find new languages and new creative ways of preaching Christian values in today's continuously changing world, to enable this preaching to be heard and properly understood. The sphere of culture is the area in which constructive dialogue between the Church*

---

[16] Rod Dreher, *The Benedict Option: A Strategy for Christians in a Post-Christian Nation* (New York: Sentinel, 2017), 1-5.

[17] Idem, 144.

[18] *Manhattan Declaration: A Call of Christian Conscience*, 2009.

*and society can be the most effective, and I see here an opportunity for fruitful cooperation between Christians who uphold traditional values. In the first place, I mean the cooperation between the Roman Catholic Church and the Orthodox Church, which have a common social and economic view of the pressing problems of social and economic ethics, bioethics, the family, and personal morality. Our common Christian tradition, commitment to dialogue, and readiness for cooperation can and must become a driving mechanism of mutual rapprochement.*[19]

In conclusion, it is clear the eleventh hour is upon us and the time to act is urgent. In our history as Christians we can reflect upon a pattern of a 500-year cycle of crisis beginning with the fall of Rome and the Dark Ages. With the Great Schism of 1054, followed the Protestant Reformation 500 years later. In our day we are in yet another time of cultural collapse and chaos. Christians are divided and a type of martyrdom has begun yet again. Matters of faith and conscience demand our attention as individuals and corporately by those who know Christ as Lord and Savior. His own testimony will see us through dark times:

*He who is unjust, let him be unjust still; he who is filthy, let him be filthy still; he who is righteous, let him be righteous still; he who is holy, let him be holy still.*

*And behold, I am coming quickly, and My reward is with Me, to give to every one according to his work* (Rev. 22:11-12).

---

[19] Chad Hatfield, ed., *Patriarch Kirill in His Own Words* (Yonkers: SVS Press, 2019), 195-196.

# How the Church Can Protect Religious Freedom and Rights of Conscience

## R. R. Reno

The temptation to theocracy is born in charity, not malice. What greater good can one do for another than secure his eternal salvation—or at least increase the odds? To that end the theocratic-minded seek to establish religion, using the state's power to institute particular doctrines as authoritative, even obligatory. A religious test for public office provides a carrot to promote establishment, for only members of the established church can ascend to high positions of public leadership. The same theological impulse leads to policies limiting the free exercise of religion. This is the stick that punishes, making dissent painful.

Our country's founders understood the temptation of theocracy. They carefully crafted the first right of the Bill of Rights: "Congress shall make no law respecting the establishment of religion, or prohibiting the free exercise thereof." Article Six of the Constitution stipulates, "No religious Test shall ever be required as a Qualification to any Office or public Trust under the United States." Thus, the basic elements of our noble American tradition of religious freedom: no establishment, no sticks to punish dissent, and no carrots to encourage conformity.

Paradoxically, as Christianity's influence over American society has waned over the last two generations, the temptations of theocracy have waxed. Our society faces two threats. One comes from those who wish to use government power to establish the religion of secularism, complete with punishments for those who dissent and religious tests for public office. To meet that threat we need good lawyering, political influence, and clarity about the threats we face. The second threat comes from within our hearts. Worldly powers always seek to enslave us. The established church of progressivism seeks to cow us into retreating from the public square. To resist we must deepen our faith.

## The New Theocrats

The negative view of the role of revealed religion in society has origins in the Enlightenment. It regards faith as a threat to human flourishing. Voltaire, the French *philosophe*, wrote to Frederick II of Prussia that Christianity "is assuredly the most ridiculous, the most absurd and the most bloody religion which has ever infected this world. Your Majesty will do the human race an eternal service by extirpating this infamous superstition." Instead of Christianity as the leaven of society, Voltaire envisioned a society governed by Reason.

The reign of Reason did not have a good track record in the 20th century. Nazism and Fascism drew ideological resources from modern science, especially evolutionary theory. Marxism presented itself as a science of history. Nevertheless, the judgment that Christianity is the source of our social ills has endured, updated in the 20th century with theories about religion's role in forming the "authoritarian personality." According to this theory, Nazism and Communism are actually "religious" in nature, and ideological fanaticism is a subspecies of dogmatism. It supposedly blossoms when people have strong convictions about moral and spiritual truths, which Christianity encourages. Religious commitment is regarded as a source of blind obedience. Notice, progressives describe Christian morality as "patriarchal" and "homophobic," not as a rich tradition with roots in the Bible and classical philosophy.

This view of Christianity as the vehicle for pernicious ideologies triggers an aggressive mentality among progressive leaders. Minority religions are not chief objects of their ire. Jews and Muslims may suffer discrimination in some respects, but they are not seen as large-scale threats to secular American society. Judaism and Islam often get a pass, while Christianity, a major cultural and political force throughout our nation's history, becomes the target of hostility. Recent Senate hearings for judicial candidate Brian Buescher saw the airing of concerns about the "extremism" of the Knights of Columbus, a Catholic fraternal organization. This made sense politically, because unlike Jewish or Muslim organizations, the Catholic Church (along with Evangelical Christian organizations) has played a pivotal role in the pro-life movement.

But progressive concerns are broader. Secular liberals believe they must protect their fellow citizens from "authoritarian" Christians who nurture "hateful" views on gays and lesbians, impose patriarchal norms on women, and refuse to accept the sexual revolution. For progressives, these are not forms of legitimate dissent. They are "heresies" threatening the new theology of our time.

There is no authoritative scripture or creed for this new theology. But we have all sensed the hardening of progressivism into a cultural dogma over the last generation. Its leading motifs are diversity and openness. Pope Benedict XVI spoke of it as a cultural regime: the dictatorship of relativism. This relativism is not a philosophical position, but a catechism that prevents us from drawing sharp boundaries between right and wrong. Political correctness serves as its latter-day Inquisition that roots out heresies of "exclusion." The new theology's eschatology is best captured by the ideals of multiculturalism, a utopia of inclusion in which there are no authoritative norms and all will be acknowledged and affirmed as they wish to be acknowledged and affirmed. Transgenderism is in this respect an important vanguard ideology, which is why it has become so important for progressives.

The theology of openness and inclusion is ascendant, dominating our universities and fashioning the moral imaginations of elites who work hard to establish it as our national religion. In this new theology, traditional religious expressions and practices become dire threats to the common good, engines of exclusion that must be driven out of public life—and suppressed as far as possible in citizens' private lives. The ambition of secular leaders today is to create a perfect society, a City on the Hill that realizes the multicultural ideal.

## Religious Freedom Redefined

The new theology of progressivism promotes a reinterpretation of the Constitution's commitment to religious freedom. This advances in two ways. The first involves extending an extreme anti-establishment juris-prudence. The second develops a diminished view of the free exercise of religion. Both serve the ultimate end of establishing the new theology as our national religion.

*Non-establishment.* Some of the Founding Fathers were not orthodox Christians. Yet, they regarded religious belief and practice as beneficial to society. In their view, good political leadership finds fitting ways to sup-port and encourage religiosity among the citizenry. This understanding of the benefits of religiosity led to a qualified understanding of non-estab-lishment. The government was not to promote any particular doctrine or empower clergy to become lawmakers, but the government rightly created conditions congenial to religion.

In practice, this led to prayer and Bible reading in public schools and other forms of state-sponsored religious practices. Legislators created tax exemptions and other legal forms that indirectly supported religious institutions. In the 20th century the mingling of religion and civic insti-tutions became controversial. The boundaries between state-sponsorship and religious practices and symbols were sharpened and pushed back significantly. This was, perhaps, a necessary adjustment as our society became more religiously pluralistic. After 1945, however, American constitutional law evolved in the direction of increasing anxiety about public support for religion. Various cases came before the Supreme Court involving public funding for salaries, supplies, and other costs at reli-giously founded schools. Other cases concerned Christmas displays in town squares, crosses on public property, and prayers offered at school graduations and legislative sessions. In each instance, those bringing the lawsuits claimed a wrongful "establishment of religion."

I leave it to constitutional scholars to sort out the Supreme Court's current doctrine of non-establishment. For my purposes, it is more impor-tant to note a strict and ideological doctrine of non-establishment—the "wall of separation"—tends toward the suppression of religion in the public square. This suppression has been the goal of anti-establishment activists since 1945. They have sought to reframe religious freedom as freedom from religion, a right to live without having any contact with traditional faiths.

More recently, a cultural politics has emerged to suppress religion in public life. As seen in the case of Brian Buescher, an important new progressive tactic has been to re-describe moral and political resistance to their agenda as "religious," and thus a wrongful "establishment of religion."

This tactic was used by Federal District Court Judge Vaughan Walker when he overturned Proposition 8, the California ballot measure defining marriage as the union of a man and a woman. In his judicial opinion, Walker cited the lack of a rational basis for thinking only men and women can marry: "The evidence shows conclusively that Proposition 8 enacts, without reason, a private moral view that same-sex couples are inferior to opposite-sex couples." He continues by observing that many supporters of Proposition 8 were motivated by their religious convictions, which amounts to an unconstitutional attempt to establish their religion. Walker was drawing on earlier legal reasoning by Justice Anthony Kennedy. In striking down Texas sodomy laws, he noted that moral censure of homosexuality has "been shaped by religious beliefs," and was thus constitutionally suspect.

In cultural politics, we are sure to see further re-description of our moral and political positions as "religious," and thus illicit and illiberal. This will be a powerful tool for suppressing Christianity in public life. All traditional views of marriage, sex, family, and society in the West are tinctured with Christian concepts and reasoning, given the West's history. Therefore, the progressives can make arguments that opposition to the tenets of their new theology—which is post-Christian—are "religious" in character and thus not in keeping with our liberal tradition of non-establishment. Over the next few years, we should expect further development of this line of argument. It will be used to establish the new theology of progressivism as the only legitimate basis for participation in public life.

*Free exercise.* Non-discrimination gives legal form to the new theology's doctrine of inclusion. This legal principle will be used to argue for a much narrower understanding of the free exercise of religion.

Some recent Supreme Court cases about the free exercise of religion turned on non-discrimination. In 2005, a former teacher at Hosanna-Tabor Evangelical Lutheran Church and School in Redford, Michigan, filed an employment lawsuit, claiming discrimination based on disability. The Hosanna-Tabor leaders argued otherwise, saying she was fired for violating St. Paul's teaching that Christians should not bring their disputes before secular judges. The case revolved around whether or not a religious institution could invoke a theological principle that overrides our secular laws of non-discrimination. As the dispute came before the Supreme Court, the Obama administration argued that non-discrimination should hold sway, even at the expense of the Lutheran school's freedom to run its affairs in accord with its theological principles.

In the event, the Lutheran school won a decisive victory for the free exercise of religion. But legal scholars refer back to an earlier case concerning interracial dating at Bob Jones University. In that case, the Supreme Court judged the imperative of non-discrimination so important it overrode the free exercise of religion. Drawing on that precedent, Martha Nussbaum, who teaches at the University of Chicago Law School, has suggested today's anti-discrimination laws should be applied to prevent colleges and university run by the Catholic Church from requiring their leaders to be ordained, because doing so runs afoul of the prohibition against discriminating against women. Another law professor, Chai Feldblum, has written about the conflict between gay rights and religious liberty. With admirable frankness she admits, "I'm having a hard time coming up with any case in which religious liberty should win."

Many of the current threats to the religious liberty of Christians stem from our refusal to affirm every aspect of the sexual revolution. Our unwillingness to embrace abortion, sodomy, gay marriage, and transgenderism is recast by the new progressive theology as discriminatory in intent and consequence. This sin against inclusion makes us heretics, and we are treated accordingly, deplored in public as "haters" and subject to boycotts and lawsuits whenever possible.

## Addressing the Legal Threats

The Becket Fund for Religious Liberty defends all religions against encroachments on their liberty. This principled stand is culturally astute. Progressives target Christianity—not Judaism, Islam, or other religions. They do so because Christianity is a powerful cultural force in our society. Since the Religious Right appeared on the scene in the 1970s, conservative Christianity has become a potent political force as well. Progressivism may not like conservative Islam or Orthodox Judaism, but it can accommodate these communities, because they pose no threat to the hegemony of progressive theology. Moreover, minority religions have sacred

141

significance as part of the multicultural mosaic. Christianity is different. It cannot be accommodated because our communities are too large and too powerful. In the progressive theology, we are "hegemonic," not part of the diversity of society, which means we are evil.

In this context, clear alliance with and defense of our fellow religious believers, whatever their faiths, clarifies the differential treatment of Christianity. It undermines the progressive strategies of developing extreme interpretations of non-establishment, because even-handed application of that extreme interpretation will harm religious minorities. It also hinders the diminution of free-exercise, for it, too, harms religious minorities.

Principled and culturally astute lawyering will take us only so far, however. As Mormons know from their history, our courts form a branch of government that will bend to powerful political forces, less immediately and completely than elected officials, perhaps, but eventually and to some degree. Therefore, it is essential to make religious freedom a political priority. This means voting for candidates who affirm the proper role of religion in public life. We need to make our voices heard in politics—not just as citizens, but as believers.

Winning elections matters for our freedom. The best protection of religious freedom comes from elected officials and appointed bureaucrats who do not kowtow to the progressive theologians. If those running our government do not try to use their power to oppress us, we won't need lawyers to argue our cases. The second best protection comes from judges who understand the positive role religion plays in sustaining a healthy, free society. This too depends upon winning elections, for those elected nominate and approve judges. In this regard, Donald Trump's election marked a decisive victory for religious freedom. With further Supreme Court appointments, a sound doctrine of religious freedom may remain the law of the land for decades to come.

## The Danger of Dhimmitude

When United States senators raise questions about membership in conventional religious organizations such as the Knights of Columbus, the effect can be chilling. The same is true when corporate boards and university admissions departments let it be known traditional religious views are disqualifying. When the owners of Chick-fil-A are attacked as "bigots," when corporate executives gang up on state legislatures passing legislation buttressing religious freedom and major newspapers editorialize how "hate" has no place in our society, it becomes tempting to retreat into private belief, putting a bushel basket over the light of faith.

European scholars who studied the Middle East in the late 19th century coined a term for this retreat: dhimmitude. It comes from the Arabic word *dhimmi*, which means non-Muslims. In a traditional Muslim society, Jews and Christians are allowed to survive, but only insofar as they accepted Muslim dominance and control of society as whole. Dhimmitude refers to the mentality of submission that evolved over the centuries among Jews and Christians under Muslim dominance.

In 21st-century America, the greatest threat to our religious freedom is not external. Our constitutional system works against the anti-establishment extremism of progressives who want to establish their theology of inclusion. The doctrine of free exercise may be chipped away, but it is unlikely to be eviscerated. Far more probable will be collective Christian retreat and resignation—acceptance of *dhimmi* status in a culture dominated by the progressive theology and policed by political correctness. We'll want to advance professionally, send our kids to elite universities, and move easily on the upward path of success. Insofar as the *New York Times* tells us to hide our Christianity, we'll do so. This is the way of dhimmitude, and it is the gravest threat to religious liberty. For there is no need to defend freedoms people don't claim.

The danger, in a word, is we'll allow ourselves to be silenced and marginalized. Or worse, we'll be seduced into policing our faith communities by denouncing more courageous Christians as enemies of "inclusion." This self-monitoring will be done in the vain effort to prove to our progressive overlords we can be trusted. At root, this is a spiritual danger, not a political one. It requires a spiritual response.

Some years ago, I attended a lecture by Rabbi Jonathan Sacks that outlined the best response to threats to religious liberty. It concerned the Passover celebration of liberation from captivity in Egypt. Sacks taught me an important lesson about freedom, one that opens the inner meaning of St. Paul's call for us to take up the freedom for which Christ has set us free.

The Hebrews of the Old Testament had two straightforward words for freedom. *Chofesh* is used in Exodus 21:2, which stipulates a Hebrew slave must be set free after six years of servitude. (The same word appears in the Israeli national anthem, expressing the hope the Jewish people will be free in their own land.) *Dror* is used in Leviticus 25:10. This verse is inscribed on the Liberty Bell in Philadelphia: "Proclaim LIBERTY throughout all the Land unto all the inhabitants thereof." The same word is used in Isaiah 61:1: "He sent me to bind up the brokenhearted, to proclaim liberty to the captives."

But Sacks observed the Passover Seder does not use either word for the festival of freedom, preferring instead *herut*. This seems a peculiar choice. *Herut* appears only once in the Bible, in 1 Kings 21:8. Most translations render it "elders" or "ministers." Its literal meaning is "those consecrated." This does not bring the notion of freedom to mind.

But things get stranger still, as Sacks explained. In Exodus 32 we find the account of Moses's descent from Mount Sinai with the two tablets of the Ten Commandments. In verse 16 we read these words are carved or engraved on the stone. The Hebrew word for "engraved" is *harut*. The Torah scrolls from which Jews read this passage are written in ancient Hebrew without vowel markings. This opens a possibility exploited by the rabbinic tradition, which teaches when reading one should pronounce *harut* as *herut*, "consecrated" rather than "engraved," which is then exported for use as "freedom" in the Passover festival.

Christianity tends to present its teachings in explicit creedal form. Judaism is different, often using verbal substitutions like this one to convey foundational truths of the faith. In this case, the notion of being consecrated into God's service (*herut*) is being defined as having God's commandments engraved (*harut*) on one's heart. This, as Rabbi Sacks pointed out in his lecture, is exactly the freedom God promises in Jeremiah 31:33: "I will put my law within them, and I will write it on their hearts." Through this play of words, the Passover receives its definitive theological interpretation within the Jewish tradition. The Seder does not just celebrate the physical liberation of the Israelites. More profoundly, it celebrates the spiritual freedom from knowing and obeying God's word—having it written on your heart. (This theological judgment is echoed in the fact that the biblical text that serves as the foundation for the Passover Seder comes from Deuteronomy 16, a commandment to be fulfilled, not the Exodus account, which is a narrative.)

The New Testament proclaims this Passover view of freedom as God's word engraved on our hearts. Jeremiah 31:33 is quoted in Hebrews 8:10, and St. Paul evokes the verse in 2 Corinthians 3:3 when he calls the Christian faithful in that city, "a letter from Christ delivered by us, written not with ink but with the Spirit of the living God, not on tablets of stone but on tablets of human hearts." This, therefore, is the freedom for which Christ has set us free: to have the law of his love engraved on our hearts. His way is the fulfillment of the law, which is the law of liberty (James 1:25). The more perfect our obedience, the more perfect our liberty.

We are living in a time of profound bondage. The progressive theology of secularism promises inclusion, the freedom to live as we please without fear of censure. We can even become men or women—the choice is ours, we're told. A punitive political correctness comes with these promises, but that's the least of our captivity. As the progressive theology drives biblical norms from society—norms about sex, consumption, status, and much more—our fellow citizens fall into bondage to the principalities and powers enslaving men. I won't recount the statistics about suicide, drug overdose death, and declines in life expectancy. They are but stark indicators of our thoroughgoing captivity to sin and death. More subtle, but more powerful, are the false gods of success, wealth, and celebrity.

We do need to defend religious liberty, but much more is at stake. Progressive theology proclaims that freedom means doing what we want. In this, the paladins of our time are half right. But they are entirely wrong about where that freedom comes from, thinking it is merely a matter of removing external impediments. In truth, the profound and bitter slavery is internal, not external, just as the more dire threat to our religious liberty is self-enforced dhimmitude, not Human Rights Campaign lawsuits and misguided judges.

Genuine freedom requires the power to say *no* to worldly powers coercing us into doing what *they* want. And the power to say *no* comes from saying *yes* to truths that transcend us. The free man is the one who can look in the eyes of those who imagine themselves all-powerful, saying "I will *not*." In a fallen world, these are the first words of liberty. We are truly free when we can say with St. Paul, "I am sure that neither death, nor life, nor angels, nor principalities, nor things present, not things to come, nor powers, nor height, nor depth, nor anything else in all creation, will be able to separate us from the love of God in Christ Jesus our Lord" (Romans 8:38–39). This is the freedom of the martyrs.

Without the freedom for which Christ has set us free, the world's best lawyers and most sympathetic politicians will be of no moment. The First Amendment is but parchment freedom if we lack the interior liberty to stand and speak as Christians, with love, yes, but also in truth. Cowed by political correctness, in bondage to false gods of wealth, security, celebrity, and hedonism, our age needs the witness of freedom. We must be those witnesses as followers of Christ who say *no* to the culture of death, the false promises of the sexual revolution, and the false gospel of "inclusion."

# The Child in Relation to Family and State

*Bruce Ashford*

*Just as every man owes his creaturely existence to the fact that two individuals, a man and a woman, became one, every man, at the root of his existence is part of a community. This community, however, is not the state, but the family. The one community without which human life cannot be imagined in any circumstances is the family.*

—EMIL BRUNNER, *Justice and the Social Order*[1]

## Our Secular Age

In conformity with Nietzsche's prophecy, the modern West is experiencing a radical desacralizing of the social order, unprecedented in world history. The great theologian Dietrich Bonhoeffer described it as a "world come of age," an era in which Westerners had learned to understand themselves and manage their lives without recourse to the "working hypothesis" known as "God."[2] American sociologist Philip Rieff referred to it as one in which the social order and cultural institutions have been severed from their roots in religion, leaving Western

---

[1] Emil Brunner, *Justice and the Social Order*, trans. Mary Hottinger (San Francisco: Harper, 1945), 135.

[2] Dietrich Bonhoeffer, "Letter to Eberhard Bethge (June 8, 1944)," in Dietrich Bonhoeffer, *Letters and Papers from Prison*, Dietrich Bonhoeffer Works 8, ed. John W. De Gruchy, trans. Isabel Best, Lisa E. Dahill, Reinhard Krauss, and Nancy Lukens (Minneapolis: Fortress, 2010), 425–27.

society without a transcendent matrix of meaning or a normative code of permissions and prohibitions.[3]

But it is Canadian philosopher Charles Taylor who, perhaps better than any other, has explored the existential and societal implications of modern life. In *A Secular Age*, Taylor describes our era as one in which Westerners consider Christianity implausible and unimaginable.[4] As Westerners, we find ourselves socialized into an "immanent" frame of reference in which theistic belief has not only been dislodged from the default position, but is positively and relentlessly contested by a myriad of other options. It is merely one option among many—and an inconceivable one at that.

Taylor argues that our era does not simply bring with it a new set of beliefs; it also fosters a new "feel" in which people of all religious and ideological persuasions are haunted by doubt. In perpetual unease, we find ourselves "fragilized," lacking confidence in our own convictions amid the profusion of options actively contesting our beliefs. We are "cross-pressured," trapped psychologically between the disenchantment of the immanent frame and moments of aesthetic enchantment that arise when we sense that there may be something more to life than the finite. Those who reach for the transcendent do so tenuously, having been socialized into a disenchanted world. Conversely, those who embrace the immanent frame nonetheless experience the "haunting" of transcendence.

This seismic social shift would not have taken place without a concurrent political shift in which the West eschewed strong forms of sacral authority, embracing instead a generic "natural" religion. This religion, uncaptivated by the beauty of the "thou shalt" and "thou shalt not," undermines Christianity's leavening influence on society and culture.[5]

## Children in a Secular Age

Taylor's account is richly suggestive, helpful for understanding the perpetual unease experienced by Christians and non-Christians alike. More to the point, it is a fecund resource for reflecting upon some of the

---

[3] Philip Rieff, *My Life among the Deathworks: Illustrations of the Aesthetics of Authority*, ed. Kenneth S. Piver, Sacred Order/Social Order Vol. 1 (Charlottesville, VA: University of Virginia Press, 2006), 1–44.

[4] Charles Taylor, *A Secular Age* (Cambridge, MA: Belknap, 2009), 83.

[5] Ibid., 234-42.

unique challenges our secular age poses for the catechesis and formation of Christian children. Taylor's exploration of the modern social imaginary helps foreground the way in which Christianity's perceived implausibility impinges upon society's view of children and of the family's primacy in a child's formation. The more Christianity becomes an "unreasonable" option in our society, the more we can expect the state to oppose aspects of Christian parental nurture.

Unenlightened by the Christian doctrine of the *imago Dei*, for example, Western society increasingly devalues human life in general and children in particular. Within a post-Christian framework of thought, ethicists can plausibly locate a child's worth in her level of consciousness or her place on the developmental spectrum, concluding that abortion and even infanticide are within the realm of reason and morality. Similarly, within a desacralized public discourse, public intellectuals and social activists can set forth—unblushingly—their view that children are bad for the Earth. Thus, as the argument goes, we are morally obliged to stop having them.

Unburdened by creation order or a normative code of permissions and prohibitions, Western society deforms human beings in general and children in particular by encouraging them to view their personal identities as self-constructed and their bodies as endlessly malleable. Increasingly, minors are encouraged to make life-altering decisions— such as hormone therapy or sex-reassignment surgeries—apart from their parent's approval.

Given that Christian catechesis is increasingly implausible and imaginable in our secular age, therefore, conflicts will inevitably arise about the extent to which families may exercise their religious convictions in the formation of their children. More to the point, we will see a competition between two social institutions—the family and the state—for primacy in a child's formation. In our Western political context in which, increasingly, the only actors of significance are the overweening state and the isolated individual, the reflexive urge of our secular age will be to "liberate" children from Christian catechesis they consider ignorant, enslaving, or even abusive.[6] This liberation could come in milder or more severe

---

[6] Richard Dawkins is famous for arguing that religion functions as a cultural virus and that religious catechesis therefore is a form of mental child abuse. Richard Dawkins, "Viruses of the Mind" in *Dennett and His Critics: Demystifying Mind*, ed. Bo Dalhbom (Malden, MA: Blackwell, 1997), 13-27.

forms, ranging from compulsory public education to other, more serious contraventions of religious liberty and of the family's integrity.

Any such attempt to displace the family, or to weaken or block the family's primacy in the formation of children, must be resisted. The family is the most basic institution of society, the first institution to appear in Scripture and in history. Families are the foundation of a society's well-being, and their flourishing is the surest indicator of a society's overall health. They are the primary and most conducive environment for a child to mature physically, psychologically, socially, morally, and spiritually.

How then can we protect the family's primacy? At a minimum, by advocating for religious liberty, promoting a vision for societal pluriformity, and exposing the pernicious effects that will flow from the family's displacement.

## Advocating for Religious Liberty

Religious liberty laws in Western democracies are an obvious line of defense in securing the family's right to shape its children and raise them to maturity.[7] In the United States, religious liberty is secured through a constitutional clause and an amendment which, together, prohibit religious criteria for public office, laws establishing religion, or laws restricting religion's free exercise. Yet, attempts are made to undermine or circumvent religious freedoms, often by reducing "religion" down to the merely private worship of a supernatural deity, thus allowing religious *exercise* to be curtailed when it impinges on public matters. One thinks of the *Obergefell v. Hodges* ruling, which prompted four Supreme Court Justices to register grave concerns about the future of "free exercise;" official documents, such as the U.S. Civil Rights Commissions' "Peaceful Coexistence," whose chairman Martin Castro suggested that Christian concerns about "religious liberty" are no more than a mask for hatred and bigotry;[8] and increasingly frequent statements by public intellectuals

---

[7] This is not to say that the rights and duties of the family are derivative in some way from liberties. The family's rights and duties are grounded in creation order. Yet in the United States, it seems prudent to develop a defense of parental right stemming from the Constitutional right to the free exercise of religion.

[8] "Peaceful Coexistence: Reconciling Nondiscrimination Principles with Civil Liberties" (Washington, D.C.: U. S. Commission on Civil Rights, September 7, 2016), http://www.usccr.gov/pubs/Peaceful-Coexistence-09-07-16.PDF. Accessed March 26, 2018.

such as the *New York Times'* Mark Oppenheimer, who argue for legal reforms that would punish Christians—financially or otherwise—for their religious convictions.[9]

And yet, as Richard John Neuhaus regularly argued, free exercise of religion is not primarily a question of First Amendment law but of the theory and practice of democratic governance.[10] A nation's claim to be a law-governed democracy rests upon its ability to guarantee justice and equality for all, which in turn requires that they secure for their citizens, "the right to ponder life's origins, meaning and purpose; to explore the deepest questions about human nature, dignity, and destiny; to decide what is to be believed and not to be believed; and, within the limits of justice for all, to comply with what one conscientiously judges to be one's religious obligations—openly, peacefully, and without fear."[11] When religious exercise is threatened, every other freedom is endangered as well.[12]

This sort of philosophical-legal argument is supported by biblical reasoning and, in Christian Scripture, we find our strongest support not from isolated texts but from God's whole way of dealing with mankind. God created man and woman in his own image, endowing us with the capacity to make morally significant choices. Though he commands and expects worship, he doesn't coerce us to do so. The God of the Bible is not interested in forcing mere outward conformity to his will and, in fact, repeatedly rejects such affectation. More to the point, the coming of God's Son—himself the very image of God—provides the supreme example, as he preached the gospel as a homeless itinerant teacher rather than decreeing it as a conquering King. It is unsurprising, then, that church history is replete with vocal Christian proponents of religious freedom.

And yet, as Christians, we cannot remain content to promote religious liberty for our own families; we must engage in religious liberty advocacy on behalf of other religious believers as well. In the words of

---

[9] Mark Oppenheimer, "Now's the Time to End Tax Exemptions for Religious Institutions," *TIME*, June 28, 2015, http://time.com/3939143/nows-the-time-to-end-tax-exemptions-for-religious-institutions/. Accessed July 17, 2015.

[10] Richard John Neuhaus, "A New Order of Religious Freedom," *First Things* 20 (February 1992): 13–17.

[11] Robert P. George. *"Leland Award Lecture by Robert P. George," The Ethics and Religious Liberty Commission*, December 13, 2013. https://erlc.com/article/leland-award-lecture-by-robert-p.-george. Accessed February 25, 2016.

[12] Timothy Shah and Matthew Franck, *Religious Freedom: Why Now? Defending an Embattled Human Right* (Princeton: The Witherspoon Institute, 2012).

18th-century Baptist preacher John Leland, "Every man must give an account of himself to God, and therefore every man ought to be at liberty to serve God in a way that he can best reconcile to his conscience. If government can answer for individuals at the Day of Judgment, let men be controlled by it in religious matters; otherwise, let men be free."[13] Similarly, 17th-century Baptist Thomas Helwys, argued regularly for religious freedom for Jews, Muslims, and Christian heretics.[14] Indeed, if we cannot promote religious liberty for other believers, as did Leland, Helwys, and countless others, our pleas for free exercise of our own religion will be received as little more than noisy gongs and clanging cymbals.

## Promoting a Vision for Societal Pluriformity

In addition to direct advocacy of religious liberty, the Christian community must argue persuasively in favor of a general philosophy of society that will secure the family's integrity and its primacy in a child's formation, while affording the state a real but limited role alongside of the family. One such philosophy is the *soevereiniteit in eigen kring* (sovereignty in each circle) paradigm anticipated by early modern thinkers and conceptualized by the Dutch theologian and social architect Abraham Kuyper and his forebears. Consonant in many ways with Catholic social teaching and with the Anabaptist emphasis on the local church as a colony of the Kingdom, Kuyper's social philosophy was built to resist the encroaching secularism of his day.[15] It thus serves as a useful conversation partner for ecumenical resistance in our own secular age.

In his inaugural speech for the founding of the Free University of Amsterdam, Kuyper identified "sovereignty" as the central issue in a Christian philosophy of society. A sovereign, he averred, is one who possesses the right and the authority to override and avenge any resistance to his will. Thus, God is the ultimate sovereign. Yet, God has delegated his authority to humans and divided life into separate spheres, each with

---

[13] John Leland, *The Rights of Conscience Inalienable* (New London, CT: 1791).

[14] Thomas Helwys, *A Short Declaration of the Mystery of Iniquity* (Amsterdam: n.p.,1612).

[15] For concise summaries of Kuyper's interface with a secularizing Europe, see *John Bolt, A Free Church, A Holy Nation: Abraham Kuyper's American Public Theology* (Grand Rapids: Eerdmans, 2001), 8-15; Peter Heslam, *Creating a Christian Worldview: Abraham Kuyper's Lectures on Calvinism* (Grand Rapids: Eerdmans, 1998), 96-110.

its own distinct reason for being and its own jurisdiction. As Kuyper summarizes:

> *Our human life, with its visible material foreground and invisible spiritual background, is neither simple nor uniform but constitutes an infinitely complex organism. It is so structured that the individual exists only in groups, and only in such groups can the whole become manifest. Call the parts of this one great machine "cogwheels," spring-driven on their own axles, or "spheres," each animated with its own spirit.*[16]

Thus, creation's normative order, with a plurality of authorities that will not be re-gathered into one until Christ, reminds us of God's sovereignty and repels human attempts to totalize.

On the spatial analogy, each God-given dimension of life possesses its own center (reason for being) and circumference (limits to its jurisdiction). *Religion,* for instance, orients the heart while *science* advances knowledge. *Art* displays aesthetic excellence while the *economic* sphere exists to steward resources. More to the point, the *state* is ordained to bring justice to the various individuals and communities under its purview, while the *family* exists as a monogamous union ordered toward having and rearing children. This array of divinely ordained sectors serves as a system of checks and balances, not at the political level by dispersing governmental power, but at the ontological level by dispersing cultural power.

The boundaries of the spheres, Kuyper noted, are not absolute, as "the divisions to be reckoned with should not be made with compass and ruler but should be derived from history and reality and should serve to nourish the vitality that is appropriate to each life-sphere."[17] The spheres have a symbiotic relationship with one another, regularly and necessarily interacting with one another. In the Kuyperian tradition this reality is described in terms of *enkapsis,* or, "structural interlacements which can exist between things, plants, animals, and societal structures."[18]

---

[16] Abraham Kuyper, "Sphere Sovereignty" in *Abraham Kuyper: A Centennial Reader*, ed. James D. Bratt (Grand Rapids: Eerdmans, 1998), 467.

[17] Abraham Kuyper, *Our Program: A Christian Political Manifesto*, trans. and ed. Harry Van Dyke, Abraham Kuyper Collected Works in Public Theology (Bellingham, WA: Lexham, 2015), 145.

[18] Albert M. Wolters, "Glossary," in L. Kalsbeek, *Contours of a Christian Philosophy: An Introduction to Herman Dooyeweerd's Thought*, eds. Bernard and Joshua Zylstra (Amsterdam: Buijten and Schipperheijn, 1975), 347-48.

Moreover, each sphere enjoys a limited transcendence vis-à-vis the other spheres. Consider the relationship of church and state. Even though the state is viewed as one cultural sphere alongside of other spheres and thus is not viewed as the supreme temporal society, it does serve as an umpire of sorts, with the right and authority to intervene in disputes involving several spheres or in instances of injustice within a given sphere. Similarly, although the church as an institution does not mediate God's authority to the other spheres but instead exists alongside of them, the church as an organism exercises influence across the spheres through its members' various callings and competencies.

In many respects, Kuyper's philosophy of societal pluriformity is consonant with Catholic social teaching, especially in relation to subsidiarity. Similar to sphere sovereignty, *Quadragesimo Anno* and subsequent iterations of subsidiarity draw upon Scripture and a combination of modern and premodern sources to articulate a philosophy of society that recognizes the value and integrity of non-governmental associations and institutions. And like sphere sovereignty, subsidiarity guards against the state's totalizing tendencies while allowing for limited state intervention when individuals or associations neglect their responsibilities.

Jacques Maritain's conception of subsidiarity, for example, promoted democracy and human rights, paving the way for the incorporation of Catholic social thought into Christian Democratic political parties. Maritain conceived of the human as a social being with obligations to God and society, a being who is not only embedded in social activity with diverse natural communities, but who possesses a divine right to conscience and religious association.[19]

Subsidiarity differs from sphere sovereignty in that its conception of society tends to be more hierarchical, with the state serving as the supreme temporal society, while other associations serve as lower parts of a larger and more organic unity. And yet, the similarities outweigh the distinctions, with both philosophies recognizing the social nature of human being, underscoring the significance of social associations and cultural institutions, and warning that democratic political arrangements succeed only when a nation's associations and institutions inculcate virtue in its citizens.

---

[19] Jacques Maritain, *Man and the State* (Chicago: University of Chicago Press, 1951).

Similarly, sphere sovereignty is consonant in many ways with contemporary discourse about "mediating" structures and institutions. As articulated by Peter Berger and Richard John Neuhaus, mediating structures are "those institutions standing between the individual and his private life and the large institutions of public life."[20] These institutions, such as churches, schools, fraternal organizations, professional associations, and even clubs, play a crucial role in society, guarding against an overweening state, on the one hand, or isolated individualism, on the other. Kuyper's sphere sovereignty is confluent with Berger and Neuhaus' concern to buttress mediating institutions, even if Kuyper was more concerned with how those institutions arise from an even more basic creational order.

Finally, sphere sovereignty secures a central concern of the Anabaptist tradition: the role of the church as a prophetic community in its own right. While Kuyper's church organic secures the magisterial Reformation's vital concern for the gospel to permeate society through cultural initiative, his conception of the church institutional secures the Anabaptist distinctive of the local church as a colony of the kingdom. When God's people gather around Word and table, they are a contrast community whose inner life and culture serve as its own powerful form of cultural witness and influence.

## Protecting the Vulnerable

Assuming some version of societal pluriformity, what, then, should be the relationship of children to the family and the state? As a general rule, the state should recognize the primacy of the family in the formation of children. The state may intervene; part of the state's unique jurisdiction, in fact, lies in its authority to intervene in other spheres. But the state must only do so in limited instances—such as abuse or gross negligence—and only then for the purpose of strengthening the family and withdrawing as soon as possible. For the government is, in Kuyper's words, "nothing but a temporary curator.... A temporary curator has the right to carry out what is absolutely necessary, but his duty is to withdraw again as soon as

---

[20] Peter L. Berger and Richard John Neuhaus, *To Empower People: From State to Civil Society*, 2d ed. (Washington, DC: American Enterprise Institute, 1995), 148.

the energy for self-rule is sufficiently aroused. Thus, he is to fulfill the role of caretaker in such a way that this energy does not weaken but rather gains in strength."[21] Parents are responsible for their children, receiving their authority from God rather than from the state, and only in extreme situations should cede their responsibility and authority to the state or other actors.

Promoting the family as the chief caretakers for their children is by no means limited to legal, philosophical, or theological rationales. Consider, for example, that multiple prominent schools of psychotherapy have demonstrated that robust legal protection of parental rights is crucial for the well-being of parents, children, and society at large. Social-cognitive approaches, for example, demonstrate that a child's formation depends heavily on imitating or modeling behaviors which are facilitated most effectively within the family unit.[22] Similarly, "object relations" and "self-psychology" theories posit that a healthy child-family relationship, especially in the first two years of the child's life, will generally lead to happy and satisfying experiences in future relationships and activities.[23] Positive early attachment experiences with primary caregivers affect a child's way of thinking, experience of emotion, conscience formation, sense of agency, gender identity, and ability to relate to others.[24] Self-determination theory posits that a child's social experiences and roles significantly influence his future goals and life activities.[25] Although these varying psychological schools differ in many regards, they all agree that the family's "internalizing" role is crucial for children's formation and, by extension, their future participation in society.[26]

Moreover, in buttressing the family, we protect not only children but also society at large. Indeed, the family is the most basic unit of society.

---

[21] Abraham Kuyper, *Our Program*, 145.

[22] A. Bandura, *The Social Foundations of Thought and Action* (New York: Prentice Hall, 1986).

[23] Phyllis Tyson and Robert L. Tyson, *Psychoanalytic Theories of Development* (New Haven: Yale University, 1990).

[24] Daniel N. Stern, *The Interpersonal World of the Infant: A View from Psychoanalysis and Developmental Psychology* (New York Basic Books, 1985).

[25] Richard M. Ryan and Edward L. Deci, "Self-Determination theory and the Facilitation of Intrinsic Motivation, Social Development, and Well-Being." *American Psychologist* 55:1 (January 2000), 68–78.

[26] That we would need to marshal the insights of psychotherapists to persuade citizens of the fact that the traditional family unit is crucial to child development is evidence of the circumambient imbecility of our secular age.

Theologically, the family is the first institution to appear in Scripture and in history, and is more fundamental than society's other institutions. Similarly, in political philosophy and sociology, a convincing case is made that the family is a relationship that is entirely independent of people's will and thus is prior to, and more fundamental than, social contracts; it is the basis for the formation of neighborhoods, cities, and ultimately nation-states.[27] Indeed, the strength and health of a society's families is the surest indicator of whether society itself will flourish. The family takes the lead in teaching its members how to balance personal integrity with social dependence, and freedom with responsibility. It is a microcosmic apprenticeship for life in broader society. Without the family, we have no civilization.

Additionally, the family's integrity and authority serve as limits upon the state. As Allan Carlson and Paul Mero argue, the West no longer recognizes the significance or meaning of the traditional family unit and thus is losing the last bulwark of liberty, the last and most important institution standing between the overweening state and the isolated individual.[28]

## Neither Blind Optimism nor Despair

In many ways, our secular age is not an ideal context for Christians who wish to raise their children in the nurture and admonition of the Lord. Many of our neighbors and fellow citizens consider Christianity implausible and even unimaginable. Many persons with cultural power are imagining society in ways that demean human life in general and children in particular. The state is expanding its reach and exercising its power in ways that may encroach upon the free exercise of Christian faith in general and Christian teaching about the family in particular. Yet, no matter how gloomy the forecast or how difficult it might be to swim against the currents of our secular age, we must embrace the moment God has given us.

---

[27] Melissa Moschella, *To Whom Do Children Belong?: Parental Rights, Civic Education, and Children's Autonomy* (Oxford: Oxford University, 2017); Scott Yenor, *Family Politics: The Idea of Marriage in Modern Political Thought* (Waco, TX: Baylor University, 2011).

[28] Allan C. Carlson and Paul T. Mero, *The Natural Family: A Manifesto* (Dallas, TX: Spence, 2007).

We know that our age is secular, and that in some ways it is arrayed against us. Yet, we also know even more surely that Christ was raised from the dead and that he will return one day to set the world aright. And having this conviction, we ought as Christians to eschew the temptation toward blind optimism or faithless despair, and instead be the heart and strength of every good movement to build up the family and protect the child.

# Religious Freedom:
# A Contemporary Review

*Kristen Waggoner*

Among America's greatest contributions to the larger world is a society and legal system dedicated to protecting religious freedom and free speech. The genius of our Founders to constitutionally protect these foundational rights is reflected in the First Amendment of the United States Constitution, in state constitutions, and in statutory law—which guarantee the right to peacefully speak, live, and learn consistent with one's religious convictions.

Indeed, the intellectual individualism, cultural diversity, and spiritual vitality Americans cherish depends on the freedom of the mind—even if this freedom comes at the price of tolerating eccentric and even offensive views.[1] When the Supreme Court held the government could not force Jehovah's Witnesses to salute the American flag (at the height of World War II) in violation of their faith, it said:

> *The very purpose of a Bill of Rights was to withdraw certain subjects from the vicissitudes of political controversy, to place them beyond the reach of majorities and officials...*

---

[1] *See Texas v. Johnson*, 491 U.S. 397, 414 (1989) ("If there is a bedrock principle underlying the First Amendment, it is that the government may not prohibit the expression of an idea simply because society finds the idea itself offensive or disagreeable."); *McCutcheon v. Federal Election Commission*, 134 S.Ct. 1434, 1449 (2014) ("The whole point of the First Amendment is to protect individual speech that the majority might prefer to restrict, or that legislators or judges might not view as useful to the democratic process.").

*Freedom to differ is not limited to things that do not matter much. That would be a mere shadow of freedom. The test of its substance is the right to differ as to things that touch on the heart of the existing order.*[2]

Today, the very heart of the existing order—our understanding of sex, marriage, and religion—is at the center of a national debate. Even if cultural and political winds shift on these issues, our constitutional rights must not shift with them.

## A "Polite" Persecution

Although many of the world's constitutions and international covenants protect religious freedom, many actively seek to reduce these critical guarantees to mere rhetoric. Our religious brothers and sisters abroad face increasingly severe persecution. In America, by God's grace, people of faith have not faced torture, rape, and death. Still, American believers and religious institutions, especially members of the Abrahamic faiths who hold orthodox beliefs about human sexuality and marriage, face a more "polite" persecution. Some of the first to experience this "polite" persecution are those who, in the everyday marketplace, serve all customers regardless of beliefs or background but decline to promote ideas that violate their religious convictions. Governments increasingly use laws and policies to elevate "sexual orientation" and "gender identity" to a protected status, and then punish differences of opinion about marriage and human sexuality as illegal discrimination.

Every American, whether or not they hold traditional views on marriage and sexuality, should be concerned about these, and any, violations of religious freedom. Allowing the government to "politely" persecute anyone—for instance, by using nondiscrimination law to compel ideological uniformity—ultimately puts everyone at risk. A government that compels a Catholic may also compel an agnostic, and a state that crushes a cake artist can crush a painter, poet, pastor, or parent. Maintaining the freedom to believe, speak, and peacefully live out our convictions requires us to defend the same freedom for those with whom we disagree.

---

[2] *West Virginia Bd. of Ed. v. Barnette*, 319 U.S. 624, 638, 642 (1943).

## Sexual Orientation Gender Identity Laws: Coercing the Religious

Public accommodation non-discrimination laws regulate how organizations serve the public. Historically, these laws forbid a relatively small class of businesses, such as hotels, from denying service "because of" someone's membership in a protected class. Protected classes have typically covered immutable characteristics irrelevant to the services provided, such as national origin, ethnicity, sex, and race. But over time, these laws have expanded. Today, they often regulate any organization offering anything to the public, for free or for money, and the scope of protected classes has also expanded to include everything from physical appearance or arrest record to political beliefs.[3] Fewer than half of the states and some local jurisdictions have public accommodation laws covering "sexual orientation" and "gender identity," but the number is growing.[4]

Officials and activists use these sexual orientation gender identity (SOGI) laws to coerce people to express messages, create art, or celebrate a view of marriage and human sexuality that violates their core beliefs. SOGI laws have inflicted personal and professional ruin on those who stand by their faith convictions—convictions held by all Abrahamic faiths for millennia.[5]

---

[3] *See*, e.g., Madison, Wisconsin, Municipal Code § 39.03(2)(mm) (defining "protected class" to include "sex, race, religion, color, national origin or ancestry, citizenship status, age, handicap/disability, marital status, source of income, arrest record or conviction record, less than honorable discharge, physical appearance, sexual orientation, gender identity, genetic identity, political beliefs, familial status, student, domestic partner, or receipt of rental assistance"). *See also Hurley v. Irish-American Gay, Lesbian and Bisexual Group of Boston, Inc.*, 515 U.S. 557, 571-72 (1995) (discussing the history of public accommodations laws growing out of common law prohibitions on discrimination by innkeepers, blacksmiths, and the like).

[4] Twenty-one states, plus the District of Columbia, prohibit discrimination on the basis of sexual orientation and gender identity by statute. Two more include these characteristics within the meaning of "sex" in their nondiscrimination statutes as a result of judicial decisions. One more prohibits discrimination on the basis of sexual orientation but not gender identity. See Map Advancement Project, *Equality Maps: State Non-Discrimination Laws*, LgbtMap.org (Jan. 29, 2019) available at http://www.lgbtmap.org/equality-maps/non_discrimination_laws (accessed Jan. 31, 2019). For a recently enacted local ordinance, see South Euclid, Ohio, Municipal Code §§ 552.01-552.99.

[5] Ryan T. Anderson, *ENDA Threatens Fundamental Civil Liberties, Heritage Foundation Backgrounder* No. 2857, 6 (Nov. 1, 2013) available at http://thf_media.s3.amazonaws.com/2013/pdf/BG2857.pdf (accessed Jan. 31, 2019).

## SOGI versus Creative Professionals

Many people of faith have faced disastrous financial penalties and even jail time for declining to create artistic expression celebrating same-sex ceremonies. Barronelle Stutzman, a seventy-three-year-old grandmother with twenty-three grandchildren and owner of Arlene's Flowers, has employed and served people from all walks of life for over forty years, including those who identify as gay or bisexual—like her customer and friend Rob Ingersoll. Barronelle designed dozens of arrangements for Rob over nine years, including for Rob to give to his partner. She knew Rob identified as gay. It made no difference. They shared a love of flowers, and over time they became friends.

Shortly after Washington changed the legal definition of marriage, Rob asked Barronelle to design the floral arrangements for his wedding. Barronelle's faith teaches her marriage is a sacred covenant between one man and one woman that represents Christ and His Church. Barronelle believed she would sin against God and undermine her Christian witness if she participated in a same-sex ceremony by creating custom wedding arrangements and assisting at the ceremony.

Taking his hand, Barronelle gently let Rob know of her convictions, kindly telling him she couldn't design his wedding arrangements because of her relationship with Christ. She then referred him to three other top local florists. They chatted about how he got engaged and his plans for the wedding, hugged, and then he left. Barronelle thought they parted as friends who simply disagreed. Soon after, the State Attorney General sued her, even though Rob had not filed a formal complaint. Later, the ACLU urged Rob and his partner to sue Barronelle. To maximize the pressure on Barronelle to violate her faith, the State and ACLU took the extraordinary step of suing not just Arlene's Flowers but also Barronelle personally. That means if Barronelle loses, she may lose not just her business but nearly all her personal assets—her home, her retirement, her savings. She won't be able to retire, and her children won't inherit her second-generation floral shop.

As an attorney from Washington State, I remember when the legislature assured us SOGI laws fostered a "live and let live" philosophy, and would not lead to government coercion. Same-sex marriage, they insisted, would not abridge religious freedom. Obviously, this is not true. Barronelle is far from the only one. Consider these other examples:

- New Mexico forced photographer Elaine Huegenin out of her photography business based on a SOGI law requiring her to create photographs and wedding storybooks that violate her conscience.

- Minnesota threatens Carl and Angel Larsen, filmmakers who love to tell God-honoring stories through the films they create, with heavy fines and ninety days in jail if they decline to create films celebrating same-sex weddings.

- Phoenix forces painter Breana Koski and calligrapher Joana Duka to choose between closing their art studio or facing up to six months in jail every time they decline a commission that violates their religious convictions about marriage.

- Colorado officials assert their SOGI law can coerce Lori Smith, a graphic and website design artist, to design wedding websites and related materials to promote same-sex weddings. They also contend the law could apply to painters and authors.

The most prominent example of a state seeking to coerce a creative professional in the wedding industry is the case of *Masterpiece Cakeshop v. Colorado Civil Rights Commission*.[6] Jack Phillips is a cake designer whose love for art and design began at an early age. Blending his skills as a pastry chef, sculptor, and painter, he opened Masterpiece Cakeshop twenty-five years ago and developed a reputation for his custom-designed wedding cakes.

Jack's deep religious faith guides his work. His beliefs inspire him to love and serve people from all walks of life, but he can only create cakes consistent with his faith. His decisions on whether to design a specific custom cake have never focused on *who* the customer is, but on *what* the custom cake will express or celebrate.

In other words, Jack is not discriminating against anyone. He creates cakes and baked goods for people regardless of a client's status, including

---

[6] 138 S.Ct. 1719 (2018).

those who identify as LGBT. But free speech guarantees Jack should be able to control what he says. In the same way, an atheist web designer can create websites for Christians but should not be forced to create websites promoting Christianity. That's not status discrimination. The web designer is serving Christians; he is merely exercising his freedom to speak only those messages consistent with who he is.

Colorado ignored this distinction and told Jack he could not decline requests for custom wedding cakes that celebrate a view of marriage in conflict with his religious beliefs. As a result, Jack was forced out of the wedding business entirely, losing 40 percent of his income and most of his employees. Colorado also ordered him to re-educate his family and demanded that he report to the government every time he declined to design a cake, and why. Their actions deprived the community's brides and grooms of a great artist.

## Coercing So Many Other Professions

SOGI laws and policies threaten those in other creative professions also. Blaine Adamson owns Hands On Originals, a company that creates promotional materials like shirts, hats, and cups. As a Christian, Blaine believes his vocation is God's calling on his life and is part of his daily worship. He believes he's accountable to God for what his company creates. Like Barronelle and Jack, Blaine believes all people have inherent dignity and deserve respect. His faith inspires him to serve everyone, but he cannot print every message or promote every event a customer requests.

In 2012, Blaine received a request to print T-shirts promoting the Lexington Gay Pride Festival. He referred the customer to another respected printer who Blaine knew would print the shirts at the same price. Government officials claim Blaine violated the SOGI law and appealed the case all the way to the Kentucky Supreme Court.

Meanwhile, East Lansing, Michigan banned organic apple farmer Country Mill Farms from its prime market, when Country Mill owner Steve Tennes mentioned on Facebook his family would only host weddings on their farm consistent with their Catholic beliefs on marriage. This despite the farm being outside the city and violating no law.

Similarly, the United States Department of Agriculture refused to pass the Vander Boon meat packing facility in its health inspection because the inspector found religious literature about marriage on a breakroom table. According to the inspector, that created a "hostile work environment."

Officials have also sought to use laws and financial strings to force churches and religious nonprofits to operate in ways that conflict with their faith, even homeless shelters.[7] Every night in Anchorage, Alaska, about sixty homeless women—many fleeing abuse—enjoy a warm, safe common sleeping room at Downtown Hope Center. If Anchorage officials have their way under the city's SOGI law, they will be cast back on the streets. When a violent, visibly injured, and intoxicated biological man in a woman's nightgown asked to sleep in the women's shelter, the Center prudently—and graciously—paid for a taxi to take the man to the hospital. Now Anchorage officials contend Hope Center violated their SOGI law by not allowing the man to sleep among the dozens of women in the shelter. The city gives the Center's Good Samaritans the choice of turning fragile, battered women out on the street—or forcing them to share their common bedroom with a biological man.

Two additional examples come from New York:

- New York City threatens fines up to $10,000 per violation on Dr. David Schwartz, a licensed psychotherapist and member of the Lubavitcher Orthodox Jewish Community, if he counsels adult patients who want to overcome same-sex attraction. Dr. Schwartz simply listens to his patients, talks with them, and offers suggestions. Most are of his same faith and many have

---

[7] The State of Maryland denies aid to economically disadvantaged students who attend religious schools whose admissions and student conduct policies reflect their religious views about sexual morality. 2017 Maryland Laws Ch. 150 (H.B. 150). The Commonwealth of Pennsylvania forbids health insurance companies from selling policies that respect religious organizations' beliefs about paying for "sex reassignment" drugs and surgeries. Pennsylvania Bulletin, *Notice Regarding Nondiscrimination*, 46 Pa. B. 2251 (Apr. 30, 2016). The Lynn, Massachusetts public school district terminated an 11-year relationship with Gordon College, a Christ-centered institution of higher education, because of its beliefs regarding sexual morality. Under the partnership, Gordon sent dozens of student volunteers into the city's poor-performing public schools. Oliver Ortega, Lynn Public Schools Sever Relationship with Gordon College, Boston Globe (Aug. 31, 2014) available at https://www.bostonglobe.com/metro/2014/08/29/lynn-public-schools-sever-relationship-with-gordon-college/aw1KwO4RGVpn284rR1jTgO/story.html (accessed Jan. 31, 2019). In December 2015, a Massachusetts court held that a Catholic school violated a state law by filling job positions with individuals who share the Church's beliefs about marriage. *Barrett v. Fontbonne Academy*, 33 Mass.L.Rptr. 287 (Mass. Sup. Ct. 2015).

achieved their personal goals. New York's law silences Dr. Schwartz and censors confidential conversations between adults.

- For over fifty years, New Hope Family Services has placed over 1,000 children into loving adoptive homes. But New York's bureaucrats have warned New Hope they will lose their license if they continue to prioritize the placement of children in homes with married moms and dads.

## Religious Freedom Protects All Americans

Remarkably, some suggest conflicts could be avoided if SOGI laws were broadly enacted that include narrow protections for churches and distinctly religious organizations. This is a false hope. While the pastor might be temporarily protected, those in the pews—the photographers, printers, bakers, farmers, teachers, social workers, doctors, and more—would face the risk of ruinous burdens like Barronelle, Jack, and so many others.

James Madison warned the abridgement of our freedoms rarely comes from violent conflicts, but through gradual and silent encroachment.[8] In the wake of the sexual revolution, those gradual encroachments on religious freedom accumulate every day.

Compromising First Amendment freedoms in the SOGI context endangers freedom in *every* context: limited religious exemptions will not last. Indeed, activists have sought to remove those exemptions when they have enough political power.[9] Also, the loss of freedom in one area only

---

[8] James Madison, "Speech in the Virginia Ratifying Convention on Control of the Military, June 16, 1788," in: *History of the Virginia Federal Convention of 1788*, Vol. 1, p. 130 (edited by H.B. Grigsby ed. 1890) ("Since the general civilization of mankind, I believe there are more instances of the abridgement of freedom of the people by gradual and silent encroachments by those in power than by violent and sudden usurpations.").

[9] The California legislature came very close to removing the religious exemption in the state Equity in Higher Education Act, which forbids students from directing state student aid to schools that "discriminate" on the basis of SOGI (among other things). *See* S.B. 1146 (Cal. 2016). The District of Columbia council eliminated a decades-old religious exemption from a ban on SOGI discrimination in its Human Rights Act. D.C. Law 20-266 (2015), amending D.C. Stat. § 2-1402.41. In 2014, all the major LGBT advocacy organizations abandoned their support for the Employment Nondiscrimination Act, which would have outlawed SOGI discrimination in employment, because it included a religious exemption. Ed O'Keefe, "Gay Rights Groups Withdraw Support of ENDA After Hobby Lobby Decision," *Washington Post* (Jul. 8, 2014) available at https://www.washingtonpost.com/news/post-politics/wp/2014/07/08/gay-rights-group-withdrawing-support-of-enda-after-hobby-lobby-decision/?utm_term=.54892f66e67c (accessed Jan. 31, 2019).

leads to further loss. For example, the ACLU, Planned Parenthood, and other assisted suicide advocates have tried to leverage court decisions and laws to abridge freedom to coerce taking human life.[10]

The better way is to affirm and protect religious freedom for all. The better way is to provide the free and open debate essential to finding the truths to guide our society. The benefits of religious freedom are not esoteric, but rather secure concrete goods to society.

First, religious freedom ensures we *all* have the freedom to explore the meaning of life and to order our lives under the answers we find. It is the freedom to think, express, and peaceably act upon our deepest convictions. It is a pre-political, inalienable right that rests securely in self-evident truths. And it protects the ardent Catholic as much as the committed Muslim.

Second, a government that can destroy someone because of their religious convictions has unlimited power. Religious freedom curbs authoritarianism. People need to be able to disagree on the subjects that matter—like sex, marriage, life, death, and religion. These freedoms, when preserved and exercised well, preserve the possibility of self-government for future generations.

Third, religious freedom contributes greatly to a healthy society and economy. True faith calls us to do good and defines what good is. Knowing what is good and moral inspires volunteerism and charity. In America, religion contributes over $1.2 trillion annually to the economy—7 percent of America's GDP—and to the common good.[11]

Fourth, religious freedom permits people of all faiths to promote religious-based ideas and policies they believe will foster a moral and just nation. Christians should embrace this freedom because the teachings of our faith are true, cogent, and convincing, and provide the best

---

[10] *See, e.g., American Civil Liberties Union v. Trinity Health Corp.*, 178 F.Supp.3d 614 (E.D. Mich. 2016) (ACLU claimed that a Catholic hospital network's refusal to perform abortions violated federal law). Other useful examples include the "HHS Abortion Pill Mandate," regulations promulgated under the Affordable Care Act that compelled many religious employers to provide or facilitate access to abortifacient contraceptives, *see Burwell v. Hobby Lobby Stores, Inc.*, 134 S.Ct. 2751 (2014), and California's reinterpretation of the Knox Keene Act to compel all insurers (including many religious organizations) to pay for cover elective abortions. *See Skyline Wesleyan Church v. California Dept. of Managed Health Care*, 313 F.Supp.3d 1225 (2018).

[11] Brian Grim & Melissa Grim, "The Socio-Economic Contribution of Religion to American Society An Empirical Analysis," *Interdisciplinary J. of Research on Religion*, 12:3 (2016), 24 available at http://www.religjournal.com/articles/article_view.php?id=108 (accessed Jan. 31 2019).

opportunity for human flourishing. Put to the test in a marketplace of ideas, we can have confidence our ideas will ultimately prevail.

Fifth, religious freedom strengthens national security and stability. History shows countries diligently protecting robust religious freedom experience less poverty, war, and violence than those that do not.[12]

Sixth, civil liberties travel together. Countries protecting religious freedom are more democratic and have more robust economic freedom, freedom of the press, and protections for the vulnerable and for minorities. The threats posed to people of faith equally endanger the treasured freedoms of non-believers.[13] It's worth repeating—civil liberties travel together.

If the government can coerce Jack or Barronelle, it can force the Jewish poet to laud same-sex marriage in a wedding poem or a lesbian poet to contribute a sonnet for a rally supporting biblical marriage; force a pro-abortion filmmaker to create promotional pieces for the March for Life; or force a socialist speechwriter to write for a Republican politician. Any rule that allows those in power to suppress what they don't like today can be turned against any of us tomorrow. SOGI laws promote one view—the government's view—of human sex and sexuality. When some courts allow those laws to trump constitutional protections for religious freedom, it compromises our biblical witness and signals approval for an unbiblical understanding of the human person. Such bad precedents infiltrate our legal rights and impose radical gender ideology on an unsuspecting and ill-informed public. This ideology will affect parents and our schools, workplaces, businesses, and virtually every area of communal life.[14]

---

[12] William Inboden, "Religious Freedom and National Security," *Policy Review, The Hoover Institute*, (Oct. 2, 2012) available at https://www.hoover.org/research/religious-freedom-and-national-security (accessed Jan. 31, 2019).

[13] Thomas Farr, "Is Religious Freedom Necessary for Other Freedoms to Flourish?", *Berkely Center for Religion, Peace & World Affairs*, (Aug. 7, 2012) available at https://berkleycenter.georgetown.edu/essays/is-religious-freedom-necessary-for-other-freedoms-to-flourish (accessed Jan. 31, 2019).

[14] See The Heritage Foundation, *The Inequality of the Equality Act: Concerns from the Left*, (Heritage Organization Jan. 28, 2019) available at https://www.heritage.org/event/the-inequality-the-equality-act-concerns-the-left (accessed Jan. 31, 2019). See also Ryan T. Anderson & Melody Wood, "Gender Identity Policies in Schools: What Congress, the Courts, and the Trump Administration Should Do," *Heritage Foundation Backgrounder* No. 3201 (March 23, 2017) available at https://www.heritage.org/education/report/gender-identity-policies-schools-what-congress-the-courts-and-the-trump (accessed Jan. 31, 2019).

Again, there are concrete impacts: if religious liberty is diminished, will the pregnant women ever speak with that pro-life advocate on the sidewalk and choose life? Will the searching atheist ever chat with the Christian student in the campus quad and find the answer? Will that homeless woman be in the warmth of a shelter, or shivering in a cardboard box? We should never lose sight of the reality that robust religious freedom can cause life, healing, and eternal salvation.

## Some Good News

Standing for freedom isn't for the faint of heart. Those who stand against unjust laws also stand against the prevailing winds of culture, and the shared beliefs of their neighbors, co-workers, bosses, professors, and even fellow churchmen. Recall in his "Letter from a Birmingham Jail," Martin Luther King, Jr. was writing to churchmen who criticized his methods as unloving and ill-timed.

Courage arises when men and women place a higher value on their duty to God than the esteem of men. Their courage, manifest in humble but determined actions, eventually moved the law and the culture for all people—even those who opposed them—in the right direction.

Thankfully, that courage is evident in this generation and, thankfully, many individuals identified in this chapter have prevailed.

While we have yet to secure a broad win at the United States Supreme Court affirming the right to speak and live consistent with our convictions in the SOGI context, recent decisions by the Supreme Court bode well for the First Amendment.

In June 2018, the Court ruled 7-2 for Jack Phillips and Masterpiece Cakeshop, holding the Commission displayed clear and impermissible hostility toward Jack's religious beliefs, and identifying flaws in how Colorado applied its SOGI law.

The government, the Court ruled, cannot apply a double standard to target people of faith. The Commission treated cake designers differently, giving a free pass for those who declined religious messages but severely punishing Jack for declining a same-sex marriage message.

The Court also reiterated the free exercise clause forbids even the most subtle departures from neutrality, rebuking the Commission for suggesting faith has no place in the public square. And the Court repudiated the most vicious claim made against those who believe marriage is between one man and one woman—that it's akin to racial bigotry. To the contrary, the Court affirmed believing marriage is between a man and a woman based upon religious or philosophical grounds is decent, honorable, and deserves protection.

Also in 2018, the Court decided, in *NIFLA v. Becerra*,[15] the state of California could not compel pro-life pregnancy centers to promote the state's abortion services. The Court explained private voices cannot be co-opted by the state and it rejected the argument licensed professionals (most of us in the marketplace) have less speech protection.

The Supreme Court spoke even more forcefully against compelled speech in *Janus v. American Federation of State, County, and Municipal Employees Council*,[16] which involved whether the state can force non-union public sector employees to pay union dues. The Court explained government efforts to coerce speech violate the dignity of the speakers and force them to betray their convictions. That betrayal "is always demeaning."[17] The Court also said speech on controversial topics (including human sexuality) occupies the highest rung of the hierarchy of First Amendment values and merits special First Amendment protection.

These decisions affirm the wisdom of our Founders in protecting the free exercise of religion. They signal the Court affirms people of faith may participate fully in our civic life, and free markets and freely exercised faith are compatible with one another.

## Our Call as People of Faith

Protecting religious freedom is not just a calling for lawyers, pastors, or the select few like Barronelle and Jack. It is a call for all Christians. Justice Samuel Alito observed "the most important fight is for the hearts and minds of our fellow Americans. It is up to all of us to evangelize our fellow Americans about the issue of religious freedom."[18] We must

---

[15] 138 S.Ct. 2361 (2018).

[16] 138 S.Ct. 2448 (2018).

[17] Id. at 2464.

[18] David Porter, "Alito: US's Dedication to Religious Liberty Being Tested," *Associated Press* (Mar. 15, 2017) available at https://apnews.com/18f3eeb865d442e28486db5b7007e706 (accessed Jan. 31, 2019).

share the benefits of religious freedom in warehouses, board rooms, and at water coolers; school hallways, soccer games, and our driveways; and most important, at our dinner tables, and in our living rooms with our own children. By protecting these freedoms today and for future generations, we help to ensure all may hear and explore the full meaning of the Gospel.

# Postscript: A Contest of Worldviews

*Robert P. George*

A contest of worldviews in our time pits devout Catholics, Protestants, Orthodox Christians, Jews, and other believers against their fellow citizens who embrace secular progressive ideology and those who, while remaining within the religious denominations, have adopted essentially secular progressive ideas about personal and political morality. The contest manifests itself in disputes over abortion, embryo-destructive research, and euthanasia, as well as in issues of sex, marriage, and family life. Underlying these specific conflicts are profound differences about the nature of morality and the proper relation of moral judgment to law and public policy.

I am hardly the first to recognize the existence of this conflict of worldviews. People on both sides have noticed it, commented on it, and proposed ideas about how an essentially democratically constituted polity ought to come to terms with it. The trouble is the issues dividing the two camps are of such profound moral significance—on either side's account—merely procedural solutions are not good enough. Neither side will be happy to agree on decision procedures for resolving the key differences of opinion at the level of public policy where the procedures do not guarantee victory for the substantive policies they favor. This is not a matter of people being irrationally stubborn; rather, it reflects the considered judgment of people on both sides that fundamental and therefore nonnegotiable issues of justice are at stake.

Jürgen Habermas in Europe and the late John Rawls in the United States are perhaps the premier examples of secular thinkers who have taken the measure of the problem and proposed terms of engagement that, they believe, can be affirmed by reasonable people across the spectrum of opinion. Both single out Catholicism as an example of a non-liberal "comprehensive doctrine" that may nevertheless affirm essentially liberal terms of engagement with competing comprehensive doctrines. Indeed, they argue, one needn't be a secular person, much less a secularist or secular progressive, to endorse their teachings. There is plenty of room, they say, for religious people of various stripes to affirm the secular principles and norms that should govern political life in contemporary pluralistic democratic societies. Indeed, their goal is to identify principles and norms reasonably accepted by believers and unbelievers alike, and affirmed by people irrespective of their convictions about human nature, dignity, and destiny.

From a Christian vantage point, there is nothing startling or troubling about the quest to identify moral and political principles reasonably affirmed without appeal to theological claims or religious authority. That's one description, accurate so far as it goes, of the enterprise known as natural law theory. But there is something deeply alien to Christian thought about separating inquiry into moral and political principles from questions pertaining to human nature, dignity, and destiny.

Inasmuch as Habermas and Rawls propose theories of political morality purporting to prescind from such basic questions, there appears to be a fundamental incompatibility between their proposals and the approach to moral and political theory embraced not only by the Catholic tradition, but my most other traditions of Christian faith. This is a problem for Habermas and Rawls. Both men offer theories reasonable people of diverse faiths, including Catholics and other Christians, are supposed to be able to endorse without compromising their faith.

Moreover, for both Habermas and Rawls it is important Catholics in particular be able to endorse their theories—in part because Catholicism is the world's largest religion, and in part because contemporary Catholicism affirms and even promotes liberal democracy as a political ideal. The late pontiff Pope John Paul II repeatedly praised democracy, describing it as the political system most consistent with both man's nature as a rational creature and the principle of the equality in dignity of all human beings. Since the Second Vatican Council, popes and other Catholic officials have regularly preached the obligation of governments to respect and protect human rights, including the freedom of religion. They have been joined in this by many evangelical and other Protestant leaders as well as by leaders of the Eastern Orthodox communions. While the Catholic Church does not rule out state-established religions (such as exist in Great Britain and Israel), it does not promote them, even where Catholicism is the dominant faith, and it strictly demands respect for religious liberty, even where established religions exist.

Given these and other "liberal" dimensions of Catholic (and more generally Christian) social and political teaching, it would be particularly awkward for Rawls or Habermas if Catholics and other Christians could not, in good conscience, affirm their political theories. Indeed, the inability of these theories to accommodate Catholics and other Christians, if proven, would invite the suspicion there is something distinctly sectarian about them. It would suggest the theories are not merely secular but fully secularist.

In his influential 1971 book *A Theory of Justice*, Rawls defended what he called "justice as fairness," in which basic principles for a well-ordered society are identified as those chosen by free and equal persons in what he called "the original position." Parties in "the original position" select principles in a state of ignorance regarding their personal moral and religious convictions, social and economic status, and related factors distinguishing them from many of their fellow citizens when they emerge from behind "the veil of ignorance" to live in a society governed in accordance with the principles they selected.

In 1993, Rawls published a new book, *Political Liberalism*, which amends certain features of the theory he advanced in 1971. Most importantly, Rawls conceded the argument for "justice as fairness" in *A Theory of Justice* relied on a premise inconsistent with the theory itself: the belief "in the well-ordered society of justice as fairness, citizens hold the same comprehensive doctrine, and this includes aspects of Kant's comprehensive liberalism, to which the principles of justice as fairness might belong."

By a "comprehensive doctrine," Rawls means something like a worldview—an integrated set of moral beliefs and commitments reflecting a still more fundamental understanding of human nature, dignity, and destiny. Rawls's problem with the position he adopted in *A Theory of Justice* is liberalism (considered a "comprehensive," as opposed to a merely "political," doctrine) is not held by citizens generally in contemporary pluralistic societies. Liberalism considered as such—plainly a secularist view—competes in such societies with Catholicism, as well as with various forms of Protestantism and Judaism, and with other religious and secular comprehensive doctrines. Indeed, liberalism considered as a comprehensive doctrine is plainly a minority view in the United States. Most Americans reject secularism of any type, including secularist liberalism. In any event, Rawls's revised understanding is a plurality of comprehensive views, religious and secularist, is natural and unavoidable in the circumstances of political freedom characterizing constitutional democratic regimes. Political theorizing accepting the legitimacy of such regimes must begin, therefore, by acknowledging what Rawls calls "the fact of reasonable pluralism."

To appeal to comprehensive liberalism, Rawls concedes, would be no less sectarian than to appeal to Catholicism or Judaism. Some alternative must, therefore, be found or the social stability of such regimes would be in constant jeopardy. Everything would depend on the capacity and willingness of people with fundamentally different moral views—including radically different conceptions of justice and human rights—to reach and preserve a *modus vivendi*.

The alternative Rawls proposes is "political liberalism." Its ideal holds that "citizens are to conduct their public political discussions of constitutional essentials and matters of basic justice within the framework of what each sincerely regards as a reasonable political conception of justice, a conception expressing political values others as free and equal also might reasonably be expected to endorse."

The core of this political liberalism is the idea, whenever constitutional essentials and matters of basic justice are at stake, political actors must refrain from acting on the basis of principles drawn from their comprehensive views except to the extent "public reasons, given by a reasonable political conception, are presented sufficient to support whatever the comprehensive doctrines are introduced to support." Thus, citizens are constrained from appealing to and acting on beliefs drawn from their most fundamental moral understandings and commitments precisely at the most fundamental political level.

Rawls's political liberalism aspires, then, to be impartial with respect to the viewpoints represented by the various reasonable comprehensive doctrines competing for the allegiance of citizens. It "does not attack or criticize any reasonable [comprehensive] view," Rawls claims. "Rather than confronting religious and nonliberal doctrines with a comprehensive liberal philosophical doctrine, the thought is to formulate a liberal political conception those nonliberal doctrines might be able to endorse."

Rawls maintains that terms of cooperation offered by citizens to their fellow citizens are fair only insofar as citizens offering them "reasonably think that those citizens to whom such terms are offered might also reasonably accept them." This "criterion of reciprocity" is the core of what Rawls labels "the liberal principle of legitimacy"—the notion "our exercise of political power is fully proper only when it is exercised in accordance with a constitution the essentials of which all citizens as free and equal may be expected to endorse in the light of principles and ideals acceptable to their common human reason." When, and only when, political power is exercised in accordance with such a constitution do political actors—including voters—maintain fidelity to the ideal of "public reason."

The "liberal principle of legitimacy" and ideal of "public reason" exclude as illegitimate any appeal to principles and propositions drawn from comprehensive doctrines. At first glance, the scope of "public reason" seems to be wide. It would, to be sure, rule out as illegitimate any claim based on the allegedly "secret knowledge" of a gnostic elite or the putative truths revealed only to a select few and not accessible to reasonable persons as such. But it would not exclude any principle or proposition, however controversial, put forward for acceptance on the basis of rational argumentation.

Now, Rawls cannot accept this wide conception of public reason. His goal, after all, is to limit the range of morally acceptable doctrines of political morality in circumstances of moral pluralism to the single doctrine of "political liberalism." The wide conception of public reason will not rule out propositions drawn from comprehensive forms of liberalism. More important, it will not exclude propositions drawn from non-liberal comprehensive doctrines that content themselves with appeals to "our common human reason."

Notable among such doctrines is the broad tradition of natural law thinking about morality, justice, and human rights. This tradition poses an especially interesting problem for Rawls's theory of public reason because of its integration into Catholic teaching and its acceptance by many Christians of various traditions. So it is, at once, a non-liberal comprehensive philosophical doctrine and part of a larger religious tradition that, in effect, proposes its own principle of public reason.

If Rawls is to defend a conception of "public reason" narrow enough to exclude appeals to natural law, he must show there is something unfair about such appeals. And he must demonstrate this unfairness without appeal to comprehensive liberalism or any other comprehensive conception of justice competing with the natural law conception. In other words, he must avoid smuggling in principles in dispute among adherents to reasonable comprehensive doctrines.

This, it seems to me, he has not done and, I believe, cannot do. Rawls does not explicitly address the claims of natural law theorists. He seems, however, to have their beliefs in mind in his critique of what he calls "rationalist believers who contend that [their] beliefs are open to and can be fully established by reason." Rawls's argument rests entirely on the claim these "rationalist believers" unreasonably deny "the fact of reasonable pluralism."

But do they? Rawls's own methodological commitments mean he cannot rule out the views of natural law theorists or rationalist believers on such issues as homosexuality, abortion, euthanasia, and drugs on the grounds their views are unsound, unreasonable, or false—or else his political liberalism would have collapsed again into a comprehensive liberalism. He thus limits himself to a simple denial the claims of the rationalist believers "can be publicly and fully established by reason."

But how can this denial be sustained independently of some engagement with the specific arguments they advance—arguments Rawls's idea of public reason is meant to exclude without an appeal to their soundness and reasonableness or the truth or falsity of the principles and propositions in support of which they are offered? It will not do for Rawls to claim he is not denying the truth of rationalist believers' claims but merely their assertion these claims can be publicly and fully established by reason. What makes rationalist believers "rationalist" is precisely the belief their principles can be justified by rational argument and their willingness to provide just such rational argumentation.

Natural law theorists, whatever their religious commitments, maintain certain issues, including certain fundamental moral and political issues, there are uniquely correct answers. The question whether there is a human right against being enslaved, for example, or being punished for one's religious beliefs admits of a uniquely correct answer available in principle to every rational person. Pro-life advocates assert there is similarly a human right against deliberate feticide and other forms of direct killing of innocent human beings, irrespective of race, ethnicity, and sex, but also irrespective of disability, age, size, location, stage of development, or condition of dependency. Differences over such issues as slavery, religious freedom, abortion, and euthanasia may be "reasonable" in the sense reasonable persons can err in their judgments and arrive at morally incorrect positions. But assuming there is a truth of these matters—something Rawls cannot deny and, one would think, has no desire to deny—errors of reason must be responsible for anyone's failure to arrive at the morally correct positions.

Rawls certainly cannot declare such views unreasonable because they maintain on certain morally charged and highly disputed political questions—including questions of human rights—there are uniquely morally correct answers. The fact reasonable people can be found on competing sides of such questions in no way implies the competing views are equally reasonable. Reasonable people can be wrong, as Rawls implicitly acknowledges in his claims against the rationalist believers who are, after all, reasonable people even if their claim their beliefs can be fully and publicly justified by reason is unreasonable. There is simply no unreasonableness in maintaining otherwise reasonable people can be less than fully reasonable (sometimes culpably, other times not) in their judgments of particular issues.

In fairness to Rawls, we should acknowledge his treatment of the sources of moral disagreement in connection with what he calls "the burdens of judgment." To preserve the integrity of his political liberalism, however, we must read his account of the sources of disagreement in such a way as to avoid its collapse into relativism. If we do, Rawls's idea of "fully reasonable" views—and even "perfectly reasonable" though erroneous views—refers to false beliefs that are formed without subjective fault. I think this is what people generally have in mind when, though fully persuaded of the truth of a certain view, they allow nevertheless, "reasonable people" can disagree with them. The fact of "reasonable disagreement" in this sense is not a valid warrant for ruling out argument as to the truth of matters in dispute on the ground reasons adduced in any argument "on the merits" cannot qualify as "public reasons."

In *A Theory of Justice*, Rawls identified the basic principles of "justice as fairness" by the method of "political constructivism," which asked what substantive principles would be chosen by parties in the "original position" behind the "veil of ignorance." In a key passage of *Political Liberalism*, he says the "liberal principle of legitimacy" and the ideal of "public reason" have "the same basis as the substantive principles of justice." This basis remains insecure. Over more than thirty years, Rawls failed to provide any reason to suppose the injustice of principles of justice not selected under conditions of artificial ignorance by the unnaturally risk-averse parties in the "original position." Rawlsians seem to suppose from the proposition principles selected by such parties under such conditions are just, it follows other principles—which might well be chosen by reasonable and well-informed persons outside the original position—are unjust. But that does not follow at all.

Central to Jürgen Habermas's political thought is a distinction between "morality" and "ethics." As John Finnis has observed, in Habermas's work, this distinction "has much the same role as Rawls's untenable distinction between 'comprehensive doctrines' and 'public reasons.' The distinction, in Habermas's case, is part of what he calls an 'ethics of discourse' that "adopts the intersubjective approach of pragmatism and conceives of practical discourse as a public practice of shared reciprocal perspective taking: each individual finds himself compelled to adopt the perspective of everyone else in order to test whether a proposed regulation is also acceptable from the perspective of every other person's understanding of himself and the world." "Ethics," on this account, has to do with "how one sees oneself and who one would like to become," while "morality" has to do with the proper concern for "the interests of all." Political theory is fundamentally concerned, then, with "morality," not "ethics." And fundamental questions of the nature, dignity, and destiny of the human person are putatively excluded from the realm of political theory precisely because they are "ethical," not "moral."

According to Habermas, "Ethical questions point in a different direction from moral questions: the regulation of interpersonal conflicts of action resulting from opposed interests is not yet an issue. Whether I would like to be someone who in case of acute need would be willing to defraud an anonymous insurance company just this one time is not a moral question, for it concerns my self-respect and possibly the respect others show me, but not equal respect for all, and hence not the symmetrical respect everyone should accord the integrity of all other persons."

Finnis has put his finger on the problem here: "The compatibility of self-respect with this dealing with the insurance company cannot…be rationally assessed without making 'moral' judgments about the conditions on which property rights are justly respected and justly overridden, and about the injustice of fraud, and so forth." But if that is true, the distinction begins to collapse.

Worse still, Habermas employs the distinction in a way implicitly answering the question much disputed in our culture of who is to count as within the "all" whose interests must be taken into account in making moral judgments, while purporting to lay aside the evaluation of certain types of homicide as merely ethical. Writing in a law-review symposium devoted to his work in legal and political theory, Habermas raised the questions of abortion and euthanasia as cases involving "ethical" judgment and not "morality."

Of course, the claim of pro-life citizens is that a just law will protect the lives of the unborn and the frail or disabled precisely because justice requires respect for the fundamental interests of "all." No human being may be excluded from the community of the commonly protected on the basis of age, size, stage of development, disability, condition of dependency, or any other grounds on which supporters of abortion and euthanasia seek to exclude some human beings in order to justify these practices. The discourse into which pro-life people invite their fellow citizens is precisely a discourse about the reasonableness or unreasonableness of such exclusion. People on the pro-life side offer rational grounds— public reasons—for protecting the unborn and the disabled from being killed. They offer to show the exclusion of the unborn and the disabled from the protections of the law is arbitrary and, as such, unjust.

Habermas, however, expressly speaking of Catholics, suggests pro-life citizens are bound to accept legal abortion and euthanasia precisely because these are ethical questions, concerned with what is the best way to live, and not moral questions, concerned with the interests of all. Indeed, he implies morality requires pro-life citizens to refrain from acting on the basis of their ethical judgments, not because these judgments are in any way unsound, untrue, or unreasonable, but because they are ethical. The abstention is required, in other words, by a due regard for "the interests of all."

Yet, on what ground are the interests of the unborn or the severely disabled to be excluded from consideration? If the question of who is to count as within the all whose interests must be taken into consideration is an ethical one, then it is clear moral questions depend on ethical judgments—judgments regarding the nature and dignity of the human person—that cannot be avoided or relegated to the domain of the private.

There is in John Rawls's later work an almost exact parallel to Jürgen Habermas's error on this point. In *Political Liberalism*, Rawls raises the issue of abortion in a footnote—the one concrete contemporary political issue Rawls uses to illustrate the application of his doctrine of public reason. He asserts, "as an illustration," "any reasonable balancing" of the political values of respect for human life, "the ordered reproduction of political society over time," and women's equality would "give a woman a duly qualified right to decide whether or not to end her pregnancy during the first trimester" and perhaps beyond. For the law to protect the life of the human being in the early stages of development would be to impose, according to Rawls, a "comprehensive doctrine" in defiance of the strictures of political liberalism.

Like Habermas, Rawls offers no argument as to why the developing human being should be excluded from the law's protection. He does not offer reasons to rebut those scientific and philosophical arguments and fully public reasons offered in defense of the rights of the unborn by pro-life citizens. (In the end, as Rawls later acknowledged, he merely expressed an opinion, not an argument.) Also, like Habermas, he eventually gets around to addressing "Catholics," as such on the issue:

> *Some may, of course, reject a decision, as Catholics may reject a decision to grant a right to abortion. They may present an argument in public reason for denying it and fail to win a majority. But they need not exercise the right of abortion in their own case. They can recognize the right as belonging to legitimate law and therefore do not resist it with force. To do that would be unreasonable: It would mean their attempting to impose their own comprehensive doctrine, which a majority of their fellow citizens who follow public reason do not accept. Certainly Catholics may, in line with public reason, continue*

*to argue against the right of abortion. That the Church's nonpublic reason requires its members to follow its doctrine is perfectly consistent with their honoring public reason.*

Even if interpreted generously as granting advocacy of the strict prohibition of abortion can be consistent with public reason, Rawls's admonition to Catholics here is awkward. Plenty of American Catholics and other pro-life people, the vast majority of whom reject resorting to violence to protect the unborn from the injustice of abortion, reasonably refuse to recognize the right to abortion as "belonging to legitimate law." Rather, they believe any law recognizing a right to abortion is so gravely unjust as to be illegitimate in principle. As such, any law of this type should be opposed resolutely by people who understand its grave injustice.

As Finnis observes, "[T]he argument of [pro-life] citizens is the killings whose legalization Rawls and Habermas defend are a radical basic injustice imposed on people deprived or to be deprived of the protections of citizenship. The responses suggested by the argumentation of Rawls and Habermas would run something like: 'You free citizens need not exercise the right to [own slaves] [abort your children] in your own case, so you can and must recognize our law as legitimate as it applies to the rest of us (and as we will enforce it against you if you interfere).' 'You people need not do any of this [slave owning] [killing] yourselves, so your integrity is undamaged and so you ought (and will be compelled) to stand aside to allow us, in the exercise of our prior right of coexistence with you, to ['coexist' with our slaves] [terminate our coexistence with these unborn children/fetuses and with people whose lives are not worth living].'"

In fact, advocacy of the right to life against the forces advancing abortion and euthanasia is an example of how Christians and others honor public reason (though not Rawls's artificial and unreasonably restricted conception of it) and promote an "ethics of discourse" (though not Habermas's artificial and biased version of it). Natural law, as Christians and others who embrace it understand the matter, truly demands "the interests of all" be taken into account.

This is the implication of the principle each and every human being is fashioned in the image and likeness of the divine creator and ruler of the universe and, as such, shares a fundamental dignity with others, including those exercising the highest worldly authority, are bound in reason to respect and protect.

Moreover, natural law is nothing other than a doctrine of public reasons, as Finnis puts it, "would command a universal consensus under ideal conditions of discourse and meanwhile are available to, and could be accepted by, anyone who is willing and able to give them fair and adequate attention." These reasons can be, and have been, affirmed by people who know nothing of, or do not accept, Jewish or Christian revelation or the authority of the Church or any other institution. Respect for these reasons as reasons accounts for the honored place of dialectic in the tradition of natural law theory and the emphasis of contemporary natural law theorists on full and fair debate in the forums of democracy on such issues as abortion, euthanasia, embryonic stem-cell research, human cloning, and marriage.

That is why, from the Christian vantage point, there is something scandalous in the effort of theorists such as Rawls and Habermas to remove such issues from public debate by arbitrarily restricting reasons on one side of the debate over the nature, dignity, and destiny of the human person. There is nothing "liberal," "democratic," "reasonable," "moral," or "ethical" about that.

# About the Contributors

**Randy Alcorn** is the founder and director of Eternal Perspective Ministries, a nonprofit organization dedicated to teaching biblical truth and drawing attention to the needy and how to help them. A *New York Times* bestselling author, Randy has written nearly fifty books, including *Courageous*, *Heaven*, *The Treasure Principle*, and Gold Medallion winner *Safely Home*. He has also served as a pastor and a part-time faculty member at Western Seminary and Multnomah University.

**Ryan T. Anderson** (Ph.D., University of Notre Dame) is the William E. Simon senior research fellow at The Heritage Foundation, and the founder and editor of *Public Discourse*, the online journal of the Witherspoon Institute of Princeton, New Jersey. He is the author of *When Harry Became Sally: Responding to the Transgender Moment and Truth Overruled: The Future of Marriage and Religious Freedom*, and he is the co-author of *What Is Marriage? Man and Woman: A Defense and Debating Religious Liberty and Discrimination*. Anderson's research has been cited by two U.S. Supreme Court justices, Justice Samuel Alito and Justice Clarence Thomas, in two Supreme Court cases. He received his bachelor of arts degree from Princeton University, graduating Phi Beta Kappa and magna cum laude.

**Bruce Ashford** (Ph.D., Southeastern Baptist Theological Seminary) is provost and professor of Theology & Culture at Southeastern Baptist Theological Seminary. He is also a research fellow at the Ethics and Religious Liberty Commission, a fellow in theology at the St. George's Center for Biblical and Public Theology and a participant in the Dulles Colloquium of the Institute on Religion & Public Life. Dr. Ashford has been teaching at Southeastern since 2003 and became the provost in 2013. His goal in teaching is to encourage his students to bear witness to the truth, goodness and beauty of the gospel and to work out its implications in all facets of their lives and in all dimensions of culture. Ashford defended his dissertation on "Ludwig Wittgenstein's Impact on Anglo-American Theology," is the co-author of *One Nation Under God: A Christian Hope for American Politics*, the author of *Every Square Inch: An Introduction to Cultural Engagement for Christians*, and is the editor of *Theology and Practice of Mission*. His primary interest is public theology; his secondary interests include philosophy of education, theology of mission, theological method, and contemporary theology.

**Charles W. "Chuck" Colson** (1931–2012), the Founder of Prison Fellowship, was widely recognized as one of the outstanding and influential Christian leaders during the final decades of the 20th century and the early years of the 21st. The author of more than thirty books, he was also the founder of the Colson Center for Christian Worldview. Chuck Colson was the visionary leader for *The Manhattan Declaration*.

**David S. Dockery** (Ph.D., University of Texas system) serves as the 15th president of Trinity International University and is now serving in his 24th year as a university president. Highly regarded as one of the outstanding leaders and senior statesmen in the world of Christian higher education, Dockery served as president of Union University for nearly two decades before coming to Trinity. Having authored or edited more than thirty volumes, and contributed to more than seventy other books, he is best known for his works in the area of Christian higher education, Baptist studies, and biblical interpretation. In 2018, Dockery was recognized with the John R. Dellenback Global Leadership Award for his work in Christian higher education.

**Timothy Cardinal Dolan** is an American cardinal prelate of the Roman Catholic Church. Appointed by Pope Benedict XVI, Dolan serves as the tenth and current Archbishop of New York. Dolan served as the president of the United States Conference of Catholic Bishops from 2010 to 2013. He is an alumnus of the Pontifical University of St. Thomas Aquinas Angelicum from which he earned the degree of Licentiate of Sacred

Theology. Dolan is the author of a number of books including *To Whom Shall We Go?: Lessons from the Apostle Peter.*

**Mary Eberstadt** currently serves as a senior research fellow at the Faith and Reason Institute. Previously, she was a research fellow at the Hoover Institution and a senior fellow at the Ethics and Public Policy Center in Washington, D.C. Eberstadt focuses on issues of American society, culture, and philosophy. She has written widely for various magazines and newspapers, including *Policy Review*, the *Weekly Standard*, *First Things*, the *American Spectator*, *Los Angeles Times*, *London Times*, and the *Wall Street Journal*. Her most recent books are *It's Dangerous to Believe: Religious Freedom and Its Enemies* (2016); *How the West Really Lost God: A New Theory of Secularization* (2013); *Adam and Eve After the Pill: Paradoxes of the Sexual Revolution* (2012). Between 1998 and 1990, she was executive editor of the *National Interest* magazine. From 1985 to 1987, she was a member of the Policy Planning Staff of the U.S. State Department, a speechwriter for former secretary of state George P. Shultz, and a special assistant to Ambassador Jeane J. Kirkpatrick at the U.S. Mission to the United Nations. She was also managing editor at the *Public Interest*. A four-year Telluride Scholar at Cornell University, Eberstadt graduated magna cum laude.

**Michael Farris** (J.D. Gonzaga University School of Law) currently serves as CEO and general counsel for Alliance Defending Freedom. He is also the founder of the Home School Legal Defense Association and the former president of Patrick Henry College.

**Timothy George** (Th.D., Harvard University) has been the dean of Beeson Divinity School since its inception in 1988. As founding dean, he has been instrumental in shaping its character and mission. In addition to his administrative responsibilities, George teaches church history and doctrine. He is a life advisory trustee of Wheaton College, is active in Evangelical–Roman Catholic Church dialogue, and has chaired the Doctrine and Christian Unity Commission of the Baptist World Alliance. He serves as senior theological advisor for Christianity Today, and is on the editorial advisory boards of *First Things* and *Books & Culture*. George is the general editor of the *Reformation Commentary on Scripture*, a twenty-eight-volume series of 16th century exegetical comment. A prolific author, he has written more than twenty books and regularly contributes to scholarly journals.

**Robert P. George** (J.D. and M.T.S., Harvard University; D.Phil., Oxford University) holds Princeton's celebrated McCormick Chair in Jurisprudence and is the founding director of the James Madison Program in American Ideals and Institutions. He served as chairman of the United States Commission on International Religious Freedom (USCIRF), and before that on the President's Council on Bioethics and as a presidential appointee to the United States Commission on Civil Rights. He also served as the U.S. member of UNESCO's World Commission on the Ethics of Scientific Knowledge and Technology (COMEST). He is a former Judicial Fellow at the Supreme Court of the United States, where he received the Justice Tom C. Clark Award. He is the author of *In Defense of Natural Law; Making Men Moral: Civil Liberties and Public Morality; The Clash of Orthodoxies: Law, Religion and Morality in Crisis; Conscience and Its Enemies: Confronting the Dogmas of Liberal Secularism*; and co-author of *Embryo: A Defense of Human Life; Body-Self Dualism in Contemporary Ethics and Politics; What is Marriage? Man and Woman: A Defense; and Conjugal Union: What Marriage Is and Why It Matters.*

**Chad Hatfield** (D.Min., Pittsburgh Theological Seminary) is the President of St. Vladimir's Orthodox Theological Seminary. Prior to his appointment at St. Vladimir's, Archpriest Hatfield was at St. Herman Seminary in Alaska, where he was serving as the dean. He presently serves as a member of the Metropolitan Council of the Orthodox Church in America (OCA). His experience in various pastoral, teaching, and administrative roles, spread over some thirty years of ordained ministry, are now blended into his ministry at the seminary.

**Frederica Mathewes-Green** is a wide-ranging author, whose work has appeared in such diverse publications as the *Washington Post, Christianity Today, Smithsonian*, the *Los Angeles Times, First Things, Books & Culture, Sojourners, Touchstone*, and the *Wall Street Journal.* She has been a regular commentator for National Public Radio (NPR), on Morning Edition and All Things Considered. She has published ten books, including

*Welcome to the Orthodox Church* (Paraclete Press, 2015), *The Jesus Prayer* (Paraclete, 2009), *Facing East: A Pilgrim's Journey into the Mysteries of Orthodoxy* (HarperCollins, 1997) and *The Illumined Heart: The Ancient Christian Path of Transformation* (Paraclete, 2001). She has published over 700 essays.

**Jennifer Roback Morse** (Ph.D., University of Rochester) is the founder of the Ruth Institute, a global non-profit organization that defends the family at home and in the public square and equips others to do the same. She is passionate about equipping family advocates with the knowledge and confidence to defend the family at home and in the public square. Doctor Morse was a campaign spokeswoman for California's winning Proposition 8 campaign, defining marriage as the union of a man and a woman. She has authored or co-authored five books and spoken around the globe on marriage, family, and human sexuality. Her newest books are *The Sexual Revolution and Its Victims* and *101 Tips for Marrying the Right Person*, co-authored with Betsy Kerekes. She taught economics at Yale and George Mason Universities. Doctor Morse and her husband are parents of an adopted child, a birth child, a goddaughter, and were foster parents for San Diego County to eight foster children.

**Russell Moore** (Ph.D., The Southern Baptist Theological Seminary) is president of the Ethics & Religious Liberty Commission of the Southern Baptist Convention. The ERLC is the moral and public policy entity of the nation's largest Protestant denomination. Prior to his election in 2013, Moore served as provost and dean of the Southern Baptist Theological Seminary in Louisville, Kentucky, where he also taught theology and ethics. He currently serves as distinguished professor of Christian ethics at Southern Seminary, and as a visiting professor of ethics at Southeastern Baptist Theological Seminary and New Orleans Baptist Theological Seminary. He also is an affiliate faculty member at Trinity International University. His recent book, *The Storm-Tossed Family: How the Cross Reshapes the Home*, was named the *Christianity Today* Book of the Year.
R. R. Reno (Ph.D., Yale University) is the editor of *First Things* magazine. Formerly a professor of theology and ethics at Creighton University, he is the author of several important books, including *Resurrecting the Idea of a Christian Society, Fighting the Noonday Devil – and Other Essays Personal*

and *Theological, In the Ruins of the Church, Redemptive Change*, and a theological commentary on the Book of Genesis.

**John Stonestreet** (M.A., Trinity Evangelical Divinity School) is President of the Colson Center for Christian Worldview and a sought-after author and speaker on faith and culture, worldview, education and apologetics. John is the daily voice of *BreakPoint,* the nationally syndicated commentary on faith and culture founded by the late Chuck Colson, and is an ordained deacon in the Convocation of Anglicans in North America (CANA). John has co-authored four books, including *A Practical Guide to Culture* (David C. Cook) and *Restoring All Things* (Baker).

**Joni Eareckson Tada**, the founder and CEO of Joni and Friends International Disability Center, is an international advocate for people with disabilities. A diving accident in 1967 left Joni Eareckson, then seventeen, a quadriplegic in a wheelchair, without the use of her hands. After two years of rehabilitation, she emerged with new skills and a fresh determination to help others in similar situations. Her bestselling autobiography *Joni* and the feature film of the same name have been translated into many languages, introducing her to people around the world. Mrs. Tada has served on the National Council on Disability and on the Disability Advisory Committee to the U.S. State Department. Joni has written over fifty books and is a regular columnist in several magazines.

**Kristen Waggoner** (J.D., Regent University School of Law) serves as the senior vice president of U.S. legal division and communications with Alliance Defending Freedom. In this role, Waggoner oversees the U.S. legal division, a team of one hundred attorneys and staff who engage in litigation, public advocacy, and legislative support. Since she assumed this role, ADF has prevailed as lead counsel in eight U.S. Supreme Court victories. She brings to this role extensive experience in civil litigation, employment, education, nonprofit, and constitutional law.

**Andrew Walker** (Ph.D., Southern Baptist Theological Seminary) is the director of research and senior fellow in Christian Ethics at the Ethics and Religious Liberty Commission. In his role, he researches, speaks, and writes about the intersection of Christian ethics, public policy, and the church's social witness. He also oversees the ERLC's academic initiatives and directs the ERLC's Research Institute.

**Rick Warren** is the founding pastor of Saddleback Church, the author of *The Purpose-Driven Life* (2002), which is the bestselling hardcover non-fiction book in history (over thirty-two million copies), and the second-most translated book after the Bible. He is widely recognized as one of the most influential evangelicals in the United States.

**Trevin Wax** (Ph.D., Southeastern Baptist Theological Seminary) is Bible and reference publisher for LifeWay Christian Resources and has served as managing editor of *The Gospel Project*, a gospel-centered small group curriculum for all ages. A contributor to numerous publications including the *Washington Post, Religion News Service, Christianity Today*, and *World,* Trevin writes daily at Kingdom People, a blog hosted by The Gospel Coalition. A former missionary to Romania, Trevin was recently named by *Christianity Today* as one of thirty-three millennials leading the next generation of evangelicalism. He is the co-host of the *Word Matters* podcast that explores difficult and contested passages of Scripture.

# ADDENDUM

## *The Manhattan Declaration*
## A Call of Christian Conscience

### Preamble

Christians are heirs of a 2,000-year tradition of proclaiming God's word, seeking justice in our societies, resisting tyranny, and reaching out with compassion to the poor, oppressed and suffering.

While fully acknowledging the imperfections and shortcomings of Christian institutions and communities in all ages, we claim the heritage of those Christians who defended innocent life by rescuing discarded babies from trash heaps in Roman cities and publicly denouncing the Empire's sanctioning of infanticide. We remember with reverence those believers who sacrificed their lives by remaining in Roman cities to tend the sick and dying during the plagues, and who died bravely in the coliseums rather than deny their Lord.

After the barbarian tribes overran Europe, Christian monasteries preserved not only the Bible but also the literature and art of Western culture. It was Christians who combated the evil of slavery: Papal edicts in the 16th and 17th centuries decried the practice of slavery and first excommunicated anyone involved in the slave trade; evangelical Christians in England, led by John Wesley and William Wilberforce, put an end to the slave trade in that country. Christians under Wilberforce's leadership also formed hundreds of societies for helping the poor, the imprisoned, and child laborers chained to machines.

In Europe, Christians challenged the divine claims of kings and successfully fought to establish the rule of law and balance of governmental

191

powers, which made modern democracy possible. And in America, Christian women stood at the vanguard of the suffrage movement. The great civil rights crusades of the 1950s and '60s were led by Christians claiming the Scriptures and asserting the glory of the image of God in every human being regardless of race, religion, age or class.

This same devotion to human dignity has led Christians in recent decades to work to end the dehumanizing scourge of human trafficking and sexual slavery, bring compassionate care to AIDS sufferers in Africa, and assist in a myriad of other human rights causes—from providing clean water in developing nations to providing homes for tens of thousands of children orphaned by war, disease, and gender discrimination.

Like those who have gone before us in the faith, Christians today are called to proclaim the Gospel of costly grace, to protect the intrinsic dignity of the human person and to stand for the common good. In being true to its own calling, the call to discipleship, the church through service to others can make a profound contribution to the public good.

## Declaration

We, as Orthodox, Catholic, and Evangelical Christians, have gathered, beginning in New York on September 28, 2009, to make the following declaration, which we sign as individuals, not on behalf of our organizations, but speaking to and from our communities. We act together in obedience to the one true God, the triune God of holiness and love, who has laid total claim on our lives and by that claim calls us with believers in all ages and all nations to seek and defend the good of all who bear his image. We set forth this declaration in light of the truth that is grounded in Holy Scripture, in natural human reason (which is itself, in our view, the gift of a beneficent God), and in the very nature of the human person. We call upon all people of goodwill, believers and non-believers alike, to consider carefully and reflect critically on the issues we here address as we, with St. Paul, commend this appeal to everyone's conscience in the sight of God.

While the whole scope of Christian moral concern, including a special concern for the poor and vulnerable, claims our attention, we are especially troubled that in our nation today the lives of the unborn, the disabled, and the elderly are severely threatened; that the institution of marriage, already buffeted by promiscuity, infidelity and divorce, is in jeopardy of being redefined to accommodate fashionable ideologies; that freedom of religion and the rights of conscience are gravely jeopardized by those who would use the instruments of coercion to compel persons of faith to compromise their deepest convictions.

Because the sanctity of human life, the dignity of marriage as a union of husband and wife, and the freedom of conscience and religion are foundational principles of justice and the common good, we are compelled by our Christian faith to speak and act in their defense. In this declaration we affirm: 1) the profound, inherent, and equal dignity of every human being as a creature fashioned in the very image of God, possessing inherent rights of equal dignity and life; 2) marriage as a conjugal union of man and woman, ordained by God from the creation, and historically understood by believers and non-believers alike, to be the most basic institution in society and; 3) religious liberty, which is grounded in the character of God, the example of Christ, and the inherent freedom and dignity of human beings created in the divine image.

We are Christians who have joined together across historic lines of ecclesial differences to affirm our right—and, more importantly, to embrace our obligation  to speak and act in defense of these truths. We pledge to each other, and to our fellow believers, that no power on earth, be it cultural or political, will intimidate us into silence or acquiescence. It is our duty to proclaim the Gospel of our Lord and Savior Jesus Christ in its fullness, both in season and out of season. May God help us not to fail in that duty.

## Life

*So God created man in his own image, in the image of God he created him; male and female he created them.* Genesis 1:27

*I have come that they may have life, and have it to the full.* John 10:10

Although public sentiment has moved in a pro-life direction, we note with sadness that proabortion ideology prevails today in our government. Many in the present administration want to make abortions legal at any stage of fetal development, and want to provide abortions at taxpayer expense. Majorities in both houses of Congress hold pro-abortion views. The Supreme Court, whose infamous 1973 decision in Roe v. Wade stripped the unborn of legal protection, continues to treat elective abortion as a fundamental constitutional right, though it has upheld as constitutionally permissible some limited restrictions on abortion. The President says that he wants to reduce the "need" for abortion-a commendable goal. But he has also pledged to make abortion more easily and widely available by eliminating laws prohibiting government funding, requiring waiting periods for women seeking abortions, and parental notification for abortions performed on minors. The elimination of these important and effective pro-life laws cannot reasonably be expected to do other than significantly increase the number of elective abortions by which the lives of countless children are snuffed out prior to birth. Our commitment to the sanctity of life is not a matter of partisan loyalty, for we recognize that in the thirty-six years since *Roe v. Wade*, elected officials and appointees of both major political parties have been complicit in giving legal sanction to what Pope John Paul II described as "the culture of death." We call on all officials in our country, elected and appointed, to protect and serve every member of our society, including the most marginalized, voiceless, and vulnerable among us.

A culture of death inevitably cheapens life in all its stages and conditions by promoting the belief that lives that are imperfect, immature or inconvenient are discardable. As predicted by many prescient persons, the cheapening of life that began with abortion has now metastasized. For example, human embryo-destructive research and its public funding are promoted in the name of science and in the cause of developing treatments and cures for diseases and injuries. The President and many in Congress favor the expansion of embryo-research to include the taxpayer funding of so-called "therapeutic cloning." This would result in the industrial mass production of human embryos to be killed for the purpose of producing genetically customized stem cell lines and tissues. At the other end of life, an increasingly powerful movement to promote assisted suicide and "voluntary" euthanasia threatens the lives of vulnerable elderly and disabled persons. Eugenic notions such as the doctrine of *Lebensunwertes Leben* ("life unworthy of life") were first advanced in the 1920s by intellectuals in the elite salons of America and Europe. Long buried in ignominy after the horrors of the mid-20th century, they have returned from the grave. The only difference is that now the doctrines of the eugenicists are dressed up in the language of "liberty," "autonomy," and "choice."

We will be united and untiring in our efforts to roll back the license to kill that began with the abandonment of the unborn to abortion. We will work, as we have always worked, to bring assistance, comfort, and care to pregnant women in need and to those who have been victimized by abortion, even as we stand resolutely against the corrupt and degrading notion that it can somehow be in the best interests of women to submit to the deliberate killing of their unborn children. Our message is, and ever shall be, that the just, humane, and truly Christian answer to problem pregnancies is for all of us to love and care for mother and child alike.

A truly prophetic Christian witness will insistently call on those who have been entrusted with temporal power to fulfill the first responsibility of government: to protect the weak and vulnerable against violent attack, and to do so with no favoritism, partiality, or discrimination. The Bible enjoins us to defend those who cannot defend themselves, to speak for those who cannot themselves speak. And so we defend and speak for the unborn, the disabled, and the dependent. What the Bible and the light of reason make clear, we must make clear. We must be willing to defend, even at risk and cost to ourselves and our institutions, the lives of our brothers and sisters at every stage of development and in every condition.

Our concern is not confined to our own nation. Around the globe, we are witnessing cases of genocide and "ethnic cleansing," the failure to assist those who are suffering as innocent victims of war, the neglect and abuse of children, the exploitation of vulnerable laborers, the sexual trafficking of girls and young women, the abandonment of the aged, racial oppression and discrimination, the persecution of believers of all faiths, and the failure to take steps necessary to halt the spread of preventable diseases like AIDS. We see these travesties as flowing from the same loss of the sense of the dignity of the human person and the sanctity of human life that drives the abortion industry and the movements for assisted suicide, euthanasia, and human cloning for biomedical research. And so ours is, as it must be, a truly consistent ethic of love and life for all humans in all circumstances.

## Marriage

*The man said, "This is now bone of my bones and flesh of my flesh; she shall be called woman, for she was taken out of man." For this reason a man will leave his father and mother and be united to his wife, and they will become one flesh.* Genesis 2:23-24

*This is a profound mystery-but I am talking about Christ and the church. However, each one of you also must love his wife as he loves himself, and the wife must respect her husband.* Ephesians 5:32-33

In Scripture, the creation of man and woman, and their one-flesh union as husband and wife, is the crowning achievement of God's creation. In the transmission of life and the nurturing of children, men and women joined as spouses are given the great honor of being partners with God Himself. Marriage then, is the first institution of human society—indeed it is the institution on which all other human institutions have their foundation. In the Christian tradition we refer to marriage as "holy matrimony" to signal the fact that it is an institution ordained by God, and blessed by Christ in his participation at a wedding in Cana of Galilee. In the Bible, God Himself blesses and holds marriage in the highest esteem.

Vast human experience confirms that marriage is the original and most important institution for sustaining the health, education, and welfare of all persons in a society. Where marriage is honored, and where there is a flourishing marriage culture, everyone benefits—the spouses themselves, their children, the communities and societies in which they live. Where the marriage culture begins to erode, social pathologies of every sort quickly manifest themselves.

Unfortunately, we have witnessed over the course of the past several decades a serious erosion of the marriage culture in our own country. Perhaps the most telling and alarming-indicator is the out-of-wedlock birth rate. Less than fifty years ago, it was under 5 percent. Today it is over 40 percent. Our society—and particularly its poorest and most vulnerable sectors, where the out-of-wedlock birth rate is much higher even than the national average—is paying a huge price in delinquency, drug abuse, crime, incarceration, hopelessness, and despair. Other indicators are widespread non-marital sexual cohabitation and a devastatingly high rate of divorce.

We confess with sadness that Christians and our institutions have too often scandalously failed to uphold the institution of marriage and to model for the world the true meaning of marriage. Insofar as we have too easily embraced the culture of divorce and remained silent about social practices that undermine the dignity of marriage we repent, and call upon all Christians to do the same.

To strengthen families, we must stop glamorizing promiscuity and infidelity and restore among our people a sense of the profound beauty, mystery, and holiness of faithful marital love. We must reform ill-advised policies that contribute to the weakening of the institution of marriage, including the discredited idea of unilateral divorce. We must work in the legal, cultural, and religious domains to instill in young people a sound understanding of what marriage is, what it requires, and why it is worth the commitment and sacrifices that faithful spouses make.

The impulse to redefine marriage in order to recognize same-sex and multiple partner relationships is a symptom, rather than the cause, of the erosion of the marriage culture. It reflects a loss of understanding of the meaning of marriage as embodied in our civil and religious law and in the philosophical tradition that contributed to shaping the law. Yet it is critical that the impulse be resisted, for yielding to it would mean abandoning the possibility of restoring a sound understanding of marriage and, with it, the hope of rebuilding a healthy marriage culture. It would lock into place the false and destructive belief that marriage is all about romance and other adult satisfactions, and not, in any intrinsic way, about procreation and the unique character and value of acts and relationships whose meaning is shaped by their aptness for the generation, promotion and protection of life. In spousal communion and the rearing of children (who, as gifts of God, are the fruit of their parents' marital love), we discover the profound reasons for and benefits of the marriage covenant.

We acknowledge that there are those who are disposed towards homosexual and polyamorous conduct and relationships, just as there are those who are disposed towards other forms of immoral conduct. We have compassion for those so disposed; we respect them as human beings possessing profound, inherent, and equal dignity; and we pay tribute to the men and women who strive, often with little assistance, to resist the temptation to yield to desires that they, no less than we, regard as wayward. We stand with them, even when they falter. We, no less than they, are sinners who have fallen short of God's intention for our lives. We, no less than they, are in constant need of God's patience, love and forgiveness. We call on the entire Christian community to resist sexual immorality, and at the same time refrain from disdainful condemnation of those who yield to it. Our rejection of sin, though resolute, must never become the rejection of sinners. For every sinner, regardless of the sin, is loved by God, who seeks not our destruction but rather the conversion of our hearts. Jesus calls all who wander from the path of virtue to "a more excellent way." As his disciples we will reach out in love to assist all who hear the call and wish to answer it.

We further acknowledge that there are sincere people who disagree with us, and with the teaching of the Bible and Christian tradition, on questions of sexual morality and the nature of marriage. Some who enter into same-sex and polyamorous relationships no doubt regard their unions as truly marital. They fail to understand, however, that marriage is made possible by the sexual complementarity of man and woman, and that the comprehensive, multi-level sharing of life that marriage is includes bodily unity of the sort that unites husband and wife biologically as one. This is because the body is no mere extrinsic instrument of the human person, but truly part of the personal reality of the human being. Human beings are not merely centers of consciousness or emotion, or minds, or spirits, inhabiting non-personal bodies. The human person is a dynamic unity of body, mind, and spirit. Marriage is what one man and one woman establish when, forsaking all others and pledging lifelong commitment, they found a sharing of life at every level of being—the biological, the emotional, the dispositional, the rational, the spiritual—on a commitment that is sealed, completed and actualized by loving sexual intercourse in which the spouses become one flesh, not in some merely metaphorical sense, but by fulfilling together the behavioral conditions of procreation. That is why in the Christian tradition, and historically in Western law, consummated marriages are not dissoluble or annullable on the ground of infertility, even though the nature of the marital relationship is shaped and structured by its intrinsic orientation to the great good of procreation.

We understand that many of our fellow citizens, including some Christians, believe that the historic definition of marriage as the union of one man and one woman is a denial of equality or civil rights. They wonder what to say in reply to the argument that asserts that no harm would be done to them or to anyone if the law of the community were to confer upon two men or two women who are living together in a sexual partnership the status of being "married." It would not, after all, affect their own marriages, would it? On inspection, however, the argument that

198

laws governing one kind of marriage will not affect another cannot stand. Were it to prove anything, it would prove far too much: the assumption that the legal status of one set of marriage relationships affects no other would not only argue for same sex partnerships; it could be asserted with equal validity for polyamorous partnerships, polygamous households, even adult brothers, sisters, or brothers and sisters living in incestuous relationships. Should these, as a matter of equality or civil rights, be recognized as lawful marriages, and would they have no effects on other relationships? No. The truth is that marriage is not something abstract or neutral that the law may legitimately define and re-define to please those who are powerful and influential.

No one has a civil right to have a non-marital relationship treated as a marriage. Marriage is an objective reality—a covenantal union of husband and wife—that it is the duty of the law to recognize and support for the sake of justice and the common good. If it fails to do so, genuine social harms follow. First, the religious liberty of those for whom this is a matter of conscience is jeopardized. Second, the rights of parents are abused as family life and sex education programs in schools are used to teach children that an enlightened understanding recognizes as "marriages" sexual partnerships that many parents believe are intrinsically nonmarital and immoral. Third, the common good of civil society is damaged when the law itself, in its critical pedagogical function, becomes a tool for eroding a sound understanding of marriage on which the flourishing of the marriage culture in any society vitally depends. Sadly, we are today far from having a thriving marriage culture. But if we are to begin the critically important process of reforming our laws and mores to rebuild such a culture, the last thing we can afford to do is to re-define marriage in such a way as to embody in our laws a false proclamation about what marriage is.

And so it is out of love (not "animus") and prudent concern for the common good (not "prejudice"), that we pledge to labor ceaselessly to preserve the legal definition of marriage as the union of one man and one woman and to rebuild the marriage culture. How could we, as Christians, do otherwise? The Bible teaches us that marriage is a central part of God's creation covenant. Indeed, the union of husband and wife mirrors the bond between Christ and his church. And so just as Christ was willing, out of love, to give Himself up for the church in a complete sacrifice, we are willing, lovingly, to make whatever sacrifices are required of us for the sake of the inestimable treasure that is marriage.

## Religious Liberty

*The Spirit of the Sovereign LORD is on me, because the LORD has anointed me to preach good news to the poor. He has sent me to bind up the brokenhearted, to proclaim freedom for the captives and release from darkness for the prisoners.* Isaiah 61:1

*Give to Caesar what is Caesar's, and to God what is God's.* Matthew 22:21

The struggle for religious liberty across the centuries has been long and arduous. Religious liberty is not a novel idea or recent development, but is grounded in the character of God Himself, the God who is most fully known in the life and work of Jesus Christ. Determined to follow Jesus faithfully in life and death, the early Christians appealed to the manner in which the Incarnation had taken place: "Did God send Christ, as some suppose, as a tyrant brandishing fear and terror? Not so, but in gentleness and meekness…for compulsion is no attribute of God" (Epistle to Diognetus 7.3-4). Thus, the right to religious freedom has its foundation in the example of Christ Himself and in the very dignity of the human person created in the image of God—a dignity, as our founders proclaimed, inherent in every human, and knowable by all in the exercise of right reason.

Christians confess that God alone is Lord of the conscience. Immunity from religious coercion is the cornerstone of an unconstrained conscience. No one should be compelled to embrace any religion against his will, nor should persons of faith be forbidden to worship God according to the dictates of conscience or to express freely and publicly their deeply held religious convictions. What is true for individuals applies to religious communities as well.

It is ironic that those who today assert a right to kill the unborn, aged and disabled and also a right to engage in immoral sexual practices, and even a right to have relationships integrated around these practices be recognized and blessed by law—such persons claiming these "rights" are very often in the vanguard of those who would trample upon the freedom of others to express their religious and moral commitments to the sanctity of life and to the dignity of marriage as the conjugal union of husband and wife.

We see this, for example, in the effort to weaken or eliminate conscience clauses, and therefore to compel pro-life institutions (including religiously affiliated hospitals and clinics), and pro-life physicians, surgeons, nurses, and other health care professionals, to refer for abortions and, in certain cases, even to perform or participate in abortions. We see it in the use of antidiscrimination statutes to force religious institutions, businesses, and service providers of various sorts to comply with activities they judge to be deeply immoral or go out of business. After the judicial imposition of "same-sex marriage" in Massachusetts, for example, Catholic Charities chose with great reluctance to end its century-long work of helping to place orphaned children in good homes rather than comply with a legal mandate that it place children in same-sex households in violation of Catholic moral teaching. In New Jersey, after the establishment of a quasi-marital "civil unions" scheme, a Methodist institution was stripped of its tax exempt status when it declined, as a matter of religious conscience, to permit a facility it owned and operated to be used for ceremonies blessing homosexual unions. In Canada and some European nations, Christian clergy have been prosecuted for preaching Biblical norms against the practice of homosexuality. New hate-crime laws in America raise the specter of the same practice here.

In recent decades a growing body of case law has paralleled the decline in respect for religious values in the media, the academy and political leadership, resulting in restrictions on the free exercise of religion. We view this as an ominous development, not only because of its threat to the individual liberty guaranteed to every person, regardless of his or her faith, but because the trend also threatens the common welfare and the culture of freedom on which our system of republican government is founded. Restrictions on the freedom of conscience or the ability to hire people of one's own faith or conscientious moral convictions for religious institutions, for example, undermines the viability of the intermediate structures of society, the essential buffer against the overweening authority of the state, resulting in the soft despotism Tocqueville so prophetically warned of. Disintegration of civil society is a prelude to tyranny.

As Christians, we take seriously the Biblical admonition to respect and obey those in authority. We believe in law and in the rule of law. We recognize the duty to comply with laws whether we happen to like them or not, unless the laws are gravely unjust or require those subject to them to do something unjust or otherwise immoral. The biblical purpose of law is to preserve order and serve justice and the common good; yet laws that are unjust—and especially laws that purport to compel citizens to do what is unjust—undermine the common good, rather than serve it.

Going back to the earliest days of the church, Christians have refused to compromise their proclamation of the gospel. In Acts 4, Peter and John were ordered to stop preaching. Their answer was, "Judge for yourselves whether it is right in God's sight to obey you rather than God. For we cannot help speaking about what we have seen and heard." Through the centuries, Christianity has taught that civil disobedience is not only permitted, but sometimes required. There is no more eloquent defense of the rights and duties of religious conscience than the one offered by Martin Luther King, Jr., in his "Letter from a Birmingham Jail." Writing from an explicitly Christian perspective, and citing Christian writers such as Augustine and Aquinas, King taught that just laws elevate and ennoble human beings because they are rooted in the moral law whose ultimate source is God Himself. Unjust laws degrade human beings. Inasmuch as they can claim no authority beyond sheer human will, they lack any power to bind in conscience. King's willingness to go to jail, rather than comply with legal injustice, was exemplary and inspiring.

Because we honor justice and the common good, we will not comply with any edict that purports to compel our institutions to participate in abortions, embryo-destructive research, assisted suicide and euthanasia, or any other anti-life act; nor will we bend to any rule purporting to force us to bless immoral sexual partnerships, treat them as marriages or the equivalent, or refrain from proclaiming the truth, as we know it, about morality and immorality and marriage and the family. We will fully and ungrudgingly render to Caesar what is Caesar's. But under no circumstances will we render to Caesar what is God's.

### Drafting Committee

*Robert George, Professor, McCormick Professor of Jurisprudence, Princeton University*
*Timothy George, Professor, Beeson Divinity School, Samford University*
*Chuck Colson, Founder, the Chuck Colson Center for Christian Worldview (Lansdowne, VA)*